Handley Page
Victor

The Crescent-Winged V-Bomber

Phil Butler and Tony Buttler

An imprint of
Ian Allan Publishing

Handley Page Victor
© 2009 Tony Buttler and Phil Butler

ISBN 978 1 85780 311 2

Published by Midland Publishing
4 Watling Drive, Hinckley, LE10 3EY, England
Tel: 01455 254 490   Fax: 01455 254 495
E-mail: midlandbooks@compuserve.com

Midland Publishing and Aerofax are imprints of
Ian Allan Publishing Ltd

Worldwide distribution (except North America):
Midland Counties Publications
4 Watling Drive, Hinckley, LE10 3EY, England
Telephone: 01455 254 450   Fax: 01455 233 737
E-mail: midlandbooks@compuserve.com
www.midlandcountiessuperstore.com

North American trade distribution:
Specialty Press Publishers & Wholesalers Inc.
39966 Grand Avenue, North Branch, MN 55056
Tel: 651 277 1400   Fax: 651 277 1203
Toll free telephone: 800 895 4585
www.specialtypress.com

Design and concept
© 2009 Midland Publishing and
Stephen Thompson Associates
Layout by Russell Strong

Printed in England by
Ian Allan Printing Ltd
Riverdene Business Park, Molesey Road,
Hersham, Surrey, KT12 4RG

Visit the Ian Allan Publishing website at:
www.ianallanpublishing.com

Contents

Introduction 3
Glossary 4

Chapters

 1   Beginnings. 5
 2   Test Beds, Prototypes and Mark 1s . 19
 3   Production Mark 2s and
     Unbuilt Proposals 43
 4   Service History. 61
 5   Trials Aircraft 77
 6   Detail Description 83
 7   What Was It Like? 99

Appendices

 1   Contracts and Airframe Histories . . 109
 2   Victor Flying Units 118
 3   Victor K Mk.2 Conversion Programme 120

Bibliography. 120
Victors in Colour. 121
Unit Badges 144

Title page: **English Electric Lightnings XR723 and XS932 are seen receiving fuel from an unidentified Victor tanker.**

Below: **Victor K.2 XL190 of No.55 Squadron, seen landing at Fairford during the 1989 RIAT Display.**
Gerry Manning

Introduction

The Handley Page Victor is in all probability the least well known of the three V-Bombers. This aircraft always seems to come last in the coverage given to the V-types in books and magazines, always behind the ever popular Avro Vulcan and, because it was the first of the three types to enter service and thereby broke new ground, the Vickers Valiant. In fact, nothing like enough space has been allocated to the Victor in comparison to many RAF aeroplanes and this is most unfair because Handley Page's V-Bomber completed a highly successful career with the Service. However, it is hoped that, alongside a major two-volume work written about the aircraft by Roger R. Brookes and published by Pen & Sword in 2007 (*The Handley Page Victor: The History and Development of a Classic Jet – Volumes I and II*), this imbalance has now partly been addressed. With this book the Publisher also completes a series of Aerofaxes covering the individual V-Bombers.

As we have explained in previous titles in this series, the Aerofax style, written essentially for enthusiasts and modellers, prevents us from putting together a truly in-depth account. Nevertheless, there is still scope to include previously unpublished information and another fine selection of high-quality photographs and illustrations, many in colour. There is information on variants that failed to win contracts and detailed histories for each aircraft built, and documents held by the National Archives and by the Handley Page Association have again permitted a full account to be made for the design and development period.

Once again, putting together a book of this nature has required the assistance of many people and we would like to thank the following for their vital contributions – Flt Lt John Allam OBE, Air Vice-Marshal Nigel Baldwin CBE, Peter Berry, Sir George Cox, Richard Curtis, Chris Gibson, Harry Fraser-Mitchell (who does such a great job running the Handley Page Association), Mike Hooks, Graham Hopkin, David Howley, George Jenks, Barry Jones, Gerry Manning, Ken Nevinson, Terry Panopalis, Flt Lt Andy Pugh, Clive Richards, Air Vice-Marshal

Victor B Mk.2 in silhouette. Handley Page

Mike Robinson, Phil Spencer, and the staff of the National Archives.

The V-Force dominated British defence policy for a number of years and in their heyday these aircraft served as strategic weapons systems that were designed to deliver nuclear bombs after a high-speed penetration to their targets. Once the original concept of a high flying nuclear bomber had been made extremely vulnerable by more advanced defensive systems the three types continued to build up a fine career in other roles. In some ways the Victor is the unsung hero of the V-Force, and yet perhaps it has a claim to have been the most successful of them all. It was the most sophisticated of the three designs, and great credit must go to Handley Page for developing such an outstanding aeroplane.

Phil Butler and Tony Buttler
December 2008

Glossary

A&AEE Aeroplane and Armament Experimental Establishment, Boscombe Down
AAM Air-to-air missile
AFB Air Force Base (US Air Force)
AFC Air Force Cross
AFEE Airborne Forces Experimental Establishment
AIEU Armament and Instrument Experimental Unit, based at Martlesham Heath
AoA Angle of attack, the angle at which the wing is inclined relative to the airflow
ARI Airborne Radio Installation
ASM Air-to-surface missile
Aspect ratio Ratio of wingspan to mean chord, calculated by dividing the square of the span by the wing area
AVM Air Vice-Marshal
AW/CN Awaiting Collection
BAC British Aircraft Corporation
BCDU Bomber Command Development Unit
BDR Battle Damage Repair
BOAC British Overseas Airways Corporation
C(A) Controller of Aircraft (UK – MoS post)
CAS Chief of the Air Staff (Air Ministry post)
CENTO Central Treaty Organisation
Centre of Pressure The point, or line, through which an aerodynamic force is considered to act
CinC Commander in Chief
chord Distance between centres of curvature of wing leading and trailing edges when measured parallel to the longitudinal axis
CofG Centre of gravity
Critical Mach No Mach number at which an aircraft's controllability is first affected by compressibility, i.e. the point at which shock waves first appear
DFC Distinguished Flying Cross
DFM Distinguished Flying Medal
DMARD Director of Military Aircraft Research & Development (MoS post)
EAS Equivalent Air Speed (a rectified figure incorporating a compressibility correction)
ECM Electronic Countermeasures

EMC Electro-Magnetic Compatibility
ETPS Empire Test Pilots School
FF Fire Fighting
F/H Flight Hours
GI Ground Instruction
GPI Ground Position Indicator
HC High Capacity bomb
HE High Explosive
HF High Frequency
HP Handley Page
HRS Heading Reference System
HSAL Hawker Siddeley Aviation Ltd
HDU Hose Drum Unit
IAS Indicated Air Speed
IFR In-Flight Refuelling
IFF Identification Friend or Foe
ILS Instrument Landing System
IMN Indicated Mach Number
Incidence Angle at which the wing (or tail) is set relative to the fuselage
IR Infra-red
JSTU Joint Services Trial Unit
LORAN Long Range Aid to Navigation
MC Medium Capacity bomb
MinTech Ministry of Technology
MoD Ministry of Defence – created in the late 1940s to co-ordinate the policy of the three Armed Services. In April 1964, the MoD was reconstituted to absorb the functions of the Air Ministry, Admiralty and War Office, the Air Ministry (the civilian body that had governed the RAF) ceasing to exist.
MoD(PE) Ministry of Defence (Procurement Executive)
MoS Ministry of Supply – provided stores for the RAF from 1946 onwards. Disbanded and reconstituted as the Ministry of Aviation in 1959
M/S Major Servicing
MU Maintenance Unit
NAE National Aeronautical Establishment
NATO North Atlantic Treaty Organisation
NBC Navigation and Bombing Computer
NBS Navigation and Bombing System
NGTE National Gas Turbine Establishment (merged with RAE, 1983)
nm Nautical Mile
OC Officer Commanding
OCU Operational Conversion Unit
ODM Operating Data Manual
OR Operational Requirement

'q' feel The term for artificially-induced loads into a control circuit, so that the pilot 'feels' a load on the control even though the actual load is not being fed back to him. For example, the control is being moved by a hydraulic ram in response to a movement that the pilot makes, but he/she cannot know what the actual aerodynamic load is on the item being moved. 'q' is the accepted letter for dynamic pressure.
PDTD(A) Principal Director of Technical Development (Air) (MoS post)
PE Position Error: tests to determine the accuracy of an aircraft's airspeed indicators.
PR Photo Reconnaissance
QRA Quick Reaction Alert
RAAF Royal Australian Air Force
RAE Royal Aircraft Establishment, Farnborough
RATO Rocket-Assisted Take-Off
RATOG Rocket-Assisted Take-Off Gear
RCM Radio Countermeasures
RoS Repair on Site
rpm Revolutions per Minute
RRE Royal Radar Establishment
R/T Radio Telephony
RTP Reduced to Produce
SBAC Society of British Aircraft Constructors (now Society of British Aerospace Companies)
SLAR Side-Looking Airborne Radar
SoC Struck Off Charge
SoTT School of Technical Training
SRIM Service-Engineered Radio Installation Modification
TACAN Tactical Aid to Navigation
TACEVAL Tactical Evaluation
TAS True Air Speed (Actual velocity relative to the surrounding air mass)
t/c Thickness/chord ratio
TFR Terrain-Following Radar
TI Trial Installation
TMB Target Marker Bomb
TOD Take Off Director
TRE Telecommunications Research Establishment, Malvern (became RRE)
TTF Tanker Training Flight
USAF United States Air Force
VHF Very High Frequency
VTF Victor Training Flight

Chapter One

Beginnings

The V-Bomber Force was one of the most powerful of all of the weapons handed to the RAF since its formation in 1918. Each of the aeroplanes that operated within it – the Avro Vulcan, the Handley Page Victor and the Vickers Valiant – were fine flying machines and all of them were capable of delivering nuclear or conventional weapons. However, their stay as the front line of the country's nuclear deterrent was short because these bombers were designed to operate at high altitude and the introduction of far more capable defensive systems in the Soviet Union soon made their task of nuclear delivery over enemy territory near impossible. During the 1960s the nuclear role was passed to the Royal Navy with its Polaris submarines and the Valiants were withdrawn after fatigue problems had been discovered in their wings. But the Vulcan and Victor soldiered on and Handley Page's aircraft remained in service until 1993 to complete thirty-five years of service. However, the start of the Victor story goes right back to the second half of the 1940s.

Specification

In the period following the end of World War Two the Air Staff showed a strong desire to acquire a long-range jet bomber but in due course studies indicated that this type of aeroplane, which might weigh as much as 200,000 lb (90,720kg), would be very expensive to put into service. The long-range requirement came together as OR.230 and one of the designs prepared at this time was the HP.72A project from Handley Page. The company's design team, led by Godfrey Lee, had used the HP.72A and the HP.75A designations as camouflage to screen their work on large high-speed jet bomber designs. The original HP.72 number had covered a piston-engine transport project that was eventually abandoned, while the HP.75 was a small flying-wing research aircraft flown in 1943. The HP.75A project featured a 'front rider plane' and was soon dropped (and no information on it appears to have survived) but the HP.72A was continued and eventually renumbered HP.80.

A beautiful image of an early production Handley Page Victor XA918 in silver finish.
Handley Page

The HP.72A/HP.80 drawings showed an aircraft powered by four 5,600 lb (24.9kN) thrust, scaled-down Rolls-Royce AJ.65 jet engines which had a wingspan of 122ft (37.2m) and an all up weight of 90,000 lb (40,824kg). The wing was highly swept but, at this stage, except for a slight reduction just outboard of the engine bays, the leading edge sweep angle was constant across the full span. The aircraft was designed to carry a 10,000 lb (4,536kg) bomb load at 520 knots (599mph/963km/h) and in the spring of 1946, a brochure was prepared which was submitted to the Ministry in June. Handley Page's staff unofficially called this project the 'Flatfish' but, although fine for flying at high speeds, its highly swept wing of near constant angle would not work very well at slow speeds. Tests showed that there would be a big drift of boundary layer towards the wing tips and this

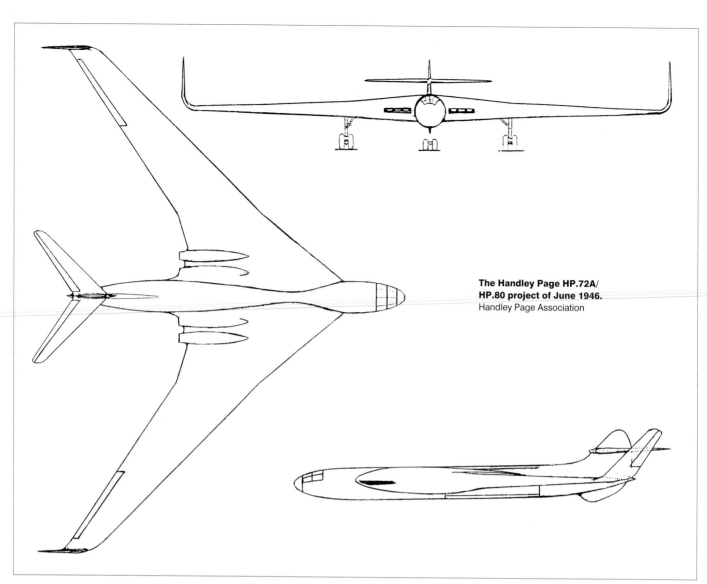

**The Handley Page HP.72A/
HP.80 project of June 1946.**
Handley Page Association

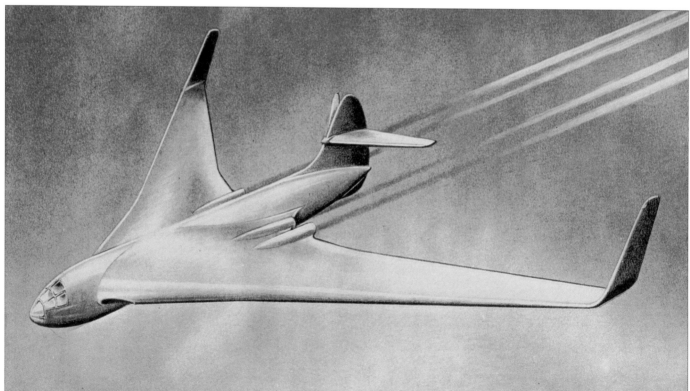

would create dramatic stall characteristics with a horrendous nose-up pitch.

Soon afterwards, when it was realised that the long-range bomber would be too big a step at this time, the Air Staff replaced its requirements with an alternative medium bomber programme. This was covered by Operational Requirement OR.229 and Specification B.35/46. The draft OR.229 was circulated on 7th November 1946 and the approved OR was issued to industry for a tender design competition on 7th January 1947. The requirements were still very severe and detailed an aeroplane that had to be able to hit a target at distances as far away as 1,500 nautical miles (nm) (2,778km), anywhere in the world, while cruising at a continuous 500 knots (576mph/926km/h) and at altitudes up to 50,000ft (15,240m). The medium bomber's all up weight was not to exceed 100,000lb (45,360kg) and when it had 10,000lb (4,536kg) of bombs aboard its still-air range had to be at least 3,350nm (6,210km).

The aircraft was to be capable of carrying up to 20,000lb (9,072kg) of bombs, composed of either two 10,000lb concrete piercing, two 10,000lb HC (high capacity), four 5,000lb (2,268kg) HC or twenty 1,000lb (454kg) MC (medium capacity) iron bombs, twenty 1,000lb incendiary and fragmentation clusters or one 'special' (nuclear) gravity bomb. The aircraft's cruise ceiling had to be 50,000ft (15,240m) and this was to be reached inside two and a half hours from take-off. In fact, the flight plan would involve flying at a constant speed with a gradual climb as the weight decreased due to fuel being burnt off. Defensive armament would not be carried but warning devices would be available for the bomber's crew of two pilots, two navigator/bomb aimer/radar operators and one wireless/warning and protective device operator. The nuclear store, later christened Blue Danube, was of course the most important item on the weapon list. From now on and for many years hence the ability to deliver strategic nuclear weapons over the Soviet Union would be the dominant factor in Western bomber design.

The resulting design competition brought forth six different proposals. They were the AW.56 flying wing project from Armstrong Whitworth, Avro's delta wing Type 698, a fairly conventional design from English Electric, the Handley Page HP.80 (a new design which reused the number), the Short S.B.1 (another flying wing) and a relatively conventional six-engine project from Vickers. Detailed descriptions of all of these proposals are given in another book published by Midland called *British Secret Projects: Jet Bombers Since 1949* but the main elements of Handley Page's May 1947 brochure for the HP.80 were as follows.

Handley Page HP.80

By 1946 the firm of Handley Page based at Cricklewood in north London had built up a strong tradition for supplying bombers to the RAF. The first of these had been the O/100 and O/400 built during World War One but it was the World War Two Halifax that cemented the company's position as a designer and producer of outstanding bombers. This four-engine piston aircraft was manufactured in great numbers and, although never quite eclipsing Avro's Lancaster in the front line (and in the publicity stakes), it was highly successful and also proved to be a most versatile aeroplane.

The new HP.80 project was a complete redesign of the original proposal of 1946 and at 95,000lb (43,092kg) maximum weight (to comply with B.35/46) was actually heavier than the earlier aeroplane. Undoubtedly the biggest feature of this proposal was the wing. Three of the B.35/46 competitors had used advanced wing shapes in the form of a swept wing with no tail or a delta but the HP.80 introduced a new planform to British jet aircraft design called the crescent wing. This had evolved through extensive wind-tunnel research and the resulting combination of sweepback and wing thickness was expected to give a high critical Mach number together with good stalling and stability characteristics, plus low structure weight and freedom from shock-wave formation.

The HP.80's wing had its semi-span divided into three approximately equal parts with the angles of sweepback at ¼ chord set at 48.25°, 37.5° and 26.75° respectively from the centreline of the aircraft to the tip. Its structure consisted of a single spar with concentrated light alloy flanges situated at 40% chord, a torque box with front and rear webs and closely spaced ribs. The skin forward of the spar was made of sheet sandwich construction whilst aft of the spar single skinning was used, and this arrangement was expected to ensure the best possible surface for laminar flow. Wing tip fins and rudders were employed which were structurally integral with the wings, the junction being carefully faired. The wing had leading-edge slats over the outer 50% of its semi-span in conjunction with rear slots at 60% of the chord. The elevons, which occupied 50% of the semi span, had plain round leading edges with balance tabs and there were no mass balances. The flaps extended under the jet engine fairings to the side of the fuselage, the flying controls were power operated and there was complete duplication by two independent systems. There would be no mechanical feedback.

The bomber was to be powered by four Metropolitan-Vickers F.9 axial flow jet engines with, at the time, an assumed thrust of 7,500lb (33.3kN) each, although the Rolls-Royce AJ.65 (later called the Avon) could be installed as an alternative once it had been developed to the same required thrust and specific fuel consumption. These power units were mounted two per wing in separate fireproof compartments that were divided by a spanwise bulk-

head situated between the engine compressor and jet pipe. The wing leading-edge air intakes were adjacent to the root fillet while the jet pipes exhausted over the trailing edge, the inboard pipe facing slightly outboard to keep the exhaust gases from fouling the fuselage side.

The fuselage had a circular cross-section with a maximum diameter of 9ft 10in (3.0m) and was divided into three parts:

1. The front fuselage contained the crew stations, nose wheel and H2S scanner. This was constructed with longitudinal stringers and hoop frames and the aft end terminated in a spherical bulkhead ahead of the wing leading edge. Here, the stressed skin was replaced by tubular bracing members that carried the front fuselage on a series of single-pin joints. The entire crew cabin could be jettisoned by removing these pins. A shallow streamlined blister was provided under the H2S scanner which, together with the nose skin (and the aft end of the rear fuselage), was made of resin-impregnated glass-fibre sandwich material.

2. The fuselage centre section consisted of a structural hoop fairing on top of the wing centre section. On the wing underside a fairing 'skirt' was fitted on each side that extended down to the forward bomb bay doors. These forward doors, actuated separately from the main bomb bay doors, extended back to the wing spar.

3. The rear fuselage was joined to the fuselage centre section by a 'pipe' joint in the plane of the wing spar and to the wings by four steel joint fittings, two per side. This section housed the main bomb bay which had hinged doors that opened by retracting into the sides of the fuselage. The bomb floor was on the same level as the top spar boom and was built up with cross beams skinned on the underside, while the aft part of the bomb bay was made from hoop frames and stringers. A short vertical fin was built integral with the rear fuselage and carried a small swept back horizontal tailplane.

The tailplane was rotatable about a spanwise axis to provide variable incidence and was built in three parts comprising a fixed centre section and movable outer sections. It was built with a single spar, closely spaced ribs and metal skinning. This surface was available to give additional damping in pitch and to provide longitudinal trimming at cruising and climbing speeds without recourse to trimming the elevons. Trimming by elevons alone would impair the retention of laminar flow over the outer part of the wing and increase induced drag. The crew's cabin was small but there was enough space for five crew, it was pressurised and air-conditioned and, as noted above, jettisonable as a unit. There was a prone visual bombing station with an optically flat aiming panel in the nose.

The HP.80's fuselage accommodated all of the specified operational equipment and bomb loads and had enough room for a maximum of twenty-one 1,000lb (454kg) MC bombs. Alternative loads were one 10,000lb (4,534kg)

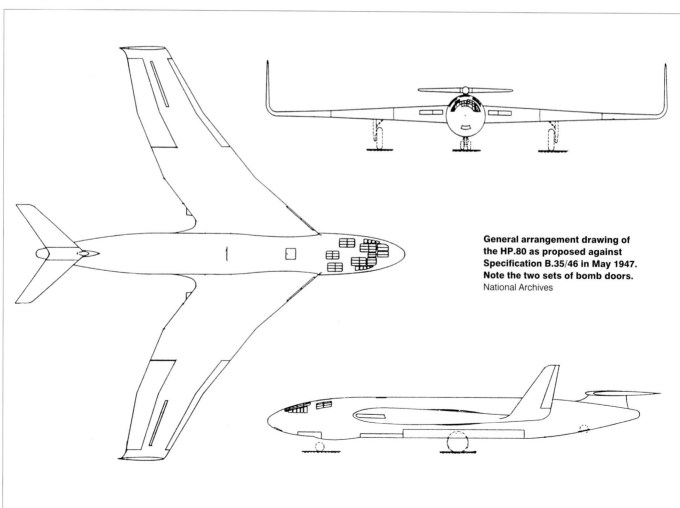

**General arrangement drawing of
the HP.80 as proposed against
Specification B.35/46 in May 1947.
Note the two sets of bomb doors.**
National Archives

'special' (the term used in brochures in those days to describe the nuclear store), two 10,000 lb HC or three 6,000 lb (2,722kg) HC bombs. The normal height of the fuselage was such that the largest bomb could be wheeled into position under the bomb bay without the necessity for pits or other special devices. A total of 3,092gal (14,059lit) of fuel was housed in the wings and another 1,240gal (5,638lit) of auxiliary fuel could be carried in rear fuselage tanks above the bomb bay. Span was 100ft (30.5m), overall length 91ft 6in (27.9m) and overall height 21ft (6.4m). Gross wing area was 2,000ft^2 (186m^2), the thickness/chord ratio at the wing root was 14% and at the tip 8%. There was a tricycle undercarriage with two small wheels on the nose leg and a large single wheel on each main gear. The undercarriage track was 43ft 2in (13.2m).

The estimated performance figures included the required 500 knots (576mph/927km/h) cruise speed at 50,000ft (15,240m), a sea-level rate of climb at maximum all up weight of 6,200ft/min (1,890m/min) and a range when carrying 10,000 lb (4,534kg) of bombs of 3,350nm (6,208km); with 20,000 lb (9,072kg) of bombs aboard the range became 2,140nm (3,965km). The mean cruising height with the 10,000 lb load over a whole sortie was actually 51,000ft (15,545m) and the absolute ceiling after one hour's 'normal flying' with one engine stopped and the other three set at maximum thrust was estimated to be 44,000ft (13,411m).

Theory of the Crescent Wing

Regardless of what type of aeroplane might be under consideration, the efficiency of its performance was primarily dependent on its wing design. In a case like the Victor where long range was important, the design of the wing was in fact paramount. Compared to someone working on an airliner, however, a bomber designer would get an advantage because he had a far less demanding payload to cope with – a passenger fuselage created far more drag than even a nuclear weapon and its associated equipment and services.

The crescent wing was chosen for the HP.80 on performance grounds. The design team realised that no single layout could meet all of the B.35/46's requests for range, load-carrying, high subsonic cruise and high cruising altitude. In general a moderately high aspect ratio would be required with a high angle of sweepback to give the high critical Mach number. However, unfavourable pitching behaviour at the stall would result from the high aspect ratio and high sweep, and tip-stalling problems would become particularly acute. The crescent wing was therefore a working compromise between two methods of overcoming these problems – that is between high sweep with a low aspect ratio, and moderate sweep on a thin wing of reasonably high aspect-ratio. Unlike many compromises, with the crescent this fact was externally quite obvious.

On the crescent wing the relationship between thickness/chord ratio and sweepback was varied progressively along the span to give, approximately, a constant critical Mach number over its entire surface. (The fuselage and tailplane had to be equally well designed so that they matched the wing's critical Mach number.) The HP.80's wings had been given a high degree of sweepback to delay the drag rise due to shock wave formation and yet have a reasonable thickness. The sweepback was at its greatest at the centre and least at the wing tips so that, even with a high sweep angle, the centre section was thick enough and possessed the strength to house the engines and main wheels. Without sweepback the wings would be so thin that the structure weight would be prohibitive and the undercarriage, powerplants and fuel could not be housed inside them. In addition a wing with a large uniform sweepback was expected to be excessively heavy or have poor stalling properties. However, the reduction in sweepback at the tip of the crescent wing had to be limited because of the danger of a loss of aileron effect, but the aileron power at low speeds was actually found to be an improvement over that of the 'straight' swept wing.

The combination of the crescent's leading-edge slats and rear slots would control the

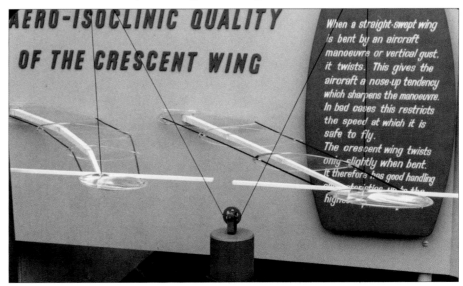

AERO-ISOCLINIC QUALITY OF THE CRESCENT WING

When a straight-swept wing is bent by an aircraft manoeuvre or vertical gust, it twists. This gives the aircraft a nose-up tendency which sharpens the manoeuvre. In bad cases this restricts the speed at which it is safe to fly. The crescent wing twists only slightly when bent. It therefore has good handling characteristics up to the highest...

Below: **Another artist's impression, this time showing the HP.80 as it stood in January 1948 after a conventional tail and single fin had been introduced.** Handley Page

boundary layer on the outer wing so that flow breakdown, which was normally associated with large sweepback, was delayed until the general stalling angle was reached. On a straight wing of equivalent sweepback, leading-edge and rear slots alone would be inadequate to prevent premature tip stalling. Leading-edge slats were chosen in preference to nose flaps because they were a little more effective, had well-known properties and were easier to install. Tests of the crescent wing with and without tip fins had shown that fitting these brought reductions in drag without detriment to the tip stalling properties, so the proposed HP.80 had tip fins and rudders for directional stability and control. Handley Page's interest in a wing which featured a progressive reduction of sweep had begun in 1946, and the determination of the most suitable wing geometry and the pressure distributions across it had involved a considerable volume of calculation and experimental work. Some high-speed tunnel tests had been performed by the Royal Aircraft Establishment (RAE) at Farnborough.

In 1959, Godfrey Lee was interviewed by *Flight* and asked about the development of the crescent wing. His team had studied the three alternative concepts that were available to obtain the necessary lift/drag ratio for this type of bomber, i.e. using a plain thin swept wing with engine pods, a compound sweep (crescent) wing with buried engines, and a tail-less delta with both engines and load buried inside. All three could fulfil the requirements but there were variations in weight and drag which favoured one or the other. However, assuming equal critical Mach numbers, Lee concluded by saying, "The operational heights of the crescent and the delta are both better than that of the podded layout, which suffers from its high wing-loading. This will reduce cruising height and will badly restrict manoeuvrability at altitude." He added, "The take-off and landing performance of the crescent and delta is satisfactory in both cases, and is much better than the podded layout which suffers, again, from its high wing loading." In the end Handley Page chose the crescent, while Avro opted for the delta for its Vulcan.

Godfrey Lee, the man considered to be the 'father' of the Victor, joined Handley Page in 1937 as a stress man. Three years later he succeeded Dr Gustav Lachmann as the head of the Research Department and one of his early tasks was the development of a small swept wing and tail-less research aeroplane driven by two pusher propellers. That was the Manx that has been referred to earlier in this chapter after it received the designation HP.75 and it gave Lee and the team experience in swept wings along with the confidence and knowledge that a swept wing aeroplane could be flown. This, coupled with a considerable amount of information on such wings and also high-speed aerodynamics which Lee acquired in Germany in the winter of 1945/46, enabled the team to begin studies for a swept wing jet bomber: that of course crystallised into the HP.72A/HP.80 projects and then the Victor. (Lee had been a member of a technical team, composed of representatives from both the aircraft industry and Ministry of Aircraft Production, which had visited Germany to study that country's work on swept wing and tail-less aeroplanes.) At the time of the Victor's birth Lee was officially the company's Assistant Chief Designer but many of his colleagues considered him to be the key man, although Lee himself always said it was a team effort. In a distinguished career Godfrey Lee achieved many more successes, and his final design for Handley Page was the small HP.137 regional airliner that flew as the Jetstream. He died in 1988 at the age of 84.

Gustav Lachmann was a German aeronautical engineer and Lee filled his position in the Handley Page design team after he was interned as an enemy alien following the outbreak of World War Two. However, Lachmann was permitted to return to the company and continue his work after the end of hostilities. In fact he stayed with the firm for the rest of his career and contributed much to the Victor's development. Handley Page's chief designer during the Victor's design phase was Reginald Stafford who had replaced George Volkert in this position when the latter retired at the end of the war. Handley Page assembled two teams to solve the complex problems presented by Specification B.35/46 and Stafford had control over both, their staffs working together very closely. However, Stafford himself had little to do on the Victor; he was not a high-speed swept wing expert but he was skilled in picking the right people to do the job that was required. He allowed Lee to lead the HP.80 design effort within the company's aerodynamic group while the airframe and systems design group was led by Charles Joy, another top-class engineer.

Decision Time

On 28th July 1947 a meeting was held at the Ministry of Supply (MoS) to discuss the six B.35/46 proposals and select a winner. The event's official title was Tender Design Conference. It marked the end of several weeks of assessment and was attended by 32 people including experienced RAF personnel now on the Air Staff and a variety of experts from the Ministry and RAE. It was chaired by Stuart Scott-Hall who was the MoS's Director of Technical Development (DTD). However, thanks to the advanced nature of the aerodynamics employed on some of these designs, choosing a winner was far from easy. The discussions regarding the HP.80 and the three more aerodynamically advanced submissions from Armstrong Whitworth, Avro and Shorts raised several points. It was difficult to assess the stability and control of each of the four projects but on general performance they were all much the same. Nevertheless it was essential that the chosen aircraft should have the greatest possible chance of penetrating enemy airspace, even if this meant incurring development risks. Both the Avro and Handley Page projects involved a high technical risk that was not entirely removed by wind-tunnel testing and the HP.80 in particular involved a totally untried wing planform. In fact some felt that Handley Page's claims for the crescent wing were optimistic.

In addition RAE had already declared that there "are important gaps in our present knowledge of stability and control characteristics at the high speeds specified which make it impossible to declare that a particular design will be satisfactory without comprehensive wind-tunnel tests". The Establishment had also estimated that the HP.80's all up weight would be 103,650 lb (47,016kg) rather than Handley Page's brochure figure of 95,000 lb (43,092kg). There were suggestions that if these designs were chosen then flying scale models should be built in parallel with the prototype aircraft. The results from such models should be available at least a year before any full-size prototype was completed, and if they showed that major alterations were needed then these could be incorporated in the full-size machines.

It was declared that the Avro design was the most promising, that Handley Page came second and Armstrong Whitworth third, although there were objections to the latter with its weight and fuel load and the fact that it had less manoeuvrability to take evasive action. The aerodynamic issues were such that the MoS did not feel justified in making a decision on any one design without further wind-tunnel testing but it was agreed that there was a good case for placing two orders for such an impor-

Wind-tunnel models showing some of the design process which turned Handley Page's initial bomber ideas and proposals into the Victor. The last of these still requires some changes before it can match the layout that was flown.
Handley Page Association

A view of what is most likely one of the Avro Vulcan prototypes. Avro

The second Vickers Valiant prototype WB215. Eric Morgan

tant class of aircraft. In the end it was decided that an order should be placed for the Avro 698 and to have a flying model of it designed and built in parallel. The RAE would undertake (with the highest priority) further high-speed tunnel work on the Handley Page crescent wing after which a decision would be made between the HP.80 and AW.56. If the HP.80 was chosen then a model would also be required. (The Armstrong Whitworth project would presumably have been covered by the trials carried out with that company's AW.52 flying-wing research aircraft which had flown for the first time in 1947.)

In due course the Avro 698 was built and flown as the Vulcan and was accompanied by a family of Avro 707 scale-model research aeroplanes. However, such was the level of concern regarding the advanced nature of Avro and Handley Page's aeroplanes with their many aerodynamic unknowns, after the Conference was over a modified version of the more conservative Vickers submission was ordered as an interim design to be in service ahead of these types and cover any delays in their development. This eventually entered service as the Vickers Valiant. Both Vulcan and Valiant have already been covered by titles in Midland Publishing's Aerofax series (*Avro Vulcan: Britain's Famous Delta-Wing V-Bomber* by Phil Butler and Tony Buttler 2007, and *Vickers Valiant: The First of the V-Bombers* by Eric B Morgan 2002).

For over two years and quite separate from the B.35/46 design competition, Short Brothers had been working on a jet-powered medium bomber with a conventional straight wing layout. This had also been ordered in prototype form in early 1947 as an insurance against the more ambitious B.35/46s. Two examples were eventually built. They were given the name Sperrin and the first of them made its maiden flight on 10th August 1951 but the development of the more advanced 'intermediate' Valiant put paid to any ideas of production for this aircraft.

Towards the end of July 1947 Scott-Hall informed Sir Frederick Handley Page that prototypes of his HP.80 would be ordered subject to the requested tunnel testing confirming the theories behind the crescent wing. The design was eventually approved in December 1947 after an Instruction to Proceed had been given on 19th November for both full- and scale-sized aircraft. However, orders were not placed for HP.80 prototypes until April 1949 but a contract was issued to Handley Page in April 1948 to build two 2/5th-scale model HP.88s. This was later sub-contracted to Blackburn Aircraft.

In between times the bomber's appearance changed somewhat. In particular there were concerns regarding the effects of flutter on the tip fins and rudders and so in January 1948 these were removed and a more conventional central fin and rudder replaced them. At the same time the span was increased to 110ft

(33.5m) and the estimated weight went up by another 500 lb (227kg). In June 1948 Lachmann studied a technical report from RAE which prompted him to recommend moving the horizontal tail to the top of the fin to take it away from the jet efflux. The new arrangement was no longer all-moving but had a small fixed section and very large elevators. The new tailplane was also given 15° of dihedral which effectively increased the fin area and there was a bullet-

fairing to cover the structural joints with the fin. As built the tailplane's leading edge sweep was reduced at the elevator joint which itself produced something resembling a crescent. This high-mounted tail arrangement would prove to be a total success from almost every point of view because, except in the extreme case of pitch-up, it was now clear of the jet stream and all of the wing-generated turbulence and airflow breakaway, even in the low-speed stall.

The first Shorts Sperrin prototype was VX158 that made its first flight in August 1951. The Sperrin had straight wings, which aerodynamically put it behind all of the V-types. Short Bros

Had further wind tunnel testing on the HP.80 project's crescent wing proved unsatisfactory then the Armstrong Whitworth AW.56, shown here in model form, may well have been built instead of the Victor. The AW.56 came third in the B.35/46 design competition and was another beautiful design. Ray Williams

V-Bomber Complexity

Before moving to the 'hardware' part of the Victor story it is worth stopping to consider a few of the problems that went into creating the V-Force and its aircraft. (Note: some of this text has previously been published in the February and March 2008 issues of *Aviation News*.)

During World War Two the variety, size and destructive power of RAF bombs grew substantially but that did not affect very much the aircraft that were designed to carry them. These aircraft were still powered by piston engines and that kept their maximum speed and altitude over a target within a relatively limited flight envelope. In due course the Avro Lancaster, the spearhead of Bomber Command, was adapted to carry the heavy earthquake bombs (the 12,000 lb [5,443kg] 'Tallboy' and 22,000 lb [9,979kg] 'Grand Slam') that had been designed by Barnes Wallis, the famous aircraft designer working for Vickers in Surrey. In 1941 Wallis designed a high-altitude bomber (sometimes called the 'Victory Bomber') specifically to carry these bombs and this was one of the first occasions (in Britain at least) where a new aircraft had been proposed exclusively to carry a new type of bomb. To reach the required altitudes the 'Victory' would have needed another new invention, the pressure cabin, which allowed aircrew to fly in much thinner air. This, however, was never fitted on the Lancaster and so the 'Grand Slams' had to be dropped from lower altitudes than had been hoped for at the beginning. The 'Victory'

was never built, but the seeds had been sown.

What provided the water to make them grow were the jet engine and the atom bomb. In due course, after a period of development and maturity which took them into the postwar years, jet engines became capable of supplying sufficient power and performance to propel a bomber at 500 knots (576mph/927km/h) and altitudes up to 50,000ft (15,240m). This would take the aircraft out of the reach of current and future enemy fighters and interceptors and, in addition, if enough fuel was stored it would be possible to reach targets well into enemy territory including the Soviet Union. Such was the power of the atomic bomb it was also now only necessary to carry one, or if possible two, of these weapons (although the early bombs were also very heavy). Not until the arrival of the later and much more powerful hydrogen bomb did the size and weight of nuclear weapons diminish.

The development of Britain's nuclear weapons moved forward relatively quickly and the first detonation of a nuclear device (beneath a retired warship) took place on 3rd October 1952. The codename given to the atomic bomb was Blue Danube and the V-Bombers were designed around this weapon. Blue Danube had a nominal yield of 20 kilotons and was housed inside a casing derived from the wartime 'Tallboy'. The first live drop was made on 11th October 1956 by a Vickers Valiant.

The technical aspects of V-Bomber development also included high-quality navigation aids

A formation of the three V-Bomber types with Victor B.1 XH620 of No 10 Squadron nearest the camera. The others are Vulcan B.1 XH479 and Valiant BK.1 XD826 of No 90 Squadron.
MoD PRB 19750 via Phil Butler

both to allow the aircraft to find its way across enemy territory, and then to pin-point the target with sufficient accuracy. Because of their destructive force one might assume that atom bombs need not be dropped with the exactitude usually required for conventional stores but navigation and accuracy of delivery were in fact very important indeed. If the target (for example a large military complex) was placed on one side of a hill and the nuclear bomb landed on the other side of that hill, the hill's peak could protect much of the target from the destructive shock wave. It is the blast wave which moves over the ground so fast that causes most of the damage, plus the heat generated by the explosion, while the much publicised nuclear fallout (dust and radiation) are really just incredibly nasty by-products. The V-Bomber's navigation aids were a modified version of a World War Two system (H2S) that was more capable than previously but which still used valve technology, so practice and experience were vital for navigators.

As specified the V-Bombers lacked defensive armament and protective armour. Investigations had revealed that carrying defensive weaponry would mean a loss in the bomber's potential speed and altitude and bring the air-

Right and below: **Scale-model testing of the crescent wing was performed by the Handley Page HP.88 research aircraft. The flying shot was taken on 26th July 1951.**
BAE Systems, Brough

Bottom: **This is believed to be the first Victor prototype WB771 flying in its original silver colour scheme.** Handley Page

craft within reach of enemy fighters. Armour was virtually useless in the face of the latest fighter armament. Finally, ensuring that the benefits of the V-type's advanced aerodynamics and higher performance were secured eventually required much more powerful jet engines to be fitted than had been developed thus far. This, on the later Victor Mk.2s and on the Vulcan respectively, resulted in the Rolls-Royce Conway and Bristol Olympus engines, both of which were a vast improvement over what had been available in 1945 and 1946.

Politics

Aircraft design and procurement has always been far more than just technical issues. There is the need for finance to pay for it (and therefore political will) and the industrial capability to produce. In fact the political desire to push ahead with the V-Bombers and the nuclear capability they would give the country was pretty well there from the start, which has not always been the case with military programmes. A key point here, however, was that after Clement Attlee's Labour Government had come to power in mid-1945 America withdrew its support and co-operation with Britain in the development of nuclear weapons. Consequently this move forced the British to go it

The second prototype WB775 roars through the sky to bring a climax to the air display at Farnborough in Hampshire on 11th September 1953. In fact, the aircraft had only made its maiden flight that morning and still lacked the main undercarriage doors. Handley Page

become rather run-down during the late 1940s, and by the early 1950s a considerable expansion was needed to get the V-Bombers and also several new fighter types into production at a sufficient rate. The outbreak of the Korean War in 1950 increased the urgency for acquiring new aeroplanes but it was several years before production lines were turning out aircraft in satisfactory numbers.

Building a V-Bomber was a substantial task in itself. In the 1940s and 1950s fighter and bomber aircraft used a lot of metal in their construction, far more than today where carbon fibre has now taken the place of a good proportion of the previously used light alloy (that is aluminium and sometimes magnesium alloy). The Valiant, Vulcan and Victor were built at a time when light alloy dominated the manufacturing of military aircraft. The age of wooden structures had passed and carbon fibre and other composite materials had still to make their mark. There are those who do not like the phrase 'metal-bashing' but when it comes to parts of a V-Bomber airframe this is actually a very apt description. Each bomber was in effect a huge lump of metal and its manufacture and construction was a complex process.

Underneath the V-Bomber's aluminium skins were very large metal components which in many cases had literally been smashed or squashed into shape. Huge forgings such as the main undercarriage legs would have been completed on heavy plant like the 12,000-ton press at High Duty Alloys (HDA) in Redditch, but the pre-forging operations that were needed to turn cast slab or billet starting stock into rough shapes were essentially the task of a blacksmith – but on a much, much larger scale using heavy hammers and just as highly skilled. When finished, these parts were heat treated to give their optimal properties – a mix of strength, ductility, fatigue and corrosion resistance – and then finish machined in readiness for assembly. For example, on the Victor B Mk.2 the larger intakes for the Conway engines required a new set of machined forgings to be introduced to replace the Mk.1's reinforced plate webs that fitted around the intake opening. These were forged into 3in (7.62cm) thick plate on HDA's 12,000-ton press and varied in size from 6ft x 5ft 9in (183cm x 175cm) to 6ft x 4ft 9in (183cm x 145cm).

Alongside the heavy metal came the vast number of 'fasteners' needed to hold the aircraft together. For example over 500,000 spot-welds were required on each Victor, although

alone both with creating the bomb itself and the means to deliver it.

For a short period after World War Two the Soviet Union was still looked on as an ally. In fact in 1945 a policy was instigated which stated that no war was likely for ten years and no substantial re-equipping would consequently be needed. As a result new equipment for the armed services would be limited but would be designed so that it could still perform its role in ten years' time. Unlike today where new aircraft and weapons are expected to stay in service for many years, back in the 1940s the operational careers of new aircraft were usually pretty short. At the time nobody could have foreseen that the Victor would survive until the 1990s (or that Britain's first jet bomber, the English Electric Canberra, would last well into the new century). The RAF however, or rather the Air Staff which formulated RAF policy, realised that its wartime bomber fleet and the piston-powered unpressurised Avro Lincoln which had succeeded the Lancaster would be made obsolete very quickly by the high performance offered by new jet fighters, regardless of who the enemy might be. The Service's bombers would be unable to run away from defending fighters, and they would be unable to climb to altitudes that took them out of the reach of interceptors.

Jet-powered bombers fitted with pressure cabins and capable of high speeds and altitudes were the solution and it was this developing situation which triggered the drafting of B.35/46. The resulting V-Bombers were classed as medium bombers but in fact they were as big and impressive as the wartime Lancaster which had been categorised as a heavy bomber. (It was the arrival of the enormous American Convair B-36 which first flew in August 1946 that brought something of a redefinition of what constituted a 'heavy'.) In the meantime the Soviet Union's potential as a possible enemy began to grow and this was confirmed when Berlin was sealed off in 1948, a move which led to the Berlin Airlift to keep the German city going. What became known as the Cold War had begun and the need to get new bombers into service was now rather urgent.

Industry and Metal Bashing

The next point to consider is industrial capacity. During the war the manufacturing capability of Britain's aircraft industry had grown beyond all recognition and, in addition, it had specialised in developing fighters and bombers whilst generally leaving other types such as transports to the Americans. Therefore the specialist bomber companies – Avro, Handley Page and Vickers – were in theory well placed to respond to any new requirements for this type of aeroplane. However, thanks to the '10 Year Policy' the industry was allowed to

B Mk.1 Victor XA927 first flew in 1958.
Handley Page

Another B.1 XA936 captured by the publicity camera, flying over a delightful land and cloudscape. Handley Page

When flying towards the camera the Victor presented a most impressive and quite intimidating sight. This shot is dated 1960 but the aircraft is unidentified. Handley Page

many of these went into the panels of honeycomb sandwich within the wing structure. Designing all of these components to fit together, and at the same time making allowances for the stresses and loads they would have to tolerate, was a substantial engineering task.

And then there were the aircraft's aerodynamics. These were analysed in the days before computer-aided design made things so much easier, although wind tunnels were becoming more common which allowed staff to predict with more confidence the behaviour of airflow over new airframes through the use of small models. Nevertheless, a new aircraft shape required masses of mathematical calculations using slide rules and other basic equipment to confirm that it was ready to fly.

A good deal of preparation and planning in other areas was also needed to put the V-Bombers into service. To begin with Bomber Command's airbases would need to be upgraded and updated. For example there was some debate as to how wide the tarmac runways should be. A 1947 Air Staff memo shows that the aircraft designed to B.35/46 would be required to operate from "Standard Heavy Bomber Airfields having runways 50yd (45.7m) wide and perimeter tracks 50ft (15.2m) wide".

It was known that such runways would generally cater for aircraft weighing only about 70,000 lb (31,752kg) and supported on two wheels, yet B.35/46 indicated a maximum weight of up to 100,000 lb (45,360kg). In fact the original proposals from Handley Page, Shorts and Vickers could have been eliminated by elements of their 'airfield characteristics'. The Vickers design for example, with four main

undercarriages and a wheel track 58ft (17.7m) wide, would have its outer legs running outside the perimeter track.

Altogether there had to be an enormous volume of testing of airframe and equipment and training for air and ground crew to get the V-Force operational, and this on aircraft that were far more advanced and complex than anything that the RAF had seen before. Plans had to

be made for operating these bombers with the most effectiveness, how to deal with targets so far away and how to handle their defences. After the V-Bombers had entered service these plans, which at the time were in part just theory, could be tried out and modified with experience.

So the scene is set. A lot of big steps and big decisions had to be taken to bring the V-Bombers into existence – if you like, the heavy engineering of aircraft construction went well beyond what had been achieved prior to 1945. From now on the nuclear bomb would be the driving force behind bomber development, and the aircraft themselves would be configured as nuclear delivery systems. Conventional weaponry was still important of course, but nuclear was the key to strategic dominance. OR.229 and B.35/46 visualised a high-speed, high-altitude, unarmed bomber built around the atomic bomb, and at this moment such a type having the greatest possible chance of penetrating enemy airspace was considered vital to the nation's defence. When the resulting proposals from industry were assessed it was felt that there should be no hesitation proceeding with the most promising designs on offer, and the winning Victor and Vulcan proved aerodynamically to be very advanced indeed. The arrival of nuclear weapons changed the function of the bomber entirely – the size and weight of the bomb became secondary to the means of ensuring its delivery.

Victor on approach – a photo taken in the 1970s, which compares the aircraft in dirty condition to the equivalent clean state in the 1960 shot.
Handley Page

The crescent wing is shown to superb effect by this Victor B Mk.2 banking towards a sunset for the benefit of the official cameraman.
Handley Page

Chapter Two

Test Beds, Protoypes and Mark 1s

When Handley Page's B.35/46 brochure was first submitted, work had already commenced on the design of a towed ¼-scale glider called the HP.87, which was to be used to check the design's low-speed characteristics in flight. In fact this project was abandoned and eventually replaced by the HP.88 scale model research aircraft requested by the Ministry and mentioned briefly in Chapter One. At the time of writing, the Handley Page Association and National Archives hold nothing in regard to the HP.87 project and so no description of the aeroplane can be given.

Aerodynamic Airframe

On 6th April 1948 a contract was placed with Handley Page to construct two 2/5th-scale model single-seat aeroplanes which were to be used to test the aerodynamics of the crescent wing. The type was designated HP.88 but the work was sub-contracted to General Aircraft at Feltham where it was designated GAL.63. At the start of 1948 however, that company had been acquired by Blackburn and so the project

was moved up to Brough where it received another designation, Y.B.2. Handley Page completed the aerodynamic work on the HP.88/Y.B.2 but it was left to Blackburn and General Aircraft to work out the detail design for the structure, full authorisation to do so being given by Handley Page to the Brough facility in November 1948.

The two aeroplanes received the serial numbers VX330 and VX337 and were built around Specification E.6/48, which was dated 12th April 1948 and issued to Handley Page on the 16th. However, the second machine was cancelled on 14th October 1949 as an economy measure. To save time and money E.6/48 stated that the HP.88 would basically be formed using a similar fuselage to the existing Supermarine Type 510 research aircraft (built to E.41/46) attached to "a 0.4 linear scale Handley Page B.35/46 wing and all-moving tailplane". As such it did not fully represent the HP.80 bomber because that aircraft had a high wing position whereas the HP.88's wing was set low down. In due course (as described

The first Handley Page HP.80 prototype WB771.
Handley Page Association

shortly) the bomber's crescent wing was subsequently modified to push its critical Mach number up to 0.86 but this occurred after the HP.88's wing had been constructed and in doing so made the test aircraft's version less representative of the full-size job. Besides having a crescent wing built to the original proportions, the HP.88's tail was placed high on the fin but not right at the top like the bomber. There was also no separate elevator hinged to the tailplane as had since been adopted for the HP.80, the HP.88's pitch being controlled by varying the tailplane incidence – the 'all-moving' tail. Finally the HP.88's airbrakes, mounted on the sides of the mid to rear fuselage, were placed further forward than the tail fuselage fittings of the HP.80.

The HP.88 would have a pressure cabin and was required "to demonstrate the stability and control of the full-scale aircraft over the full-scale speed range, its low speed handling and

Left: **A well-known but nevertheless good detailed side view of the sole HP.88 VX330.** BAE Systems, Brough

Below and opposite page: **A series of walk-around images of the HP.88 taken at Carnaby in June 1951, with the Martin-Baker seat in place. Note the deployed airbrakes and flying surfaces, and how thick the inner wing was compared to the outer surfaces.** Henry Matthews

the drag characteristics of its wing". It had to satisfy the speed and altitude requirements of B.35/46 (500 knots [926km/h] at 50,000ft [15,240m]), sufficient fuel was to be available to allow for half an hour's cruising at 50,000ft and the aircraft would also use the same single Rolls-Royce Nene 2 turbojet installation as fitted in the 510. The Type 510 was a swept-wing development of Supermarine's straight-wing Attacker jet fighter and had made its first flight in late 1948. As such its fuselage was adapted to take a swept wing but it is probably best to describe the HP.88's fuselage as an 'Attacker type'. Although it was assembled by Blackburn, Supermarine's input with its fuselage contribution gained the scale model aircraft yet another designation from that company, Type 521. In the end there were more designations than airframes ordered, which of course gives aviation authors plenty to write about.

The Type 521 fuselage was delivered from Supermarine's Hursley Park facility in late November 1950, and not without difficulty because a small amount of damage was suffered while it was being offloaded from a 'Queen Mary' trailer. This was soon fixed however, and VX330 was completed at Brough in January 1951. This was also the venue for its first taxi runs which were performed between 20th and 25th February, before the HP.88 had been painted in a splendid royal blue paint scheme. The aircraft was photographed on the ground both before and after the paint was applied (and without its Martin-Baker ejection seat installed) but sadly there are no known colour photos of the HP.88. Had it survived long enough to get to that year's Farnborough Show then one assumes some official colour images would have been made for the event.

On 14th June the aircraft was moved by road to Carnaby, a former wartime Bomber Command emergency landing strip near Bridlington which had been built for damaged aircraft to use if they could not get back to base. This airfield had a 3,000yd (2,745m) runway plus generous undershoot and overshoot extensions which in fact pushed the available 'runway' length up to 7,000yd (6,400m), far more than the 1,430yd (1,310m) on hand at Brough. Carnaby was still an active airfield serving as a satellite for an Advanced Flying School flying Gloster Meteors. It was here, after it had been reassembled, that the HP.88 resumed its preliminary taxi trials on 20th June.

On the following day, the HP.88 made its maiden flight. The pilot was Gartrell 'Sailor' Parker, Blackburn's chief test pilot, and the trip involved just a circuit and landing and lasted barely five minutes. It was realised that the rate at which the rudder could be applied by the powered controls was too slow. As a result the power unit was now by-passed to give a direct coupling between the rudder bar and rudder in order to allow the control surface to be applied more quickly. The ailerons and tailplane incidence however did continue to be operated by sideways and fore and aft operation of the control column, through the medium of the powered controls.

It was 7th July before the aircraft flew again, this time for half an hour. Parker found that the rudder control, although now heavy, had improved because it could now be applied sufficiently quickly and was effective for preventing swings during take-off. However, when the HP.88's speed reached 265mph (426km/h) it became over-sensitive to control in the pitching plane. Any disturbance, a gust for example, would set the aircraft pitching and attempts to correct this by the application of control actually made the condition worse. If the controls were held firmly or released (which with the powered system was the same as being clamped) the disturbance would damp out. A flight made on 25th July showed that above 295mph (475km/h) the aircraft was extremely difficult to control. After he had completed five

flights Parker said of the pitching oscillation, "The impression is that it could very easily get completely out of control, and is very similar to the feeling in a tail-less aircraft of being balanced on a knife edge."

In an effort to cure the problem angle pieces were added by stages to both the upper and lower surfaces of the trailing edges of the tailplane – these were the last major alterations made to the aircraft. By Flight 12 Parker could report that he was now able to stop the pitching, once it had started, except when the speed was increased to over 426mph (685km/h). He added, "It cannot be too strongly emphasised that there is a very definite impression that the pitching could get completely out of hand, since the effect of loading the 'tailevator' with angle is to increase the speed at which oversensitivity occurs. With an increase in speed there is an increase in the frequency of pitch." By Flight 20 (on 5th August) VX330's control was now satisfactory at speeds up to about 450 knots (518mph/833km/h) or Mach 0.82, at which point it was again becoming sensitive. Any pitching oscillation could be damped out after just two cycles if the pilot exerted a constant back pressure on the stick but as an interim measure Blackburn decided not to raise the limiting speed above 518mph (833km/h) for heights below 20,000ft (6,096m).

Several more flights were made from Carnaby both by Parker and by Douglas Broomfield DFM, who in September 1948 had been engaged as the assistant to Handley Page's chief test pilot Hedley Hazelden. On 23rd August VX330 was ferried to Stansted Airfield in Essex by Broomfield. The trip was the aircraft's 27th flight and this move was intended to get the HP.88 working on a flight test programme issued by Handley Page's chief designer to prepare a display routine for the forthcoming SBAC Show at Farnborough. The first flight made at Stansted from 16.50 hours on 26th August 1951 formed part of this programme but after just fourteen minutes VX330 crashed and was destroyed. The tests were intended to include flights up to a Mach number not greater than 0.85, and speeds not exceeding 550 knots (633mph/1,018km/h). (At sea level 550 knots Indicated Air Speed is equal to Mach 0.83. The authors cannot confirm if the interim speed restriction had been removed by the time of this final flight.)

Another nose view of VX330 which here shows the aircraft's drooped outer leading edges. Henry Matthews

One of the relatively few known air-to-air photographs of the HP.88. This was taken on 26th July 1951 during a manufacturer's test flight. BAE Systems, Brough

Possibly the only air-to-air picture taken showing the underside of the HP.88 research aircraft. The fairings extending aft of the inner wing trailing edges covered the aeroplane's Fowler flap actuators. Henry Matthews

After a short period of flying Broomfield informed the development engineer by R/T that some adjustments which had been carried out before the flight had proved satisfactory, and he confirmed that he had completed his flying programme. He then requested permission from Air Traffic Control to make a low run over the airfield runway. This was granted and at 17.04 VX330 approached in a shallow dive and at a speed estimated by observers to be "moderately high". Levelling out at approximately 300ft (91m), and shortly before reaching Runway 23, the aircraft was seen to begin pitching. After a second or third oscillation it assumed a violently nose-up attitude and was seen to break into pieces before Broomfield could get clear. His body was found in his ejection seat and the wreckage was strewn over a considerable area. A few small pieces also fell in fields on the north-east side of the airfield. The weather had no bearing on the accident – visibility was 15 miles (24km) with 1/8th cloud at 2,500ft (762m) and there was a 20mph (31km/h) surface wind.

VX330's total flying time amounted to thirteen hours and twenty-nine minutes, of which Broomfield had contributed one hour and fifty-one minutes in five flights. His total jet aircraft experience was about twenty-five hours in over three thousand hours of flying. The report from the Accidents Investigation Branch of the Ministry of Civil Aviation which detailed this loss (Service Accident Report No S2539) is dated 12th June 1952 and credited to Air Commodore Vernon Brown, Chief Inspector of Accidents. The first items in the wreckage trail came from the fuselage engine bay, the foremost point of which was frame 14 a little behind the wing trailing edge. Proceeding along the trail, the first major components to be found were the tail unit attached to the tail bay and fuselage frames 14 to 17. There was no evidence of a pre-crash defect or failure in any of the engine parts. It was thought that the primary failure had occurred in the region of frame 14. An analysis of the 'VG' flight recording equipment carried by this aircraft in the root of the port wing showed traces at +12g and -7g at 525mph (845km/h), and again at +7g and -5g at 475mph (764km/h).

A meeting had been held at the Ministry of Supply on 27th February 1952 to discuss the accident. No explanation could be offered as to what was the precise effect of the progressive addition of angle pieces to the trailing-edge of the irreversible power-operated tailplane but it was agreed that flight tests had shown that these additions had delayed the onset of extreme sensitivity until a higher speed was reached, when it again became apparent. RAE Farnborough was asked to undertake wind tunnel tests on an all-moving tailplane with trailing-edge pieces added. No definite cause for the accident was agreed, but S2539 gave the opinion that it was "associated with the violent oscillations in the pitching plane observed by witnesses and recorded by the vg recorder carried by the aircraft". These oscillations at low altitude resulted in accelerations beyond the Design Ultimate Factor (the maximum load that a structure was designed to withstand without breaking) and the consequent failure of the fuselage structure at about frame 14. Type records for the HP.88 showed that frame 14 was indeed the critical point and the Ultimate Factor here was 8.2g. The precise reason for the oscillations was not determined.

On 16th July A. E. Woodward-Nutt, the Principal Director of Research and Development (Aircraft) (PDRD[A]) at the MoS, wrote that the cause of the accident was not known precisely but that there were three likely possibilities:

1. Over-sensitive pitching control with a simple spring feel control allied to the small aerodynamic damping of this aircraft.
2. Interaction between the swinging bob-weight 'g' restrictor (of a different type to the HP.80) and the remainder of the power system.
3. The power system itself (which again was different to the HP.80).

Over half a century later it is understood that inertial coupling between the all-moving tail and the powered controls was the reason for the massive load on the airframe which brought about the HP.88's destruction. Fortunately for

The mass balances for the ailerons on the HP.88's outer wings appeared as small swept forward 'finlets'. Henry Matthews

The HP.88's last moments. The picture shows VX330 just after the fuselage had failed in the region of the engine bay, and the engine itself appears to be the object floating ahead of the forward fuselage. Although at this instant the wings were still attached, it was established from an examination of the wreckage that these also failed while the aircraft was still in the air but the wing failure was secondary to the fuselage failure. Vapour or smoke appears to be streaming from the aft portion. National Archives AVIA 54-121

the bomber programme, these items were not the same as those used in the HP.80, so there were no delays.

Although it had already flown at this speed at altitude, that final run appears to have been the fastest that the HP.88 reached at low level. Only twenty-eight flights had been made and little was learnt from the testing that was completed – in fact, as noted above, the HP.88 was by this time different in many ways to the HP.80 prototypes and it seems unlikely that much benefit would have accrued. Interestingly, by the time of the crash pictures of the aircraft had been published in *Flight* magazine but they had not apparently been supplied to national newspapers. Consequently, the issues published on 27th August 1951 ran headlines reporting the crash of a "Secret Jet". The HP.88 was not replaced since, by now, the crescent wing was regarded as having been proved and the construction of the prototype HP.80s was under way. Broomfield had become another of the many test pilots to be killed during the 1940s and 1950s as the frontiers of aviation moved ever forward. Fortunately publications like this help to ensure that he and his colleagues are not forgotten.

Engine Test Bed

Handley Page's test pilot for the HP.80's first flight was to be Sqn Ldr Hedley Hazelden who had a strong background in flying bomber and heavy aircraft types. He first gained this reputation while serving with Bomber Command during World War Two, before graduating from the Empire Test Pilots School (ETPS) in 1943 on what was in fact the first course to be run at the school. He then flew plenty of heavy bomber and civil types at Boscombe Down before, in April 1947, joining the civil sector himself as an employee of Handley Page. His first tasks were to test examples of the piston-powered Hermes airliner and Hastings transport but he never flew in the scale model HP.88 because quite simply he was too large to fit comfortably inside that aeroplane's small cockpit.

A second trials aircraft took part in the back-up programmes for the HP.80 Victor. This was Handley Page Hastings military transport TE583, in fact the second Hastings prototype, now fitted with a pair of Armstrong Siddeley Sapphire jet engines in its outer wing nacelles instead of the original Bristol Hercules radial piston units. One reason for this move was that Hedley Hazelden had very little experience of

flying jet aircraft and knew that he needed some, and quite obviously a Sapphire-powered type would be the most desirable. Also, experience with the engine's behaviour would be valuable to the designers and at the time there were few aeroplanes available with a Sapphire powerplant, so kitting out a Hastings was an obvious move for Handley Page to take.

TE583 arrived at the manufacturer's Radlett aerodrome on 14th June 1949 to begin its conversion to the new powerplant. The first flight with Sapphire Sa.2s installed in the outer nacelles was made on 13th November 1950, and on 30th May 1951 TE583 joined the National Gas Turbine Establishment (NGTE) at Bitteswell for trials work. The aircraft flew with this mixed Hercules/Sapphire powerplant well into 1952 and then, after being converted back to standard configuration, it assisted the Victor programme further as a trials aircraft for developments with the bomber's crew escape arrangements. Hazelden once flew TE583 at a speed of 196mph (315km/h) with just the one Sapphire running. Later he was able to gain experience of the Sapphire at higher speeds in WD933, an English Electric B Mk.2 Canberra bomber which had these engines installed in August 1951.

As first proposed the HP.80 was to have been fitted with four Metropolitan-Vickers F.9 axial flow jet engines. In fact the prototypes and Mk.1 production did use this powerplant but this was after the F.9 had become the Armstrong Siddeley Sapphire. Metropolitan-Vickers had been the original designer of the F.9, but in 1947 the development programme was taken over by Armstrong Siddeley Motors at Coventry. When the Sapphire was taken off the Secret List it was the world's most powerful jet engine, but in Great Britain it was never able to push the Rolls-Royce Avon (used in the Vickers Valiant) away from the number one spot.

Revised Requirements

In the meantime work proceeded on the design and construction of the first HP.80s. The order for two prototypes was placed on 8th April 1949 and the Mock-Up Conference for the project was held during the following December. Prior to that some redesign had been necessary to the crescent wing after high-speed tunnel testing at RAE had revealed that above Mach 0.8 the increase in drag was too great. This rise in drag needed to occur above the wing's design cruise speed (0.86) and the problem here was that the thickness/chord ratio at the tip was too high. As a result the designers reduced the outer wing's thickness down to 6% from the original 8%. However, another problem surfaced when it was realised that the wing root

The 'Sapphire Hastings' TE583 photographed just after the installation of its jet engines in very smooth and streamlined nacelles. They make an interesting comparison to the Hercules piston engines retained in the inboard nacelles.
Handley Page Association

Progress with the manufacture of prototype WB771's fuselage had reached this stage by January 1952. Handley Page Association

By March 1952 WB771 was beginning to resemble a Victor. The sign by the door says "No unauthorised person allowed in this aircraft". Handley Page Association

section needed to be thicker to provide enough space to house the engines and fuel. To compensate for this, and the increased taper ratio that came with it, Lee and his design team had to increase the outer wing chord by 20%.

The modifications worked – any instability that the revised wing thickness brought with it was balanced by the additional chord – and tunnel tests indicated that the aircraft would stall in a satisfactory manner. However, the changes to the wing meant that the crescent's outer kink was now further inboard, and it was these alterations that made the HP.88's version of the crescent no longer representative of the full-size wing. On the HP.80 and Victor B Mk.1 the thickness/chord ratio was 16% at the root, 10% at the first kink, 8% at the second kink and 6% at the wing tip.

In July 1952 Handley Page and the Ministry of Supply estimated that the aircraft's basic range could be extended from 3,350nm to 5,000nm (6,210km to 9,265km) for a loss of just 200ft to 300ft (61m to 91m) in height over the target. This was subsequently accepted by the Air Staff, and the updated Issue 3 of OR.229 and a new Specification B.128P were completed on 25th September 1952 to embrace these changes. Additions for reconnaissance and flight refuelling were made in 1953. B.128P proved to be the production specification for the Victor B Mk.1 and requested the following:

1. The original basic requirement laid down in B.35/46 and OR.229 (a still-air range of 3,350nm [6,210km] when cruising at a speed of 500 knots [576mph/927km/h] at a minimum height of 50,000ft [15,240m] with a 10,000 lb [4,536kg] bomb load) was retained, but the increased range of 5,000nm (9,265km) with the same load was now requested. This was to be achieved without appreciably penalising the performance of the basic aircraft or adding any weight to the permanent structure. External tanks could be used to achieve the additional range.

2. The aircraft was required to fulfil the strategic medium bomber role by delivering the 10,000 lb (4,536kg) bomb by night but, should the need arise, it was also to be capable of supplementing the tactical bomber force by delivering high explosive bombs by night and possibly by day. The bomb-carrying requirement was eventually expanded to cover the maximum number of 1,000 lb (454kg) bombs which could be carried over a range of 1,200nm (2,225km), again without appreciable penalty to the basic aeroplane.

3. The highest possible degree of manoeuvrability was to be provided, particularly at high altitude.

4. The aircraft had to be capable of cruising at maximum continuous cruising power at heights between 35,000ft (10,668m) and 50,000ft (15,240m). In the interests of saving structure weight a speed restriction below 25,000ft (7,620m) was agreed with the Air Staff for the prototype.

5. The aircraft should be able to fulfil the reconnaissance role by day or night. In 1954 it was confirmed that PR (day and night) conversion packages would enable Handley Page's aircraft to be switched between its bomber and PR roles at short notice. This would not necessarily apply to all production aircraft but it was required for the early production batches. (In fact, apart from Mk.1 XA920, which served as a trials aircraft, all of the reconnaissance Victors were converted Mk.2s.)

6. Every aircraft had to be capable of a simple conversion to either receive or transfer fuel in flight. Fixed fittings were to be built into all production aircraft and conversion sets supplied to special order. In addition to their use in the V-Bomber Force, by 1954 both the Victor and Avro Vulcan were being envisaged as tankers for a new breed of bombers and PR projects that were currently being studied.

The jettisonable nose cabin was also deleted at this time and, in addition, the new document stated that the aircraft was now required in service in 1955, a target which in fact would not be achieved. Right from the time of the submission of the B.35/46 brochure it had been intended to make the HP.80's nose cabin jettisonable as a complete unit. In an emergency the crew's cabin would be detached from the rest of the aircraft, and in the original brochure all five crew members would then escape using ejection seats. However, by 1952 it was becoming evident that the technical difficulties involved in producing a jettisonable cabin could not be resolved within the timescale available for the development of the aircraft. Therefore in November 1952 the concept was abandoned.

In the HP.80 and production Victors (and also in the Valiant and Vulcan) only the pilots were to be given ejection seats. As a result Martin-Baker, the company which has designed so many ejection seats for the RAF since the 1940s, built a special rig to demonstrate a method for ejecting the three rear crew members out of a stricken V-Bomber. Because the cabin was pressurised it was not possible for each man to have his own escape hatch, so Martin-Baker decided that the chaps at the back would use a single, central hatch. To avoid collisions a command system was to be employed that automatically sequenced the departure of each rear crewman in the shortest possible time. Once the central occupant had left, the crew members seated outside his position would in turn be canted sideways into the centre position to leave through the same hatchway. A nose section from a scrapped Avro Vulcan was used by Martin-Baker to test

Part of WB771 being ferried from Radlett to Boscombe Down in May 1952.
Handley Page Association

this arrangement; it worked well and was demonstrated to the RAF and the Ministry. However, the latter decided against the idea and for the rest of their lives the V-Bombers never had rear crew ejection seats. This has always been a most controversial decision and lives were lost because of it.

After the naming of the Vickers Valiant and Avro Vulcan jet bombers, the Air Council continued the trend for 'V' names by announcing, at around the time the HP.80 made its first flight, that Handley Page's new bomber would be called the Victor. The construction of the first HP.80 prototype took place in Handley Page's new Park Street Experimental Shop at Radlett. Parts also came from the firm's Cricklewood factory and, in addition, sub-assemblies such as the ailerons, elevators, rudder and outer

flaps were forthcoming from Handley Page's Woodley facility.

In May 1952 the airframe was transported in pieces by road to Boscombe Down because, at the time, Radlett's runway was considered to be too short to provide a sufficient safety margin. The fuselage was covered in a huge piece of white canvas and marked GELEYPANDHY SOUTHAMPTON to suggest that this was a new boat hull on its way to the coast. The motorcycle police escort might have suggested it was something a bit more important however, and anyone who was good at solving anagrams might soon have spotted the name of the parent company (with a 'Y' replacing one of the 'A's). It took several journeys to get the various sub-assemblies to A&AEE's airfield, and then the time taken to reassemble the air-

craft and prepare it for flight was badly hampered by a fire on 19th September. This occurred in the hydraulic system at the rear end of the fuselage and Eddie Eyles, an electrician working on the airframe, was tragically killed. The repairs took some time, particularly from having to replace the fin because the base of the original had been damaged by the flames. Nevertheless, on 22nd December fast taxi trials were made along the Boscombe runway.

Flight Testing
The first flight of prototype HP.80 WB771, of seventeen minutes' duration, took place from Boscombe Down on 24th December 1952. Sqn Ldr Hazelden was accompanied on the trip by test observer Ian Bennett. Prior to releasing the brakes, the engines were run up to 7,000rpm, and then to 7,500rpm for the take-off and climb at 121mph (195km/h). The flaps and undercarriage were left extended during the entire flight, while iron ballast had to be carried in the empty radar bay beneath the flight deck to offset the discovery that the centre of gravity was too far aft. (The solution to this CofG problem was to lengthen the forward fuselage of production aeroplanes.) The trip triggered the start of a period of intensive development flying, which ran in conjunction with a full programme of strength testing using full-sized components.

WB771 completed fourteen handling flights from Boscombe before returning to Radlett on 25th February 1953, the runway at Handley Page's airfield having in the meantime been

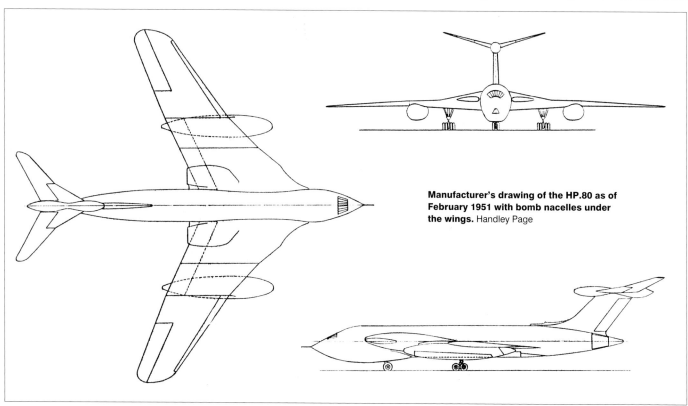

Manufacturer's drawing of the HP.80 as of February 1951 with bomb nacelles under the wings. Handley Page

The first Handley Page HP.80 Victor prototype WB771 photographed when about to begin a test flight, probably in the late spring of 1953. It still has its original silver-grey finish. Handley Page Association

One of the first photographs of WB771 to be released to the press was this shot taken at Boscombe Down, possibly just before its first flight on Christmas Eve 1952. The photo was released on 27th December. Phil Butler

Rear fuselage detail of WB771 in another Boscombe Down view. Phil Butler

extended to 7,000ft (2,134m) to permit production Victors to make their test flights from the factory. On 15th July the prototype made a semi-public appearance when it took part in a flypast during the Coronation Review at RAF Odiham. Overall the flight testing programme proceeded pretty smoothly until the last day of the year when, while making an approach to land, WB771 lost an inboard leading edge flap, although the crew were unaware that this had happened until after they had landed. Hazelden had experienced the start of a roll but thought this was a problem with the flap actuator – not that the entire assembly had departed the aircraft.

It was also found that the prototype was facilitated to a remarkable degree by its ability to land itself off a correct approach with no movement of the elevators, trimmers or throttles. This was done regularly during trials with WB771 and the capability arose from the combination of the swept crescent wing and a high tail. Ground effect started at about 50ft (15m) and caused the aircraft to round out into a landing attitude and to hold this attitude just above the runway while the speed fell off. After touching down on the main wheels the pilot would close his throttle and runway reaction would then provide a nose-down movement that reduced incidence and allowed the aircraft to settle firmly on the runway. As long as the aircraft was lined up accurately, it would not require flareout action by the pilot when it entered the ground effect cushion during the final stages of the approach. The high tail position meant that this flying surface was kept well clear of the ground and consequently the tail downwash was not destroyed just before touchdown by the ground's close proximity. Normally when that happened there was a nose-down moment but here the tail retained its full authority in keeping the nose up until the machine touched the runway. In fact the designers had suggested that the aeroplane would be able to do this before it flew. On production Victors the height of the fin and rudder were reduced and that pretty well eliminated this most unusual capability.

During the winter of 1953/54 flights at the higher end of the speed range appeared to show great potential. A Handley Page report written in January 1954 noted that WB771's rate of roll at low altitude, with the undercarriage and flaps raised and the aircraft travelling at between 184mph and 190mph (296km/h and 306km/h) EAS, was 30°/sec. Another produced in July reported how flight tests had shown that the requirements of Specification B.128P could be met as follows:

1. At the normal take-off weight of 160,000 lb (72,576kg), and with a mean cruising speed of 500 knots (576mph/926km/h), the still air range was 4,850nm (8,982km) when dropping a 10,000 lb (4,536kg) bomb from 50,800ft (15,484m).
2. Carrying the same bomb load at the overload weight of 190,000 lb (86,184kg), the range was 6,170nm (11,427km) at a mean cruising height of 50,200ft (15,300m).
3. In level flight a corrected Mach number of 0.930 had been registered at 46,500ft (14,173m), and for a short period WB771 had flown at Mach 0.985.
4. The prototype had been subjected to manoeuvres at height. Accelerations of 2g were applied at 46,500ft (14,173m) at a Mach number of 0.93 and the aircraft had behaved normally.
5. After taking off at a weight of 160,000 lb (72,576kg), 45,000ft (13,716m) was reached in twenty-three minutes using climb power.

Between February and June WB771 was grounded for a major inspection to be carried out and to receive minor modifications. Then tragically, on 14th July the first HP.80 Victor was lost when it crashed at the College of Aeronautics aerodrome at Cranfield in Bedfordshire.

chief flight test observer), Bruce Heithersay (flight observer) and Albert Cook (flight observer). Everything happened so quickly that the crew would have known nothing. The similarity of these events to the loss of the HP.88 must have been horrifying to all, although this was not a fuselage failure in the form that had stricken the scale model aeroplane.

Ecclestone had flown with Bomber Command in 1944; he spent periods with one of the Bomber Defence Training Flights which were attached to many Bomber Command training and conversion units, and afterwards the Central Bomber Establishment at Marham. He then passed through the ETPS test pilots' course. After that for over two years he had been with the Aerodynamics Flight at RAE Farnborough where he worked in the field of stability and transonic flight. When he died he had been with Handley Page for less than a month. Bennett had been with the company since 1946 and had much to do with the development of the Hastings and Hermes. He had also gone on WB771's first flight. Both Heithersay, an Australian who had previously worked with Commonwealth Aircraft in Melbourne, and Cook, who had earlier worked with Gloster Aircraft, had joined Handley Page at the same time in 1953.

The next day the remains of WB771 were removed to Farnborough for examination and the reason for the tailplane breaking off was eventually determined to be the failure of the three attachment bolts used to keep it in place. It was flutter on the tailplane that led to the formation of cracks around these bolts, and on later aircraft the fittings were modified by the addition of a fourth bolt and by the substitution of sandwich skin instead of the original plain sheet to cope with the stresses experienced by the fin and tail. To back this up a full programme

At the time WB771 was performing a set of low-level passes at speed across the airfield so that some ground-based camera equipment could be used to measure its ground speed accurately. Each pass was to be made at a higher air speed than the previous one and this in turn would have allowed the Position Error on the aircraft's pitot heads to be determined. The circuits had to be made at low level (at about 100ft [30.5m]) and Cranfield was chosen as the venue because it was away from large populated areas. According to one report at the time,

as the Victor approached the airfield boundary on its third run it was seen to make a slight dive, recover and then dive into the ground. In fact the tailplane and elevators had parted from the airframe and risen above the flight path and this resulted in an immediate and total loss of control. The remainder of the aircraft went straight into the ground at full power, striking the intersection of the two runways. Disintegration was complete and killed all of the occupants: Flt Lt Ronald Ecclestone DFC, AFC (Handley Page's assistant test pilot), Ian Bennett (the company's

Top: **A great shot for modellers. WB771 again at the 1953 Farnborough Show reveals underside detail for its distinctive black, red and silver finish, its wing shape and serial numbers.**
Phil Butler

Centre: **WB771 seen taxying at Farnborough.**
Handley Page

Bottom: **Film stills from the Position Error cameras at Cranfield that show the last moments of WB771. These were recovered from a waste paper bin at Radlett.** Ken Nevinson

of flutter analysis was carried out using the second Victor prototype.

The first prototype had completed just over eighty-six hours of flying and its loss undoubtedly delayed the Victor trials programme. The flight programme was already well behind schedule, due largely to mechanical troubles with the nose-flap actuators and the need to replace some of the wing-structure material (below). For these reasons a full flight test programme had still to be agreed with Handley Page but the flying achieved to date had shown no serious aerodynamic problems. Also, as noted, just prior to the accident WB771 had shown great promise by flying at Mach 0.98 and higher without any handling or buffet troubles. The powered flying controls, with 'q' feel, had also proved highly satisfactory. The only modification required to date had been an increase in the rate of aileron application to improve their control in turbulence.

WB771 had originally been fitted with four Armstrong Siddeley Sapphire 3 jets, each giving 7,900 lb (35.1kN) of thrust at sea level but before its loss Sapphire 6s had been installed.

By February 1951, well before the first flight had taken place, developments of the Sapphire were expected to increase the thrust to 9,700 lb (43.1kN) without increasing the specific fuel consumption and without having to make important changes to the installation. At that stage the designers had also made space provision to fit the alternative Rolls-Royce Avon and Conway and the Bristol Olympus. By the

end of 1953 WB771's engines had been cleared for 8,300 lb (36.9kN).

The second prototype WB775 was fitted with Sapphire Sa.6 engines rated at 7,960 lb (35.4kN) static thrust but the aircraft was later re-engined with Sa.7 (Mk.202) engines, the version used by early production Victors. When fully developed the Mk.202 was at this point expected to be rated at 11,000 lb (48.9kN)

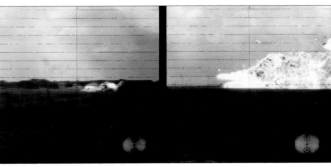

The second Victor prototype WB775 about to take off for its display at Farnborough on 9th September 1955. When first flown it was painted in the same black and silver-grey scheme as WB771 but for the 1955 Farnborough WB775 was painted overall in PR blue. Phil Butler

static thrust but, due to certain adverse features revealed during development testing, the six engines earmarked for the prototype and the first eighteen units for production aircraft were accepted initially at a rating of approximately 10,200 lb (45.3kN). At this time development was proceeding to improve the compressor throughput, the gas distribution in the combustion chamber, the blade characteristics and the cooling of the turbine, and it was hoped that these improvements would be cleared for production engines from April 1955. Further planned improvements were the Sapphire Sa.8 (an Sa.7 with an air-cooled turbine), the Sa.9 (Sa.7 with an extra compressor stage) and the Sa.10 (Sa.7 with both modifications) but, as Chapter Three explains, the Sapphire was eventually superseded by the Conway in the Mk.2 Victor. Nevertheless, in October 1959 Handley Page made some proposals to the Ministry to modify the Mk.1 Victor's engine intakes, in conjunction with some other modifications to the Sapphire engine. This was intended to restore the loss of thrust and prolong the engine life. The airframe modification was rejected but the engine changes were supported.

Progress on the programme was also hampered by a strike in the Handley Page drawing offices which began in December 1953 and lasted for four months. Then in February 1954 the Aeronautical Inspection Directorate (AID) discovered stress cracks in the wing joints of the first prototype and a full examination of this problem incurred rectifications which brought another four-month delay to the programme. Nevertheless, prototype WB775 first took to the air on 11th September 1954 from its Radlett birthplace, and that afternoon it performed a fly-past at the Farnborough Show. Later that month it appeared at some Battle of Britain 'At Home' days held at RAF bases. On 14th March 1955 the aircraft flew from Radlett to spend seventeen days at Boscombe Down to permit A&AEE's pilots to undertake some 'preview' trials. For this purpose WB775 was flown at light weight (around 100,000 lb [45,360kg]) and with its centre of gravity in an intermediate position. The aircraft was also restricted to 286mph (460km/h) IAS and 2.25g (production machines were to have a 2.7g limit), and as a prototype it was also non-representative of production aeroplanes in respect of engine thrust, keel surface geometry and cockpit layout.

In the form tested WB775 was found to be "easy and pleasant to fly and appeared to have a high potential as a bomber aircraft. No adverse features were encountered up to the maximum Mach number attained (0.95), which was reached with no rapid increase in drag being apparent." It was considered that, if possible, the transonic potential should be explored. The Victor appeared to be a "satisfactory bombing platform" but it was noted that failure of the auto-stabiliser would seriously impair the accuracy of the bomb-aiming. At this stage the Mach number/buffet threshold was thought to be adequate for the bombing needs of the first production aeroplanes but it might not be adequate for the increased operating altitudes that would be made possible by the introduction of more powerful engines. Very severe buffet was encountered near the straight stall, which caused some concern about structural safety, although the stall itself had no operational significance. Flexing of the airframe was apparent in manoeuvres at high Mach numbers and, in the light of recent experience on other aircraft types, it was thought that the structural consequences of high Mach number buffet on the Victor should be investigated. WB775's light and effective controls were particularly commended, as was the aircraft's response to control movement, the excellent infinitely variable hinged airbrake panels mounted on the tail cone and the small changes of trim with speed and change in configuration. Various aspects of the cockpit layout were however considered to be unsatisfactory, in particular crew comfort and power-control safeguards.

A new modified cockpit arrangement known as Stage 1A was approved in March 1955. However, once the Boscombe test pilots had criticised the inaccessibility of various essential switches and controls, in June the Director General of Technical Development (Air) (DGTD[A] – a Ministry of Supply officer) declared that the existing cockpit was just not acceptable and that a completely new arrangement was now required. A new layout – Stage 2 – was approved during the following month and authority was given to Handley Page to proceed with it for all production Victors. The original cockpit had been fully approved back in 1952, so this problem was unexpected and created further delay.

In July 1954 WB775 made an appearance at the Paris Air Show and in September at the annual SBAC Show at Farnborough. On 15th November 1956 the second prototype was 'Accepted Off Contract' for further development flying and it appears to have spent almost the whole of its life at Radlett – apart that is from the early visit to Boscombe in 1955 and several trips to RAE Farnborough in 1955 and 1956, either for the SBAC Show or as part of the aircraft flutter programme. The initial Victor bomb-release flight trials were made over the Orfordness range using WB775 on 15th and 16th June 1955. Nine 1,000 lb (454kg) bombs were released satisfactorily at 230mph (370km/h) and then 276mph (444km/h). Trials with inert 10,000 lb (4,536kg) atom bombs were not concluded until April 1956.

It was during 1956 and 1957 that WB775 made its greatest contribution to the programme when it completed a large number of flutter test flights, including one where part of the starboard wing broke away and most of the fuel escaped while the aircraft was flying at around 20,000ft (6,096m). WB775 became difficult to handle but pilot 'Jock' Still found that at lower speeds there was enough control to allow him to land back at Radlett. The trailing-edge box of the wing had failed and this was subsequently strengthened to ensure that there were no further problems. 'Jock' Still, with Frank Haye and Jock Ogilvy as his observers, was the principal pilot for the flutter trials and deserves the highest praise for his work, which often took WB775 very close to its safety limits. Any errors in his flying and disaster would probably have followed. These investigations also established Handley Page as a world leader in flutter research.

WB775 was grounded after its last flight on 10th April 1959, having spent its final years on specialist work and the testing of new equipment and modifications for production Victors. On 22nd August the fuselage of the now part dismantled WB775 was taken by road to RAE Farnborough to be used in some decompression tests. These were in relation to the loss two days earlier of the first Victor B Mk.2 XH668 (see Chapter Three) and were carried out in the Farnborough water tank. WB775 was finally Struck Off Charge in June 1960 and large pieces of the aircraft were eventually used as ammunition targets on the ranges at Shoeburyness.

First Production

The first Victor production order, for twenty-five aircraft, was placed in June 1952, and the first production B Mk.1 Victor XA917 made its maiden flight on 1st February 1956. Further orders followed but in the end only 84 production aeroplanes, plus the two prototypes, were to be completed. On 26th March 1956 the Minister of Supply, Reginald Maudling, officially opened a new extension to the main aircraft-assembly hall at Radlett. Five production Victors, impeccably finished all over in silver, formed the background to this special event and *The Aeroplane* described them as "looking rather like special prize-winners with unusually clean and shining faces lined up in the school hall for the headmaster's speech". After lunch one of these aeroplanes, XA918, flew briefly for the guests but it was noted that two of its undercarriage doors had still to be fitted. During the event Maudling referred to the Victor as representing the equivalent in hitting power of any bomber known at the present time.

Compared to the prototypes the Mk.1 had a forward fuselage that was longer by 42in (106.7cm), a change brought about because of an adjustment that had to be made to the centre of gravity. This was the problem mentioned earlier which had been countered by carrying iron ballast in WB771 and WB775. In addition, by taking the side door further forward of the port intake it gave a slightly better chance for any escaping aircrew to survive an emergency. There were additional windows in the cockpit roof and several other changes, including the shorter fin, modified fin/tail acorn and a set of vortex generators extending from the wing tip to just inboard of the nose flaps. Some of the early production aeroplanes were used for a number of trials and test programmes and in fact none of the first six to be built ever flew with the RAF. The first two, XA917 and XA918, were retained by the manufacturer for trials which were carried out under Controller (Aircraft) authority and in conjunction with the clearance work undertaken by A&AEE. These pair of aeroplanes spent almost their entire lives on test work and all manner of 'unusual' flying conditions were checked out, such as removing doors and hatches to ensure that a Victor would still fly satisfactorily if any of these items failed or were lost in flight.

Between 1st and 5th June 1956 a preliminary assessment was carried out by A&AEE Boscombe Down on XA917. This was made at an intermediate weight with the centre of gravity near the normal aft limit. Throughout XA917 was restricted to 300 knots (345mph/556km/h) IAS (but 0.95 IMN was permitted) and the aircraft was not representative of the expected production condition in having derated Sa.7 engines and an original Stage 1 cockpit. The aircraft also lacked automatic nose-flap operation for countering the effects of pitch-up at low to moderate Mach numbers but vortex generators were in place on the wings. The results of this preview were that the Victor showed promise in its primary role as a medium bomber. In respect of height over the target it showed considerable promise, and the figure achieved was likely to be superior to that of the other two V-types, the Valiant and Vulcan.

At this stage, however, urgent action was required to rectify certain unacceptable handling characteristics. These were:

1. Longitudinal static stability was neutral at and negative above the expected cruising Mach number range. Artificial stability was needed and, if possible, the system should have characteristics that gave an adequate warning of the approach to the limiting Mach number.
2. Further development of the yaw damping system was necessary.
3. A full flight investigation and the completion of the development of the automatic 'droop-snoot' leading-edge nose flap system was needed. A full investigation was also required into the magnitude of the structural loads induced by buffet.
4. The maximum permitted IAS needed to be increased considerably.
5. Improvements were also required in engine handling, in certain aspects of the control feel systems and to improve the braking parachute's reliability.

The first public appearance for the aircraft came on 23rd July 1956 at the Royal Review of Bomber Command at Marham, and later one of the production Victors attended the Farnborough Show in September where it made several 'touch-and-go' landings during its display. The Victor's Final Acceptance Conference was also held in September and the main criticisms to arise concerned the aircraft's electrical wiring. In its present form this was declared unacceptable and a complete reappraisal and extensive modifications would be necessary before the type could be considered acceptable for service use. Consequently, during the first half of 1957 Handley Page was engaged on a re-engineering of the electrical system and a 'final' Final Acceptance Conference was not held until the end of June.

XA917 was taken supersonic by John Allam on 1st June 1957 which made the Victor, at that

Part of the Handley Page Victor assembly line at Colney Street, Radlett, in the early 1960s.
Handley Page Association

time, the largest aircraft anywhere to be flown at Mach 1. According to the official statement issued during the following week by Handley Page, this was achieved during a normal test flight and had, indeed, been inadvertent. Officially, during a shallow dive Allam's attention "had been diverted for a moment" and when he next looked at the Machmeter it was registering more than Mach 1. The altitude at which the aircraft was flying was in excess of 40,000ft (12,192m) but the date when it achieved its sonic majority was not released. However, on 14th June *The Aeroplane* was able to report that

"on Saturday 1st June some resounding sonic bangs were heard in the neighbourhood of Radlett while a Victor was airborne". In fact, loud bangs were heard over a wide area. John Allam said that during its transonic flight the controls were perfectly normal and "the aircraft behaved in its customary stable manner". Indeed at the time he had doubted whether the speed was in fact as fast as the Machmeter had indicated, but subsequent calibration did confirm its accuracy. He confirmed that the true air speed achieved was in the region of 675mph (1,086km/h), which at the height the aircraft

was flying represented about Mach 1.02. The two other crew members on this flight were observers G. Wass and P. Langston, and in the process Paul Langston had become the first human to achieve supersonic speed travelling backwards.

Another Victor inadvertently exceeded Mach 1 in 1958 during a delivery flight from Radlett to No 232 Operational Conversion Unit (OCU) at Gaydon. However, officially, in normal service when flown by pilots of 'normal' ability, the Victor was not allowed to be taken into the supersonic regime. The aircraft was limited to around

Mach 0.95 but flying supersonically actually presented few problems.

At Farnborough John Allam was able to take the Victor through loops and slow rolls. *The Aeroplane* for 5th September 1958 also reported on the "Aerobatic Victor", describing how during a photographic sortie from Radlett (which had been organised to take pre-Farnborough air-to-air pictures) the bomber had "exhibited its lively handling characteristics by doing a barrel roll". In itself this was noteworthy for such a large aeroplane, but in point of fact two rolls were accomplished with a pause in between at around 12,000ft (3,658m) altitude

This page:

The very first production Victors were painted in a most attractive silver finish but this was soon replaced by a white scheme. This is the first production aircraft XA917. Phil Butler

XA917 flies low over the runway at Radlett, probably on 1st February 1956 during its maiden flight. It has the original pointed fuselage tail cone and an additional instrumentation pitot mast on the upper nose. Handley Page Association

Opposite page:

More Victor B.1s in final assembly at Colney Street, which was the first factory building to be built by Handley Page at Radlett. Handley Page Association

To back up its development of the Victor, Handley Page acquired some new and extensive design and experimental test facilities, research laboratories and a high-speed wind tunnel. These were concentrated in its Park Street complex at the company's Radlett aerodrome. Handley Page Association

somewhere near Huntingdonshire. The manoeuvres were described as "spectacular" and the size of the barrel "in keeping with the size of the aircraft". In performing it John Allam kept the Victor a considerable distance away from the photographic Hastings, which was being flown by his colleague Hedley Hazelden. Clearly Victor was no ordinary bomber.

XA918 flew on 21st March 1956 but the next production aircraft did not get airborne until 13th March 1957. The delay came from XA919 having been used for ground and equipment tests prior to starting its flying programme. Later this aircraft was operated by A&AEE to clear the Victor's bombing, radar and communications equipment. XA920 began its flying career on 12th May 1956 and spent much of its early life on handling and performance flying. On 15th October 1957 it went to A&AEE to begin the Victor's official performance trials and later found employment on photo reconnaissance work. XA921, after initially being used to carry out autopilot and drop-tank testing, was put on to weapons clearance work. Other examples also performed trials, but the first to reach the hands of the RAF was XA923 delivered to No 232 OCU in February 1958. The Victor had now become the third and last V-type to join Bomber Command. In 1963 XA918 took on the mantle of prototype for the three-point flight refuelling tanker Victor to be described shortly.

Back in July 1954 production Victors were expected to be equipped with rocket-assisted take-off gear (RATOG) to provide additional thrust should it be required. A de Havilland Spectre D.Spe.4 rocket motor was to be slung under each wing between the engines and jettisoned by parachute after take-off but as Chapter Five explains, this was never adopted for Handley Page's V-Bomber.

One of the first B Mk.1s, possibly XA917 again, lands at the North Orbital end of Radlett runway. Handley Page Association

The first five production Victors lined up at Radlett in readiness for the official opening of the extended main aircraft-assembly hall on 26th March 1956. Each of them has the early silver colour scheme, confirming that to begin with this was applied to five Victors. The two hatches in the cockpit roof can be seen, which would have been jettisoned prior to the pilots ejecting. None of these aircraft have wing spoilers. Handley Page

Opposite page:

An air-to-air view of the first Victor B Mk.1 XA917, now with vortex generators fitted to the outer wing upper surfaces. Note extra cabin windows compared to the prototypes. Handley Page

The fourth B.1 XA920 was used extensively for handling and performance test flying. An Orange Putter tail warning radar is fitted. Handley Page

As noted, a photograph shows that the first five production machines were finished in the silver colour scheme that was adopted at the very early stages of the V-Bomber's career but from XA922 onwards new Victors were produced in the white overall anti-radiation scheme used from then until the switch to low level and camouflage. It is understood that XA921 had also been repainted white by the time it was delivered. The Titanine all-white anti-flash coating was the result of a substantial amount of research into protecting the bombers against the powerful effects of the nuclear thermal flash created by their own bombs. It was designed to reflect away the enormous heat which radiated out from a nuclear detonation, but the aircraft's external

This page:

XA918 spent all of its life on test work and eventually became a trials aircraft for the tanker programme. It is seen at the 1957 Farnborough Show. Handley Page

XA922 was another B Mk.1 to be operated extensively on test work. Phil Butler

XA927 in white but with dark roundels and markings. Later these were switched to paler 'toned down' shades for the aircraft to perform its nuclear duties. Phil Butler

Opposite page:

In the summer of 1958 XA930 posed for a series of publicity pictures. They show many of the features of the Handley Page Victor and indeed what a handsome aeroplane it was. A nose probe for taking on fuel in flight has been installed above the cabin and the aircraft carries underwing slipper tanks, which, at the time, were a trial fitting. In fact this probe was also on trial and was the longest version to be tested; it has a bracing strut that was dropped after a redesign. Handley Page markings presented a problem. Titanine was the name of a London-based company specialising in aircraft finishes.

There were potential inherent dangers from applying national, registration and other markings to these aeroplanes in colours that had a low reflectivity value, because their exposure to a high degree of thermal flux could result in serious damage to the metal beneath these markings. Black proved to be the worst colour for conducting heat, followed closely by red, and also painting over such markings just before a nuclear operation was found to be completely ineffective. White paint on top of black or red still retained a high level of conductivity and in fact it was found that the white finish had to age for two or three months before it could be safely exposed to heavy thermal flux. In due course each of the three V-types had white colour schemes with their roundels and markings 'toned down' to paler shades for the nuclear role. Once the V-Bombers had been reassigned to low-level non-nuclear duties in the 1960s, they were repainted in disruptive green/grey tactical camouflage. This also applied to the Victors refitted as tanker aircraft.

B Mk.1A was the designation given to twenty-four 'XH' series B.1s upgraded by the inclusion of some modifications. These embraced changes in the pressure cabin (which was also strengthened) but most importantly a much better ECM fitting was introduced including the Red Steer tail warning radar in an enlarged tail cone. The early B.1s had chaff and the Orange Putter tail warning radar originally developed for the English Electric Canberra, Britain's first jet bomber, but by the time the Victor was entering production this equipment was becoming out of date. The Mk.1A brought in some other minor items and the original plans drawn up in October 1958 had called for twenty-nine ECM conversions. (At that time

B Mk.1 XH615 displays quite beautifully the Victor planform but from above, when most often the shots that show the type's wing shape are from below. The picture was taken in about 1960. Handley Page Association

respects adequate for the task of high-altitude medium bomber. The main point raised was that the maximum permitted air speed had to be raised to above 360 knots (415mph/667km/h) IAS to allow an adequate margin above the recommended climbing speed. They also requested that an aerodynamic investigation should be pursued to see if a better method of countering nose-up pitch could be developed which was simpler and lighter than the current auto nose-flap system, and finally that the engine handling characteristics had to be improved. (The modifications duly made to the wing leading edge are discussed in Chapter Three.)

The Green Satin radar was cleared for use up to 50,000ft (15,240m) in February 1958, and a month later the NBS was cleared for use in the air but for training purposes only, because at this stage no guarantee of accuracy could as yet be given. In April 1958 work on a trial installation to provide integrated wiring for the carriage of Class 'A' stores (mines) was begun on a Victor at Radlett. This was scheduled to be completed by the end of July and flight trials to clear the Yellow Sun and Red Beard nuclear stores were to take place from August through until April 1959. In June 1958 clearance was issued for Victors to be landed at weights up to 125,000 lb (56,700kg) on 3,000yd (2,743m) runways without using the breaking parachute. In April 1961 the B Mk.1 and 1A were both cleared to an all up weight of 180,000 lb (81,648kg). In the meantime the last Mk.1 Victor, XH667, had left the Radlett production line in late March 1960.

In July 1958 a meeting was held at the Ministry of Supply to establish what progress had been made in meeting some MoS requirements for rearward viewing. It became clear that the cost of installing the previously planned rearward viewing periscope retrospectively could not be justified, and that in any event the installation was not compatible with the ECM equipment. Accordingly the Air Staff ruled that all Mk.1 aircraft were to be provided with a portable periscope that would fit into the existing periscope sextant mounting. For Mk.2 Victors an attempt was to be made to provide an installation that would be compatible with the ECM and which could be fitted during production.

In September 1958 Bomber Command reported a serious shortfall in the performance it was obtaining from Victor B Mk.1 aircraft. An A&AEE assessment on a C(A) clearance Victor discussed at a meeting held on 31st October showed that the figures produced for range came within 3% of the Operating Data Manual (ODM) forecast, when Bomber Command was saying they were 10% down. In addition Boscombe Down's take-off measurements

these were actually called RCM for radio countermeasures, rather than ECM for electronic countermeasures, but the more up-to-date term has been used here to avoid confusion.)

The aircraft that were so modified were fed into the Radlett retrofit line from late February 1959 onwards and the B Mk.1A designation was decided during the same month. The trial installation aircraft was XH587, while XH613 became the first of the main run to enter the conversion process. The work proved to be slow and, like Victor production overall, fell considerably behind schedule. One of the restrictions was that only eight aircraft could be dealt with at once. XH587 made its first flight as the trials aircraft on 16th February 1960 but Treasury approval for the last five (to complete the twenty-four) was not given until February 1961. The result of this late decision was that it proved impossible to keep the line continuous, and so there was a break in deliveries after the nineteenth aircraft. XH613 proved to be the first Mk.1A delivered to the RAF and arrived at Cottesmore on 15th July 1960 to begin its acceptance checks.

In January 1957 two early production aircraft were delivered to A&AEE for the handling and radio trials required for C(A) Release. This was issued on 26th July and the Air Ministry Release to Service was sent out three days later. The initial documents cleared the Victor for speeds up to 330 knots (380mph/611km/h) between sea level and 35,000ft (10,668m) or 0.95 Indicated Mach Number at altitudes above that height, and for operations at a maximum all up weight of 160,000 lb (72,576kg). This was the weight when carrying approximately 85% internal fuel plus a 10,000 lb (4,536kg) bomb load. In essence the aircraft was cleared for the high-altitude role but not for any low flying duties, and aerobatics and spinning were prohibited. The maximum permissible landing weight was 110,000 lb (49,896kg), or 125,000 lb (56,700kg) if the breaking chute was used. At this stage there was no armament capability and the radio and navigation equipments were only partially cleared.

A&AEE's Service Release trials continued in March 1958 and the pilots reported that the Victor's handling characteristics were in all were 10% greater than that given in the ODM but Bomber Command reported that they were 14% greater. As a result A&AEE carried out two sorties on Bomber Command Victors and their results came within 1% of those the Establishment had obtained using the C(A) aircraft. It was established that Bomber Command's figures had all been made from fuel gauge readings, while A&AEE's came from using flowmeters to monitor fuel consumption and from weighing the aircraft before and after each flight. It was therefore apparent that the Victor's fuel gauge readings were very inaccurate and Handley Page accordingly proposed introducing a modification which would reduce the fuel gauge errors to acceptable limits.

Tankers

The loss of the Vickers Valiant tanker fleet in 1964/65 from a mass withdrawal following the discovery of fatigue cracks in the aircraft's wings left a void in the RAF's capability to support its fighters with in-flight refuelling. In fact, the problem of the metal used in the Valiant's wing spars (where the cracks were found) had been anticipated some time previously but it was the discovery of severe cracks which had grown 'ahead of schedule' that brought about this aeroplane's sudden retirement. That said, over two years before this event took place it was realised that the Valiants may have to be

retired early, and by February 1962 that knowledge had triggered a study for converting the Victor B Mk.1 into a tanker.

Consideration was given for converting thirty-four Mk.1 and Mk.1A aircraft into in-flight refuelling tankers and the decision to go ahead was made in November 1962. The aircraft selected to be the trial conversion was XA918 which first flew in tanker form on 8th July 1964 and began testing with A&AEE in October. The result was a three-point tanker called the K Mk.1 or K Mk.1A, depending on which version of the bomber was involved. Basically the conversion comprised the removal of the bomb doors and any equipment required for bombing; a Mk.17 hose drum unit for the centre refuel point took the available space in the rear of the bomb bay and two 16,000 lb (7,258kg) capacity fuel tanks and their piping filled up the rest of the bay. The outer refuel stations were installed in a Mk.20B pod mounted beneath each wing on a standard pylon. The Green Satin radar, H2S and the radio altimeter were retained but much of the bomber's other avionics were replaced by new equipment. The project was covered by Air Staff Requirement ASR.376 issued on 15th April 1964.

The first K Mk.1 XA937 flew on 2nd November 1965, and on 14th February 1966 this aircraft became the first production K.1 tanker to be delivered. It was followed by nine more K.1s with

'XA' serials and twenty-four K.1As from the 'XH' series. The first of these was XH650, work on her starting in September 1964, and all of these tankers were delivered during 1966 and 1967. In fact for about a year after their introduction they were actually looked on as combined bomber and tanker aircraft and to reflect this were designated B(K) Mk.1 and B(K) Mk.1A. After that the bombing role was dropped and they became K Mk.1s and K Mk.1As.

However, as a short-term replacement to lessen the impact of losing the Valiants, a selection of Mk.1A Victors were also converted into two-point tankers by the relatively simple addition of the Mk.20B pod beneath each wing, together with the two 16,000 lb (7,258kg) tanks fitted in the bomb bay. The Red Steer and much of the ECM equipment were taken out. This version was also initially categorised as the B(K) Mk.1A but was later retitled B Mk.1A(K.2P) and during 1965 half a dozen aircraft in the XH6XX series were so converted. The first, XH620, flew in this form on 28th April of that year. When three-point Victor tankers became fully available in 1967, these two-point versions were moved on to training duties.

One of the 'stopgap' B(K) Mk.1A two-point tanker conversions displays its new capability at the Colerne Battle of Britain Air Show on 18th September 1965. Handley Page

XH618 kitted out as a three-point K Mk.1 tanker while serving with 57 Squadron in the 1960s. This aircraft crashed into the North Sea in March 1975. Note the unit badge on the fin. Handley Page

K Mk.1 tanker XH616, again with its 57 Squadron number on the fin, 'refuels' two BAC Lightning fighters during a display at the Paris Air Show on 7th June 1969. The nearest Lightning is XS923. Handley Page

Chapter Three

Production Mark 2s and Unbuilt Proposals

The 1950s witnessed a phenomenal advance in the technology and capability of military aircraft, their powerplants and their weapons. Such an astonishing pace of progress left its mark on many programmes and often a new type, fighter or bomber, could be close to obsolescence soon after it had entered service. The Victor was not unaffected by this situation and, not long after the first examples had flown, work had started on finding ways of improving the aircraft or producing other versions. Some proposals were never built and are described later in this chapter, but by the mid-1950s the need to fly higher to avoid enemy fighters, and the availability of more powerful engines, meant that a Mk.2 Victor was on its way.

New Features

In 1954, at a time when the Air Staff was becoming increasingly concerned about the V-Bombers' vulnerability, both Handley Page and Avro were asked to study seriously to what extent their bombers could be developed. This was well before the first B Mk.1 Victor had flown but the estimates were indicating that Handley

Page's aircraft would meet its specification with comfort. However, anything that could increase its operational flexibility was still welcome. There was little scope for increases in speed in a subsonic aeroplane that could already exceed Mach 0.9, so the effort was concentrated on improving the height and range performance to give the aircraft something in hand tactically. By July Handley Page was investigating two separate lines of development:

1. The 'Victor II', which had the existing Mk.1 airframe, were kitted out with four more powerful Sapphire Sa.9 engines, each capable of 12,700 lb (56.4kN) of thrust. When they became available these units could be installed in place of the Sa.7s without any alteration to the airframe. The greater available power would yield a significant improvement in take-off and climb plus an additional 1,000ft (305m) of bombing height or 3% radius of action. Sea-level rate of climb at the aircraft's normal all up weight would be increased to 6,220ft/min (1,896m/min) from the Mk.1's 5,220ft/min (1,591m/min). This option was not taken up and the Sa.9 programme was eventually discontinued.

The second Handley Page Victor B Mk.2 XH669 in a well-known air-to-air photo. This was probably taken in late summer 1959 and the aircraft is devoid of serial numbers, except on the windbreak for the front access door, which was visible only when the door had been opened. This aircraft was the first Mk.2 to feature the modified intake at the fin root, and note the black walkways painted over the wing roots. Handley Page

2. The 'Victor III' looked into enlarging the basic airframe, increasing the span and employing bigger engines – in fact 15,000 lb (66.7kN) thrust Rolls-Royce Conway 6s. The current outer and intermediate wings, the rear fuselage and the bomb bay and nose (including the cabin) were all retained to go with an extended centre wing plus an extension to the main fuselage. There would be little alteration to the wing sweepback and aspect ratio so the Victor's good low speed characteristics would be preserved. The thickness/chord ratios across the wing were also the same, which enabled a similar critical Mach number to be obtained. Although the normal take-off weight would go up to 190,000 lb

The first Victor B Mk.2 (interim B.2) XH668 to the left (with the old-style fin) parked on the apron at the Park Street end of Radlett airfield in 1959 alongside prototype WB775 to the right. Handley Page Association

(86,184kg), from the Mk.1's 160,000 lb (72,576kg), it would not be necessary to alter or strengthen any of the Mk.1's major components. The take-off performance would be improved, the developed aircraft would fly rather higher than the Mk.1 for the same range and bomb load (maximum bombing height was 55,500ft [16,916m]), and when flying at the same height the range was increased by some 800nm (1,480km). A still-air range of 7,620nm (14,120km) was predicted for an overload weight of 225,000 lb (102,060kg). The estimated sea-level rate of climb at normal all up weight was 5,150ft/min (1,570m/min).

Victor III had a span of 126ft 0in (38.4m) and a length of 137ft 0in (41.7m). In due course it was revised as the Victor B Phase 3 with a span of 137ft 0in (41.7m), length 136ft 0in (41.5m) and wing area 3,267ft² (303.8m²). Powered by 16,000 lb (71.1kN) Bristol Olympus Ol.6s or 17,160 lb (76.3kN) Olympus Ol.7s, this aircraft was now expected to cruise over the target at 58,000ft (17,678m) and offer the same speed/range/bomb load as the Victor Mk.1. It is thought that Handley Page called this design the HP.104 but the brochure documents do not confirm this. This design did not proceed but the seed had been sown for introducing a new engine in the Victor.

In December 1955 agreement was given to proceed with what was called the 'Phase 2A wing' development of the Victor. Handley Page's full design proposals, made in March 1956, involved increasing the span by 10ft (3.05m), increasing in the chord and centre section and introducing larger air intakes to cater for the greater air supply required by the new engines. At this stage engine thrusts up to 17,500 lb (77.8kN) were expected and the choice was either the Conway Co.11 or the Olympus Ol.6. In due course the Conway was selected and, because its diameter was some 5in (12.7cm) fatter than the Sapphire, heavy aluminium forgings had to be added to help support the new power units. In addition the bottom intake lips were lowered. In service the type would be known as the Victor B Mk.2, and

the Phase 2A wing and the more powerful engines would substantially improve the Victor's height and range performance. In order to give maximum tactical manoeuvrability an increase in altitude was important, even for carrying the new Blue Steel stand-off bomb described shortly. The B Mk.2 would also have an AC electrical system and an airborne auxiliary powerplant.

B.128P2 was the production specification prepared for the Victor B Mk.2 fitted with the Conway Co.11 Mk.103. With the Blue Steel weapon aboard the still air range without using external tanks or flight refuelling was not to be less than 3,250nm (6,020km). The height at 40% of this range must not be less than 54,000ft (16,460ft), and an additional range of some 4,300nm (7,970km) with the same warload was required. The latter was to be achieved by using external tanks. The aircraft was also to be capable of executing a steady buffet-free turn of 1.15g at the cruising speed. The nuclear weaponry now called for was Yellow Sun or Blue Steel and there were the usual iron bomb requirements, plus PR equipment and the Yellow Aster (H2S Mk.9) radar. ECM equipment would include the Red Steer tail warning radar (signified by six small antenna blisters circling the tail cone), a fighter control communications jammer, a metric radar jammer and a passive warning receiver.

Once the Air Ministry and MoS had agreed to drop the Sapphire 9, the engines considered for the developed V-Bombers automatically became the Conway and Olympus. In 1955 it was recommended that both the Rolls-Royce and Bristol engines should be made available for the V-Bombers, with each of them acting as an insurance against the failure of the other. The Olympus was a straight turbojet, whereas the Conway was a new breed of engine – a by-pass turbojet where part of the air from the main compressor did not pass through the combustion chambers but instead was 'by-passed' around the core before rejoining the hot gases in the exhaust pipe. In 1960 the Conway was the first and at that point the only large by-pass engine in the world. It had begun life in 1948 as

the Rolls-Royce RB.80 project, designed for bomber programmes, and a prototype was built in January 1950 as the Conway Co.2. A thrust of 10,000 lb (44.4kN) was achieved in January 1953 but by then it was quite apparent that higher thrusts would be possible. Over the succeeding years a number of versions were built to satisfy the needs of both the Victor and several of the new long-range jet airliners then in development.

A weakness suffered by the Sapphires fitted in Mk.1 Victors was 'centre-line closure', a hot weather problem encountered in the Far East. When a jet engine runs at maximum power the centrifugal forces exerted on its compressor blades are sufficient to make them stretch. They are of course designed to accommodate this but when operating in the tropics this feature gets taken to its extreme and the blade tips came close to touching the outer casing. In the case of the Sapphire Victors, if the aircraft then had to pass through rain the very cold water entering the engine would cool the outer casing first and make it shrink a little. This meant that the blade tips might now hit the casing and wreck the engine, and on several occasions this did happen. The modifications eventually made to the Sapphires to affect a cure involved introducing ceramic coatings on the blades. This problem did not occur with the Conway.

B Mk.2 Progress

Aside from eight aircraft belonging to a previous order, according to the serial allocation dates all of the Victor B Mk.2 production aeroplanes were ordered in early 1956 or early 1958, and the Mock-Up Conference for the Mk.2 was held during December 1957. No prototype was requested because the flight test and clearance programmes were to rely on early production aeroplanes. However, the first B.2 XH668 did exhibit certain characteristics of

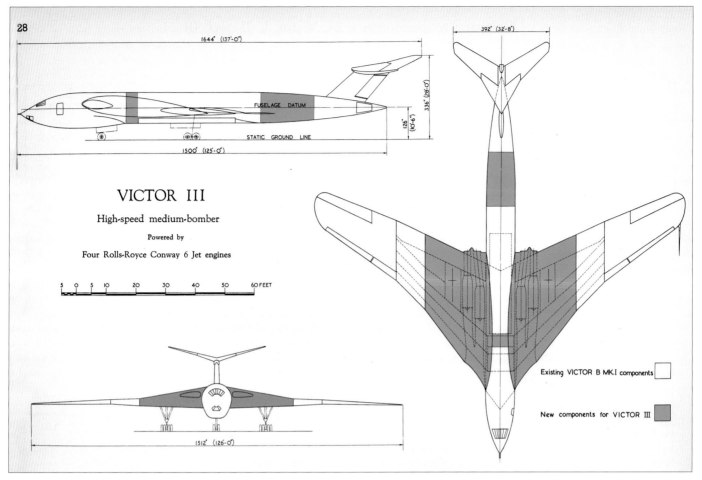

28

1644" (137'-0")

336" (28'-0")

126" (10'-6")

FUSELAGE DATUM

STATIC GROUND LINE

1500" (125'-0")

392" (32'-8")

VICTOR III

High-speed medium-bomber

Powered by

Four Rolls-Royce Conway 6 Jet engines

5 0 5 10   20   30   40   50   60 FEET

1512" (126'-0")

Existing VICTOR B MK.I components

New components for VICTOR III

General arrangement drawing of the Victor III proposal of July 1954. The white areas depict existing Victor B Mk.1 components to be used in the new design and the shaded areas represent new components.

Mk.2 Victor XL164 at rest. Note the different engine intakes to the Mk.1, and the ram-air turbine intakes raised in front of the fin.
Both Handley Page Association

This page:

The third Mk.2 was XH670 which was never used by the RAF as a bomber. Instead it spent much of its career on trials. This series of images displays several features relating to the Mk.2, or rather the (unofficial) Mk.2R, in particular the 'Kuchemann carrots' on the upper wing and the different fin root.
Terry Panopalis

Opposite page:

This image of what appears to be XL158 shows the aircraft in a pale 'nuclear' finish with very faint markings and serials. Note the Red Steer radome at the fuselage tail.
Handley Page

a prototype and it retained the Mk.1 fin. At this stage the first flight of the first Mk.2 was expected to take place during August 1958 but the programme soon fell behind schedule. Hopes for getting XH668 airborne during the December were then thwarted by surging problems with the Conway engines, which it was thought might necessitate the provision of a split air intake. That brought further delay and by May 1959 the surging problem had still not been fully resolved. Some improvements in performance were eventually achieved by providing engines with an additional 19in^2 (122.6cm^2) of by-pass area, and indeed by fitting intake splitters.

In June 1959 a policy decision was taken to install uprated Conway engines retrospectively but it was not until April 1960 that Handley Page was able to state that the Conway surging problem had been virtually solved. From January 1961 until July 1962 XL160 operated from the Rolls-Royce test airfield at Hucknall as a trials aircraft for Conway development. At one stage it had a pair of Conway Co.11 engines on one side and uprated Co.17s on the other, which allowed comparative tests to be made. Eventually it was established that localised turbulence was present inside the intake trunking.

The first Victor B Mk.2, XH668, made its first flight on 20th February 1959. John Allam was the pilot and Handley Page's own flight trials occupied the initial stages of this aeroplane's test programme. In August 1959 XH668 was delivered to A&AEE Boscombe Down for preview trials but on 20th August it was tragically lost during its first flight from the Establishment when it disappeared into St George's Channel in the Irish Sea. During this flight XH668 was to have made some high-speed turns at 52,000ft (15,850m) and then make a rapid descent to 35,000ft (10,668m) to perform some more tests. Sqn Ldr Morgan and Sqn Ldr Stockman (the pilots), Flt Lt Hannaford and Flt Lt Williams (the navigators) and Mr Williams (Handley Page's chief flight test observer) all died.

This disaster led to a lengthy investigation but this could only begin in earnest once the remains of the aircraft had been found and that took a long time. The first theory had been that an explosive decompression might have disabled the aeroplane or its crew, and this idea was the reason why prototype WB775 was sent to Farnborough for tests on its pressurised cockpit (see Chapter Two). Only after an enormous effort to recover a vast amount of wreckage from the sea bed, which lasted deep into the summer of 1960, did it finally become possible to piece together what had happened. XH668's loss was eventually pinned down to the starboard wing-tip-mounted pitot head that had detached after suffering buffeting in a steep turn. This in turn had caused a critical loss of input to various control devices, and eventually a complete loss of control with the aircraft entering an unrecoverable dive. It was a relief to learn that the crash was not brought about by a major flaw in the aircraft.

The second Mk.2, XH669, flew on 6th August 1959 and took part in that year's Farnborough Show. A report from June 1960 indicates how the early Mk.2 aircraft were utilised for trials and research. XH669 and XH670 were being used for trials which formed part of the investigation into the loss of XH668, XH671 was being equipped for radio and navigation trials which were due to commence at Boscombe Down in September, and XH672 was being fitted with engine-surge instrumentation. Engine-surge flight testing in this aircraft was due to commence in July while XH673 was being used for ground resonance testing. The tenth and eleventh Mk.2s were destined for Conway Co.17 trials and the twelfth was to be used for extensive Blue Steel trials. In November it became apparent that the completion of Mk.2s was being held back by the low delivery rate of their Conway engines.

Chapter Two reported how in 1958 the pilots at A&AEE recommended that a better method of countering nose-up pitch would be desirable, which would take the place of the complex automatic nose-flap arrangement currently in use. In fact Handley Page had by then put forward a proposal to replace the existing nose-flap system with a fixed drooped leading edge. This had been made back in August 1957 and in due course the Air Staff signified to the Ministry of Supply its support for the proposal. A decision was made to go ahead and the new leading-edge configuration was tested on prototype WB775 in 1959 before being embodied in production aircraft (this being one of WB775's last jobs before it was retired from flying). In October 1959 A&AEE recommended that, as a result of its handling trials, the fixed drooped leading edge should be introduced on the Mk.2.

In January 1960 the modification to introduce the drooped leading edge in place of nose flaps was approved for Mk.2 aircraft during production. B Mk.1A aircraft also received this modification from 1962, the work being carried out as a retrofit at their RAF bases. Early Mk.2s were similarly treated and XL159, the air-

craft engaged on low-speed handling trials with the fixed drooped leading edge in place, confirmed that there were no serious drawbacks or penalties to the Victor's performance or drag, or with its stall characteristics. However, on 23rd March 1962 XL159 was destroyed in a crash after the aircraft stalled and entered a flat spin. Pilots Paddy 'Spud' Murphy and Flt Lt Waterton ejected safely and observer John Tank was also able to get out of the stricken aircraft, but two more observers, Messrs Elwood and Evans, died together with two people on the ground. XL233 took over the test flying role vacated by the loss of XL159.

In November 1963 the aeronautical press reported that a Victor was flying with streamlined fairings above the trailing edge of each upper wing just outboard of the flaps. These only ever appeared on Mk.2 aircraft and were the result of a request to provide space for the stowage of additional equipment, and the discovery that this equipment could be stowed in fairings at the kinks in the wing trailing edges which gave a beneficial effect to drag reduction at near sonic speed. When flying at altitude these streamlined bodies, which were known as 'Kuchemann carrots' after the famous scientist Dr Kuchemann working at RAE Farnborough, reduced the aircraft's drag at around Mach 0.9. This was particularly beneficial to those Victors earmarked to carry the Blue Steel missile (below). Housed within the fairings was a large quantity of defensive chaff and flares which could now be safely released without any worries that parts of the airframe might get in the way downstream.

During late June 1960 a cut in the Mk.2 production order of fifty-nine aircraft came under consideration, and this was confirmed by the Minister of Defence on 2nd August when it was announced that the number of Mk.2s to be procured had been reduced by twenty-five aircraft. Consequently, including XH668, a total of thirty-four B Mk.2 Victors was eventually built. These aeroplanes, when also fitted with the fixed-wing leading edge, the trailing-edge bodies and with Red Steer in place, were sometimes (but apparently not officially) called B Mk.2R – the 'R' standing for 'Retrofit'. There is uncertainty about this because the official movement cards (which were used to help prepare the airframe histories in Appendix One) do not recognise a 'B.2R'. It appears that 'Retrofit' does not represent the Blue Steel conversions either, an impression given in the past by some published sources.

The full B Mk.2 was eventually powered by the Conway Mk.201 that gave over 20,000 lb (88.9kN) of thrust. However, something like the first twenty-five B Mk.2s received Conway 11s rather than the Conway 17s (Mk.103 rather than the Mk.201). In addition, not all of them had the Blue Steel modifications and as such these aeroplanes were known as the Interim B Mk.2s. As per the Mk.1s, the early production examples of the B.2 were painted white, although some machines did not have their serial numbers painted on in the usual places but instead

Photographs of Mk.2 XH674 taken in the 1970s.
HSA

had them only on the windbreak protecting the crew door.

The first Mk.2 aircraft were to enter service in the free-falling role until recalled for the Blue Steel retrofit programme (below), which was due to commence at the end of 1961. In December 1960 an Emergency Operational Clearance was issued for the B Mk.2 Victor to carry the 7,250 lb (3,289kg) Yellow Sun Mk.2 weapon. In the early days of the Mk.2, there appear to have been a number of problems shown up in regard to the bomber's capabilities. An official Ministry report revealed that:

The C(A) Release for the Victor B Mk.2 was issued on 31st August 1961 and at this time the aircraft in many respects fell far short of the Air Staff's requirements for an operational medium bomber. The poor performance shown by most of its radio and navigation equipment was described as "most disturbing", while the aircraft's limited fuel carrying capacity gave it a very restricted range. In addition the fully cleared all up weight meant that, initially, the B Mk.2 had a smaller payload than the B Mk.1

had at the time of its C(A) Release. An emergency clearance for the 2,000 lb (907kg) Red Beard tactical nuclear store and clearance for 1,000 lb (454kg) HE stores analogous with the Mk.1 were included in the Release.

Initial Service Clearance for the B Mk.2 was given on 22nd June 1962 and the limitations included as a maximum speed the lower of 330 knots (380mph/611km/h) IAS or Mach 0.85 IMN. In September 1961 each of the first thirteen Mk.2 aircraft was still engaged on flight trials, but the first B Mk.2 to be delivered to the RAF was XL188 on 1st November 1961 and the second arrived on 10th November. The last Mk.2 went into the jig at Radlett in January 1962 and by the following September Bomber Command was expected to have sixteen aircraft on strength, although still with free-falling capability only.

Mk.2 Weapons and Low Level
The V-Bombers were designed principally to deliver strategic nuclear weapons. Britain's first atomic bomb was a free-fall weapon called Blue

Danube which had a nominal yield of 20 kilotons, and this was to have been the primary armament of the Victor B Mk.1. The original specification stated that Blue Danube was not to weigh more than 10,000 lb (4,536kg). However, because the weapon was pretty well obsolete by the time it entered service only a small number of Blue Danubes had been produced prior to its withdrawal in 1962. It was replaced by Britain's first hydrogen bomb, the development of which had begun in the 1950s. A hydrogen bomb uses the fusion rather than fission of atomic nuclei and overall this produces a far more powerful and a rather lighter weapon.

Britain's first truly operational megaton-range thermonuclear weapon was codenamed Yellow Sun and the Mk 1 version weighed 7,000 lb (3,175kg) and gave a yield of ½ megaton. It was designed to arm both the Victor and Avro Vulcan B Mk.1s but again only a few were produced and these were phased out in 1963. Their withdrawal was hastened by the arrival of Yellow Sun Mk.2, which was slightly heavier at 7,250 lb (3,289kg) but gave a yield of 1 megaton. Yellow Sun Mk.2 made up the backbone of the RAF's free-fall nuclear arsenal until 1970 but for much or all of that time it could be delivered only from high or medium altitudes.

In the meantime the rapid improvement of Soviet air defences from the 1950s onwards gave an impetus to the development of weapons that would not require the carrier bomber to pass directly over its target. In Britain the final result of this work was the Avro Blue Steel air-launched missile which carried a Red Snow megaton-range warhead. This stand-off cruise missile was 35ft (10.67m) long and had a span of 13ft (3.96m) and was designed to be carried under the fuselages of both Victor and Vulcan B Mk.2s. When flying at Mach 0.8-0.9 Blue Steel's maximum range was around 200 miles (322km). However, a typical high-level launch would probably see it released from an altitude of 50,000ft (15,240m) at a distance of approximately 100nm (115 miles/185km) from its target. A 16,000 lb (71.1kN) Bristol Siddeley Stentor HTP/kerosene engine would then accelerate Blue Steel up to Mach 2.5 at 70,000ft (21,336m), after which a small sustainer motor would take over to propel the weapon for the remainder of its four-minute journey. At the end of its run the missile would pitch over into a 40° Mach 1.5+ dive towards its target.

A meeting was held at Cricklewood in April 1959 to consider the progress in the design of the Blue Steel installation in the Victor B Mk.2. It was proposed to use XH673 for the acceptance trials and the firm was required to drop two dummy stores before carriage and release clearance could be given. In fact, as Chapter Five tells, XH674 and XH675 were the aircraft that eventually took on the type's Blue Steel test programme. In due course they were joined by XL161 and in 1962 the latter aircraft went to the Weapons Research Establishment at Woomera in Australia to undertake firing trials.

In November 1961 it was confirmed that all B Mk.2s equipped with ECM were to be fed through a Blue Steel retrofit line. Of the initial feed in, to give a maximum of eight aircraft on the floor, it was expected that five examples would be fed direct from the production line and three would be given up from the Victor flight trials programme during the second and third quarters of 1962. The first Mk.2 to enter the Blue Steel retrofit line was XL164 in February 1962; by March 1964 the line was running smoothly and ten Blue Steel Victors had been produced. The first of these was delivered to the RAF in July 1963. However, as a result of an Air Council decision, the programme was reduced to twenty-one aircraft out of the original thirty designates. In due course Blue Steel was successfully adapted for release at low level to match the need for the V-Bombers to fly in at low level (below) but this brought with it a reduction in the missile's release range to about 30 miles (48km). In its new attack profile, after release the missile would zoom climb to an altitude of 17,000ft (5,182m) before diving onto the target, although at release the V-Bomber carrying it had to be climbing and also high enough to allow the Blue Steel to fall some 300ft (91m) before firing its motor.

Blue Steel was a touch more difficult to load aboard a Victor than a Vulcan because of the very limited ground clearance that was available. It was carried semi-recessed in the bomb bay and had fairings tailored to the body of the missile. After release a set of doors would close to restore the aircraft's aerodynamics around the lower middle fuselage. Yellow Sun was carried in the Victor's bomb bay, and the Mks.1 and 2 carried the same conventional ordnance load.

By the early 1960s it had become clear that Blue Steel's stand-off range would no longer be sufficient to guarantee that the bombers which carried it could reach their launch positions at high level before being attacked by surface-to-air missiles and/or Soviet fighters, even if this was well away from the target. The quality and capability of enemy defences were improving rapidly. Interceptors would soon be able to attack bombers at their operating heights and surface-to-air missiles were acquiring longer ranges and becoming more accurate. The predicted survival rates for the V-Bombers during an operation began to diminish very rapidly as did the possibility of hitting their targets. Consequently, in 1964 the Blue Steel force was switched from high to low level.

On 3rd May 1963 a 'Standard of Preparation' was issued for all Victor B Mk.2s to be adapted for low-level use following a design study made by Handley Page. After the cancellation of the Skybolt missile in December 1962 (see below), on 23rd January 1963 the Defence Committee approved the measures that would be necessary to give the V-Bombers a low-level capability, which included some modifications required for the Blue Steel missile as well. The preparations involved a considerable amount of study into the condition and potential fatigue life of the various airframes involved but in July 1964 it was considered that there was no need to improve the fatigue life of the Victor. Nevertheless, a flying programme to clear the aircraft would involve extensive low-altitude flight trials, ground trials looking into the effects of bird strikes, work on the engines to give protection against bird strikes, and the installation of terrain warning equipment.

The B Mk.2 Blue Steel Victor was given interim clearance to operate at low level for training purposes, carrying a Blue Steel training missile, with effect from 25th February 1964. Full low-level clearance for Blue Steel Victor Mk.2 was given on 21st April 1964, although later in the year the parameters covered by this approval were extended. An alternative camouflage scheme was cleared with effect from the seventh aircraft off retrofit. This comprised the original white undersides coupled with a new dark green and medium sea grey scheme plus standard 'bright' roundels and serials. The demarcation line was to run low down on the fuselage – except that is for XL513. On this aircraft the camouflage ended along the fuselage centreline and its roundels were still the old pale anti-radiation form.

Reconnaissance Developments

In April 1951, well before the first Victor had flown, Handley Page put forward a brochure for a High-Altitude Photographic Reconnaissance variant of the HP.80 bomber. It described a simple conversion where a 'PR unit' (which replaced the bomb doors) was hoisted into the bomb bay. This operation was expected to take between two and five days and was well within the capacity of RAF bases. With Armstrong Siddeley Sapphire 4 engines and a take-off weight of 160,000 lb (72,576kg) with drop tanks, the estimated range was 6,700nm (12,410km); with Rolls-Royce Conways and a 150,000 lb (68,040kg) take-off weight this became 7,100nm (13,150km). There was an alternative scheme to fit a standard bomber with a redesigned rear fuselage and no bomb bay. This would have more internal fuel and fixed provision for cameras and photoflashes, etc.

Official interest in a PR development first appeared on 16th July 1951, but it was some time before things began to happen. On 27th June 1953 a memorandum was issued by the Air Ministry which confirmed that early Victor production aircraft intended for service use were also required to operate in the photo reconnaissance role. The PR installation was to be easily removed so that the aircraft could be returned to bomber duties as and when required. The installation had to cover day, day survey and night PR operations and Handley Page was authorised to proceed with the necessary development work. The memo also indicated that prior to any quantity production an installation should be prepared and tested in the second prototype WB775. In fact, after the first prototype was lost this was not carried out and it was production aircraft XA920 that tried the PR fitting for the first time (see Chapter

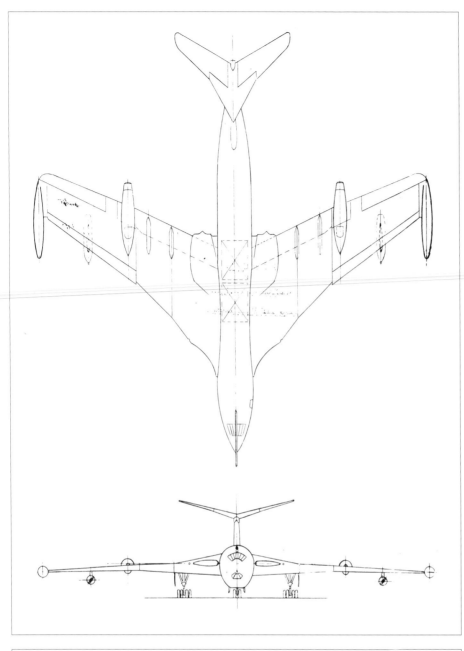

Five). In the end, however, only the Mk.2 Victor was adapted for reconnaissance work.

In May 1961 the Air Staff declared that only one squadron of Mk.2 aircraft with a PR capability would actually be required. Consequently the last nine Mk.2 Victors scheduled for the retrofit B Mk.2R programme were actually converted into B(SR) Mk.2 bomber/reconnaissance aircraft. Their equipment embraced a side-locked H2S with highly advanced mapping facility plus what is understood to be the biggest camera package ever operated by a Western air force. There were two 8,000 lb (3,629kg) cylindrical fuel tanks fitted into the front and rear of the bomb bay and the camera pallet was loaded in between these tanks. This pallet could take a mix of installations – eight F.96 reconnaissance cameras and four F.49 survey cameras for day-time operations, or F.89 cameras and three magazines with 108 photoflashes for night work – and the types of film used by them included infra-red, ultra-violet and false-colour. The magazines each held thirty-six photoflashes, and to carry all three of these in the bomb bay needed the removal of the two cylindrical fuel tanks. Both oblique and vertical photographs could be taken by these aircraft and their equipment was upgraded as required.

One aircraft, XM718, was part converted from Blue Steel standard and so retained some 'missile' features – it received only 23 of the 24 SR modifications. The reason was that this particular Victor was both the 'reserve' SR Mk.2 and Blue Steel aircraft, so one Blue Steel fitting was incorporated instead of the equivalent SR one to make it easier for the aircraft to receive all of the other Blue Steel modifications should they be needed at a later date. In fact most of the SR.2 mods were actually common to both SR Mk.2 and Blue Steel Victors, although the latter had far more changes. They were all produced on the same line, the Blue Steel examples first, and then the SR Mk.2s.

After its Blue Steel trial duties, XH675 was used at Boscombe Down to perfect the Victor B(SR) Mk.2's reconnaissance equipment right through to 1963, while XL165 performed the role of installation test airframe and flew for the first time in this configuration on 23rd February 1965. The first B(SR) Mk.2 Victor was delivered in May 1965 and these versatile machines operated in this role until they were converted into tankers in the 1970s. They were eventually redesignated SR Mk.2 because quite clearly they would not be undertaking any bombing. The tasks required of these aeroplanes were generally maritime reconnaissance at high level over the sea or coastline, plus surveying over land. Consequently they were not expected to travel over enemy territory and so some of the ECM equipment was also left out.

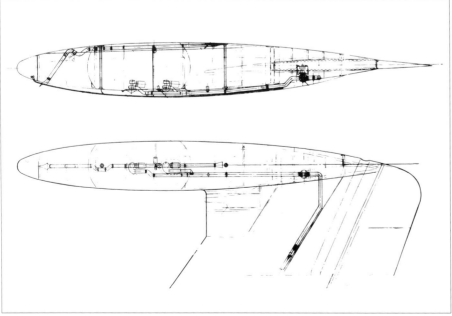

The Victor K Mk.1/1A fitted with tip tanks, as proposed in August 1966. Handley Page Association

Proposed Victor K Mk.1/1A tip tank installation and piping. Handley Page Association

Tankers

The withdrawal of the Vickers Valiants in 1965 because of metal fatigue has been described in Chapter Two. However, the same susceptible material was used in the Victor's wing and XA919, the third B Mk.1 which by now had been retired from flying and downgraded to a ground instruction airframe at Locking, was utilised as a fatigue test rig to assess the condition and the life expectancy of the Victors. In contrast to the study of this problem completed in July 1964 the results were not so good because it was clear that the Victors too would last for only a relatively short period if they were permanently employed on low-level operations. The decision was therefore taken to expand the Victor tanker conversion programme to embrace the Mk.2. This would allow them to return to high-level flying and thereby push their life expectancy back to a more reasonable figure. The Vulcan's solid delta wing planform and structure allowed that aircraft to withstand the stresses and buffeting of low-level flying rather better and so Avro's aircraft was able to perform this task for much longer.

In August 1966 Handley Page completed a design study brochure and assessment report that described a new tanker development of the Victor, for application both to the K Mk.1 and 1A and to the SR Mk.2 variants. (Note: for reasons unknown the brochure refers only to the SR Mk.2 – it is not known if these particular plans would eventually have embraced other Mk.2 aircraft.) The most visible feature was the wing-tip fuel tanks. These had in fact been proposed over a year previously and in response the Air Staff had requested that they should be examined closely. An Instruction to Proceed with a feasibility study, to assess the design problems involved and the stresses that would be experienced by the wing, had been given in January 1966. The research covered by the report also included taxi trials using XA918 that looked into the problems of the potential wing fatigue through having these tip tanks in place.

The work required to convert both marks of Victor was quite similar. The tanks were made in light alloy and mounted on fixed extensions to the outer wing structure at the wing tips and each of them had a capacity of 350gal (1,591lit). The outer wing structure required reinforcing from 'Station 480' outboard to support the tank but no additional strengthening was required inboard of this position either on the intermediate or centre wing. Connection to the existing fuel system was provided by a pipe extending through the wing leading edge structure outboard from the wing refuelling pod to the tip tank. The aircraft's existing wing tips would be removed and replaced by the fixed extensions which formed a mounting and a

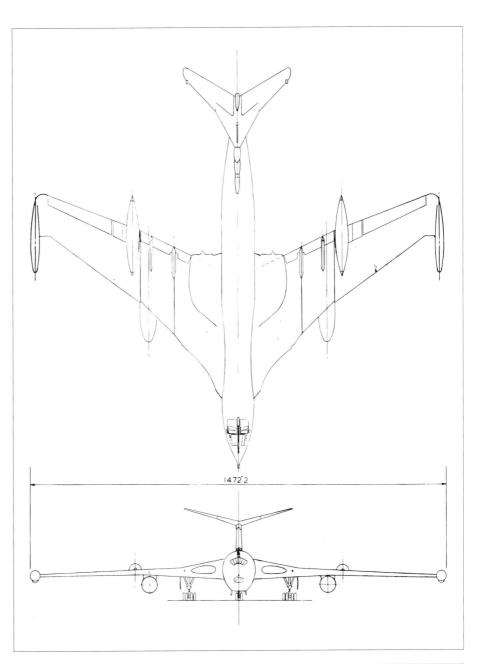

The Victor SR Mk.2 fitted with tip tanks, as proposed in August 1966. Handley Page Association

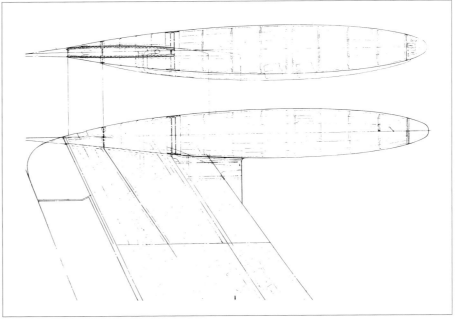

The proposed Victor SR Mk.2 tip tank installation. Handley Page Association

Victor Mk.2s undergoing conversion to K.2 tankers at Woodford in 1971/72. The aircraft in the foreground is XL188. Note the underwing tank and 'Kuchemann carrot' at the front on the floor, and the Hawker Siddeley Nimrod and airliner production lines in the background.
Handley Page Association

fairing at the rear of the tank. The estimated gross weight for the converted K Mk.1/1As was 203,000 lb (92,080kg) including 5,600 lb (2,540kg) of fuel in the tip tanks.

The aircraft's longitudinal trim, stability and control were not expected to be appreciably affected by the presence of tip tanks. Static longitudinal stability could be marginally improved by a small rearward movement of the aerodynamic centre and the lateral and directional properties would be affected by the increased rolling and yawing moments of inertia, although in the case of lateral stability the auto-stabiliser was expected to eliminate this effect. If one tip tank were full and the other empty there would be a tendency to directional swinging on applying the brakes during the landing run. There was a small increase in drag. Based on current levels of usage, Handley Page had calculated that if an aircraft was converted as the company recommended between 1968 and 1970, the wing's fatigue life would last until 1975/78 without the tip tanks in position, and until 1981/84 with tip tanks.

The SR Mk.2 would use the same conversion process with a reinforced wing structure except that the outer wing fixed extensions would have to be larger to cater for the greater span. The tanks were interchangeable with all marks of converted aircraft, and the Mk.2 tanker's gross take-off weight was 223,000 lb (101,153kg). The aerial for its Blue Diver barrage noise jammer would be remounted in the wing tip just inboard of the tip tank. Despite the Mk.2's larger span, Handley Page predicted

that the effects of having tip tanks would generally be similar to those on the K Mk.1 and 1As and would not present a serious handling problem (although they would be a little more noticeable to the pilot due to the additional effects of having the underwing tanks in place). Again the company calculated that if an aircraft was converted between 1968 and 1970, the wings would last until 1974/77 without tip tanks and to at least 1980/82 with tip tanks.

Handley Page concluded that tip tanks were feasible for both the Mk.1 tankers and Mk.2 SR aircraft and they offered a worthwhile improvement in wing fatigue life. The tip tanks gave a slightly lower rolling performance but the ailerons would provide adequate control throughout the flight envelope. Each of the six crew members – two pilots, navigator radar and navigator plotter, air electronics officer and supernumerary – would have their own ejection seats and the centre of gravity would be moved aft by about 7in (17.8cm). The presence of tip tanks effectively increased the wing aspect ratio but reduced the bending moment and thereby helped to prevent the wings from running out of fatigue life. (Stresses in a structure are proportionate to the loads, or moments, on them, so by reducing the moment, such as by reducing the length over which the load acts, the overall stress is reduced. In this case the downward moment from having a heavy tank at the wing tip tends to cancel out the upward moment produced by aerodynamic forces on the wing such as those caused by turbulent air.)

Harry Fraser-Mitchell of the Handley Page Association told the authors that had this project gone ahead the tip tanks would have needed to be empty when the Victor took off. If the Victor was fully loaded with fuel, the vibration on take-off would make the tip tanks 'bounce' and this would very quickly have strained the wings. Instead the Victor would receive the rest of its load on the climb with the fuel in the tip tanks acting as a reserve. Although the concept showed much promise, the life of the Handley Page Company was nearly over and this situation prevented these tanker conversions from going ahead in this form. In 1969 Handley Page went into liquidation and in March 1970 the company was closed.

However, it was important to the RAF to have Mk.2 Victors with their Conway engines converted to tankers because, once again, the Rolls-Royce engines offered better performance than the Mk.1's Sapphires, in this case in regard to the extra weight of fuel that could be carried. Soon after the factory closure the Mk.2 tanker conversion contract was awarded to Hawker Siddeley Aviation at Woodford, previously Handley Page's great rival Avro. It is not difficult to imagine what ex-Handley Page employees felt about this situation but work on

A K Mk.2 tanker overflies Radlett and presents the type's underside in great detail. Handley Page

A K Mk.2 tanker overflies Radlett and presents the type's underside in great detail. Handley Page

Another unidentified K Mk.2 shows off its three-point tanker facility. Handley Page

converting Mk.2 bombers, some of which had been in store, was soon under way.

Hawker Siddeley's modifications for the Mk.2 tanker were rather different to the Handley Page proposals and they dispensed with the tip tanks. The requirements had stated that the aircraft would no longer be used for any bombing and so all of the associated equipment and fittings for that task, including Blue Steel and almost all of the ECM and jamming equipment, was removed. A Blue Sage passive warning receiver was kept within the tail cone and the streamlined 'Kuchemann carrots' on the upper wings were retained. Improved navigation aids were installed, plus a TACAN beacon to help the receiving aircraft make their initial contact with the tanker. The centreline Mk.17 hose drum unit in the bomb bay and the underwing Mk.20B pods installed on the three-point Mk.1 tankers were all employed on the Mk.2. Underwing slipper tanks were available but these could not be jettisoned, and the tail cone was now used to jettison fuel. Theoretical fuel load was 127,000 lb (57,607kg), comprising 32,000 lb (14,515kg) in the wing tanks, another 32,000 lb (14,515kg) in the former bomb bay, 36,000 lb (16,330kg) carried in the rest of the fuselage and 27,000 lb (12,247kg) in underwing tanks. However, the normal load was actually 123,000 lb (55,793kg). The wingspan was reduced from 120ft (36.6m) to 117ft (35.7m) and the maximum take-off weight was 223,000 lb (101,153kg).

The prototype conversion XL231 first flew in this form (but with some modification work still required) on 1st March 1972. Woodford completed a thorough life assessment for the airframes and cleared them for an average of fourteen years of flying from conversion. In all, during the first half of the 1970s, twenty-four aircraft were converted to this K Mk.2 tanker standard, and the first to be delivered to the RAF was XL233 in May 1974. The usual Battleship Grey and Lincoln Green camouflage with white undersides was used by all Victor tankers until some examples had their undersides repainted light aircraft grey in the late 1970s. Then in 1982 each aircraft was repainted overall in a hemp colour scheme with smaller pale blue and red roundels and white serial numbers.

VICTOR DEVELOPMENT PROPOSALS

HP.98 Target Marker

The HP.98 was a November 1951 proposal from Handley Page for a high-speed target marker powered by Conway 3 engines. This was aerodynamically and structurally the same aircraft as the B Mk.1 and included the normal bomb bay to permit conversion back to a standard Victor bomber with some ease. Radar-sighted remotely controlled tail guns were to be installed for the HP.98's operations at low level. Normal all up weight was 145,000 lb (65,772kg), overload 175,000 lb (79,380kg) and the HP.98 was expected to cruise at 576mph (926km/h) but the target-marker

version of the Vickers Valiant was the design selected for prototype trials.

'Transonic' Victor B Phase 4

In October 1956 Handley Page made a tentative development proposal for a Victor Phase 4 following a study of the supersonic capabilities of the Mk.1 and 2. The application of area rule to the Victor showed that the original airframe had closely approximated to the optimum shape for minimum compressibility drag in supersonic flight. By modifying the fuselage with area rule and adding reheat to the Conway 31 engines it was possible to make the aircraft capable of Mach 1.1 on the level at 36,000ft (10,973m), and to cruise supersonically at Mach 1.06

(702mph/1,130km/h) at 65,000ft (19,812m) while over the target. When flying subsonically the design offered a potential range/load/height performance that was comparable to the B Mk.2, with an optimum cruising Mach number of 0.9. However, it was established that such an aircraft would be capable of flying at over 60,000ft (18,288m) only if it flew at Mach 1.05 – flying at Mach 0.9 would not be sufficient to push the aircraft to that altitude.

The weapon load included one 7,000 lb (3,175kg) medium capacity store, a 2,000 lb (907kg) Red Beard and one 15,000 lb (6,804kg) stand-off weapon. Normal fuel load was 11,750gal (53,426lit), the take-off weight for long-range operations was 200,000 lb (90,720kg) and the maximum range at this weight was 5,270 miles (8,480km). The reason behind this proposal was the growing threat to V-Bomber types from developments in defensive guided weapon systems; at one stage Handley Page considered six engines to try and achieve this capability but the design team realised that four afterburners would be enough. However, RAE Farnborough did not like this project and it appears that Handley Page probably only really looked at the aircraft as a stopgap. The brochure stated that it "provides an essential link in the chain of development of the 'deterrent' in the critical period 1960-66, when the subsonic 'V' Bombers may well be unacceptably vulnerable and the fully supersonic reconnaissance and bombing aircraft not yet available". No 'HP' project number was allocated to the project.

Model of the very handsome Victor B Phase 4 of October 1956. George Cox

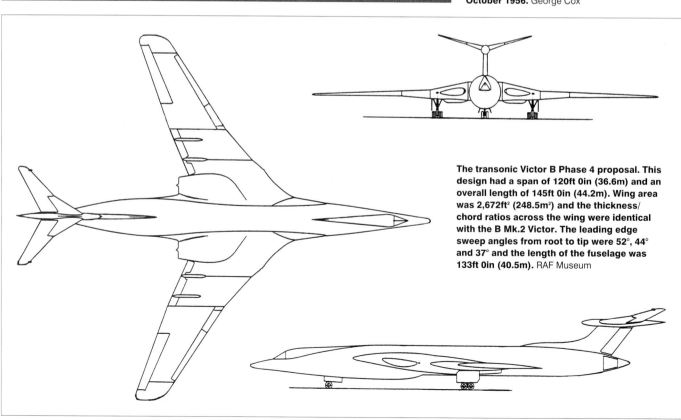

The transonic Victor B Phase 4 proposal. This design had a span of 120ft 0in (36.6m) and an overall length of 145ft 0in (44.2m). Wing area was 2,672ft² (248.5m²) and the thickness/chord ratios across the wing were identical with the B Mk.2 Victor. The leading edge sweep angles from root to tip were 52°, 44° and 37° and the length of the fuselage was 133ft 0in (40.5m). RAF Museum

Victor B Mk.2 Patrol Missile Carrier

A considerable amount of design effort went into adapting the Victor to carry examples of an American air-launched nuclear ballistic missile called Skybolt, after the Minister of Defence announced in April 1960 that the weapon was to be procured for the RAF. Avro too covered this ground with the Vulcan and actually test flew dummy missiles on wing pylons before America abandoned the weapon itself in 1962. British plans to buy Skybolt were subsequently cancelled in December of that year, which meant that Handley Page's studies never progressed beyond the drawing board.

The earliest studies for V-Bombers to carry the Douglas WS-138 missile, which became Skybolt, were made in and around July and August 1959 when the weapon looked somewhat different. In March 1960 Handley Page completed a brochure for a 'Patrol Missile Carrier' which outlined a Victor designed to carry up to four Skybolts. Such an adaptation would be much cheaper to produce than an all-new carrier aircraft and was capable of a long duration 'stand-off' patrol of some fourteen hours. A satisfactory take-off performance for all up weights up to 285,000 lb (129,276kg) would be provided by four 20,600 lb (91.6kN) thrust Conway Co.17 engines fitted with reheat, and the assistance of two Spectre rockets would push this figure up to 310,000 lb (140,616kg). The carrier would be introduced in two stages: Phase I would carry just two Skybolts at the existing drop tank positions, while Phase II would have all four. Phase I was seen as a relatively simple modification which could be done at RAF stations, while Phase II would be completed on a retrospective modification line at the factory. Handley Page estimated that a mid-1960 start would see C(A) Release for these versions in 1963 and 1964 respectively.

It was proposed to use XH670, XH673 and XL159 for C(A) flight testing, with XH670 being used for Skybolt handling, performance, engineering and release trials. This would require the fitting of modified outer wings with 1,200gal (5,456lit) tip tanks, two new bomb bay tanks containing 11,000gal (50,016lit) in total and, ultimately, new undercarriages and provision for the two additional missiles. The bomb bay doors would go and the new tanks would form the fuselage undersurface. During the early stages of XH670's programme, the handling and performance flight trials with the outer wings and tip tanks would be done by XL159. Thus XH670 would be free to cover the missile trials, while XH673 would be in reserve as an insurance aircraft and for miscellaneous trials such as radio and radar installations. The only big changes for Phase I would be the modified outer wings and tip tanks, and for conversion at

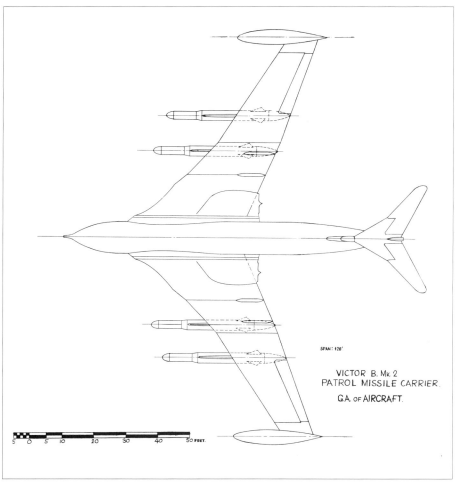

VICTOR B. Mk.2
PATROL MISSILE CARRIER.
G.A. OF AIRCRAFT.

SPAN: 128'

service stations Handley Page intended to supply replacement wings complete with tanks and piping. Some new internal structure would be needed to mount the outer missiles and this, with the tip tanks, would require additional strengthening to the outer wings. A new main undercarriage would have six-wheel twelve-tyre bogies to cope with the substantial increase in take-off weight and provide additional braking capacity. The T.4 bombsight and H2S/NBC would be removed and replaced by

a side-looking Red Neck radar and Skybolt computer.

The length was unchanged but the larger span (to reduce induced drag) was 128ft 0in (39.0m) and gross wing area 2,666ft² (247.9m²). With two missiles aboard the normal take-off weight was 260,000 lb (117,936kg); with four this rose to 310,000 lb (140,616kg). The cruise would be flown at Mach 0.7 at an altitude of around 36,000ft (10,973m), and missile launch would take place at Mach 0.85 and

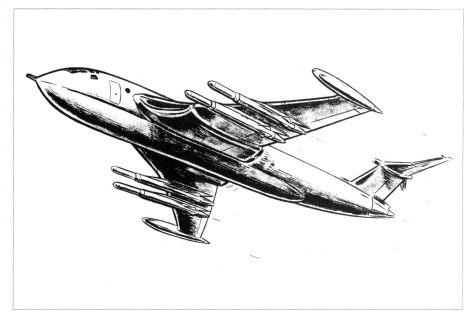

Planview drawing of the Victor B Mk.2 Patrol Missile Carrier. Handley Page Association

Artist's sketch of the Victor Patrol Missile Carrier. Handley Page Association

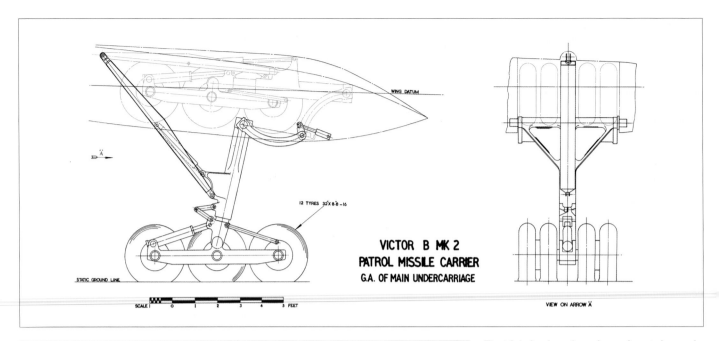

VICTOR B MK 2
PATROL MISSILE CARRIER
G.A. OF MAIN UNDERCARRIAGE

12 TYRES 32"X 8·8 – 16

WING DATUM

STATIC GROUND LINE

SCALE   0   1   2   3   4   5 FEET

VIEW ON ARROW 'A'

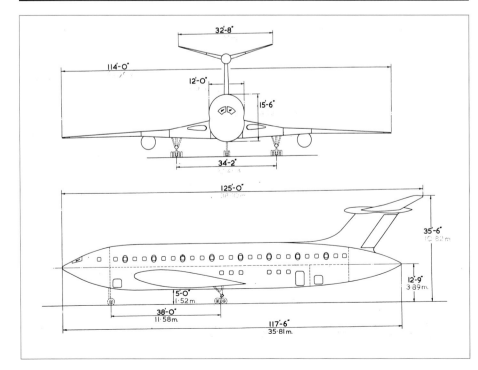

The triple-bogie main undercarriage to be used by the Victor Patrol Missile Carrier.
Handley Page Association

Model of the Patrol Missile Carrier with a full complement of four Douglas Skybolt weapons aboard. Handley Page

The HP.97 airliner proposal of February 1952.
Handley Page Association

around 45,000ft (13,716m). For Phase II with four missiles aboard the still air range was 6,000nm (11,118km); with two missiles 7,150nm (13,249km). The Air Staff formally requested that this proposal should be studied in more depth and a follow-up brochure in June covered some changes to the missile's configuration. Principally these were an increase from four to eight fins and a higher weight per round of 12,137 lb (5,505kg) from 11,450 lb (5,194kg), which contributed to the weight of the four-missile carrier going up to 318,620 lb (144,526kg). It was also now requested that the Victor's conventional free-falling weapon delivery capability should be retained, which meant that the H2S/NBC equipment with a side-looking facility was still required.

In July Handley Page told the Ministry of Aviation that after further investigation the Victor B Mk.2 could be adapted to carry two Skybolts without modifications to the airframe or missile to improve ground clearance (which had been the key issue when mating the weapon to the Victor). This was achieved by mounting the missile 18in (45.7cm) further forward on the pylon than had been done previously. However, the Skybolt Victor was not taken up and in fact it is understood that the Air Staff's plan had been to use the Avro Vulcan as its Skybolt platform and to back this up with Victors and Blue Steel. Apparently there was never a concrete programme to fit Skybolt onto the Victor. At the time the Skybolt Victor studies were highly secret and may not have been given the HP.114 number often credited to them (because the project never came to anything). The aircraft would certainly have been expensive to produce, and Handley Page never received any Skybolt rounds to try out on a Victor airframe – Avro received all of those that were available.

TRANSPORT AND CIVILIAN PROPOSALS

HP.97 Civil Transport

The HP.97 high-speed long-range civil airliner development was first proposed in February 1952. It was based on the Victor Mk.1 and the crescent wing offered not only high speeds but large payloads. HP.97 would cruise at 500 knots (576mph/926km/h) and carry 96 first class or 150 tourist passengers in a two-deck fuselage and have space for 1,000ft³ (28.3m³) of baggage and freight. The load-carrying capacity was given as 50,000 lb (22,680kg) and the freight holds and the galley were located on the lower deck. Long-range fuel was carried in external tanks (in preference to fuselage tanks). Span was 114ft 0in (34.7m), overall length 125ft 0in (38.1m), wing area 2,540ft² (236.2m²), internal fuel 4,850gal (22,052lit), external fuel (under wing) 5,000gal (22,735lit) and maximum take-off weight 170,000 lb (77,112kg) without external tanks and 190,000 lb (86,184kg) with them.

Fuselage arrangement of the 96-seat version of the HP.97. With triple seats fitted the aircraft could be reconfigured to take 150 passengers. Handley Page Association

Model of the original HP.97 proposal. George Cox

The much modified HP.97 project of October 1956. Handley Page Association

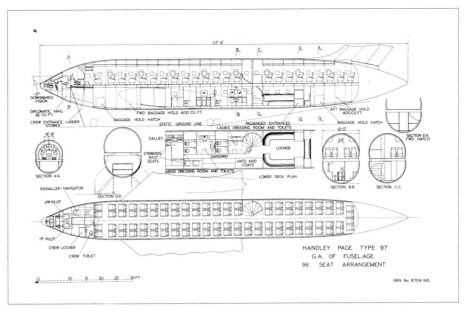

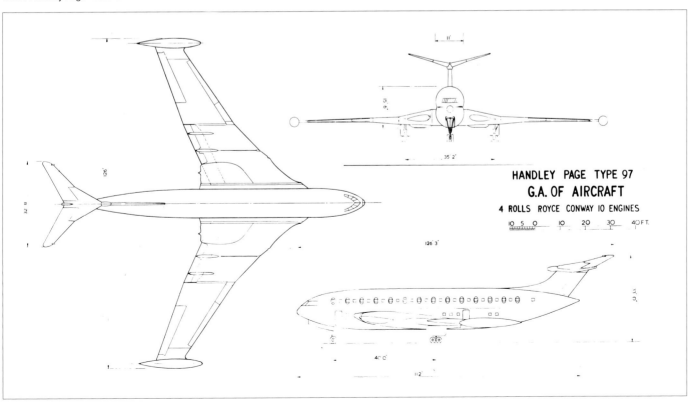

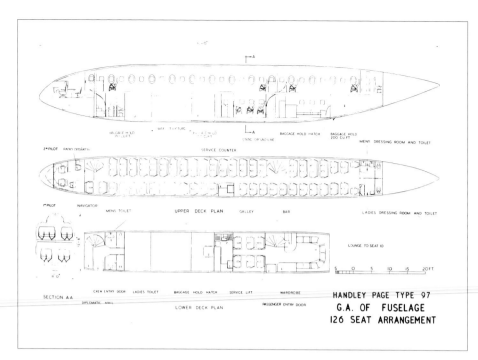

HANDLEY PAGE TYPE 97
G.A. OF FUSELAGE
126 SEAT ARRANGEMENT

Four 11,500 lb (51.1kN) jet engines would provide the power but the engine type was not specified.

In May 1953 Sir Frederick Handley Page stated in *The Aeroplane* that "our new 150-seater HP.97, an inter-continental jetliner, has profited greatly from the evolution of the Victor bomber and its crescent wing. It is capable of three [non-stop] Atlantic crossings between London and New York in a day at a direct operating cost of less than £15 per passenger." Estimates suggested that on eastbound flights 122 passengers and their baggage would be carried across in 6.5 hours; westbound there would be five fewer passengers and because of the prevailing winds the journey would take an hour longer.

The project was not taken up but in October 1956 the HP.97 reappeared in another brochure with a different double-bubble fuselage on Victor wings plus 17,500 lb (77.8kN) Conway Co.10 engines (or if required more powerful Co.30s for a greater range/load performance). These engines made this HP.97 the airliner equivalent of the Mk.2 Victor. The cruise speed at long range was the same (a little higher for short ranges) and the payload was given as 126 passengers or 30,000 lb

(13,608kg) for a still air range of 4,200nm (7,783km). The mainplane was formed from the inner, intermediate and outer sections of the Victor wing and had the same controls but there were tip tanks plus a modified centre section built integral with the transport fuselage. The engine installation was the same as the bomber but reverse thrust and jet silencing (similar to the Rolls-Royce Avon RA.29 civil engine) were under development. The empennage was identical to the Mk.2 Victor, the main undercarriage was similar but the nose gear was new. A fuselage fitted with 126 seats and a lounge bar was only one of several alternatives, and there was 800ft³ (22.64m³) of baggage space.

Span was 126ft 0in (38.4m), overall length 126ft 3in (38.5m), wing area 2,680ft² (249.2m²), wing thickness/chord ratio 16% at the root and 6% at the tip, fuel load 8,000gal (36,375lit) in the wings and 2,600gal (11,822lit) in the tip tanks, and the take-off weight was 210,000 lb (95,256kg). The fuselage was 11ft 0in (3.35m) wide and 15ft 6in (4.72m) high. The brochure included a number of route assessments and weight estimates, and the airliner was designed with BOAC Commonwealth routes in mind. Sir Frederick Handley Page's chairman's report for 1956 stated that if BOAC had been interested in the HP.97 when it was offered to the airline in 1952 it would have been in service before America's new jetliners had arrived.

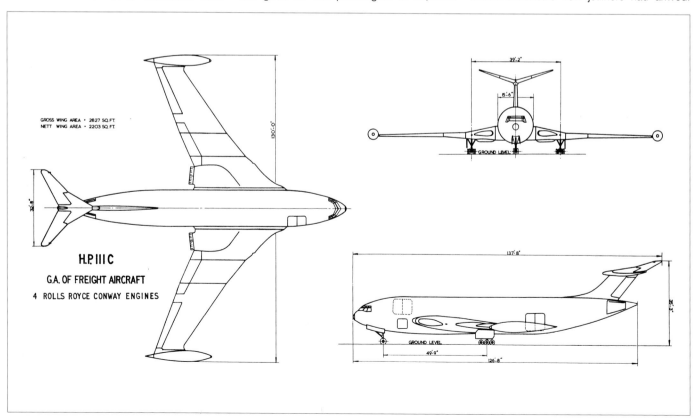

H.P. III C
G.A. OF FREIGHT AIRCRAFT
4 ROLLS ROYCE CONWAY ENGINES

GROSS WING AREA · 2827 SQ.FT.
NETT WING AREA · 2203 SQ.FT.

Internal detail of the HP.111 combined freighter and troop carrier. Handley Page Association

Civil airliner version of the Handley Page HP.111C transport. Handley Page Association

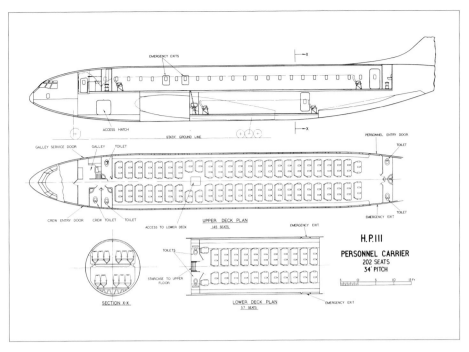

However, BOAC's new executive was now showing interest in an even more advanced civil development of the Victor (and this was why the Conway-powered HP.97 brochure was prepared). The HP.97 was still being pushed for possible orders at the September 1957 Farnborough Show but none were obtained.

HP.111

The HP.111 long-range, high-speed, general-purpose freight and personnel transport of May 1958 was intended for use in strategic and assault roles. It was powered by four 17,250 lb (76.7kN) Conway 11s fitted with thrust reversers and silencers, and as a personnel carrier could move 202 troops over a range of 3,300nm (6,115km), or 96 troops over 4,500nm (8,340km). The main freight hold was 11ft 6in (3.50m) wide, 11ft 6in (3.50m) high and 40ft (12.19m) long but there was also a forward hold 9ft (2.74m) wide, 6ft (1.83m) high and 12ft (3.66m) long. As a freighter the HP.111 could carry 53,000 lb (24,041kg) or 27,000 lb (12,247kg) of payload over the same distances as the trooper. A total of 120 paratroops could also be dropped with the aircraft flying at a speed of 132mph (213km/h). For its time the project was unique in that it offered long-range strategic operation at high speed coupled with the ability to land on 1,000yd (914m) grass airstrips. The need for such an aeroplane had

been underlined recently by an RAF airlift to Cyprus in which 3,500 men and over 90 tons of stores were flown from Britain in five days by forty-five aircraft. It was claimed that the same task could have been undertaken by six HP.111 aircraft in just two days.

Speed at altitude was Mach 0.825 (544mph/875km/h) cruising at 40,000ft to 45,000ft (12,192m to 13,716m) but Mach 0.9 (593mph/954km/h) was available for operational necessity. Maximum operating altitude was 50,000ft (15,240m). The wing thickness/chord ratio was the same as the Victor bomber, the span (including tip tanks) was 130ft 0in

(39.6m), overall length 137ft 8in (42.0m) and wing area 2,827ft² (262.9m²). The maximum diameter of the fuselage was 15ft 6in (4.72m) and internal fuel totalled 11,500gal (52,290lit); normal take-off weight off a rigid pavement was 240,000 lb (108,864kg) and for a semi-prepared runway 180,000 lb (81,648kg). With Victor drop tanks and no payload the range could be extended to 6,800nm (12,600km).

Once again the HP.111 owed much of its design to the Victor. The wing was identical to the bomber's except for the centre section across the fuselage, the main six-wheel twelve-tyre undercarriage trailing-boxes and the wing

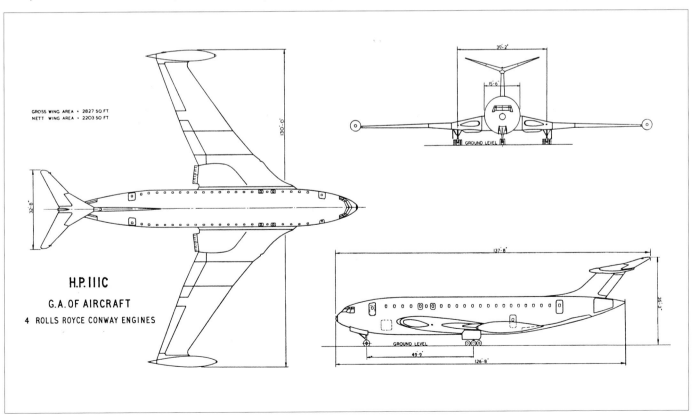

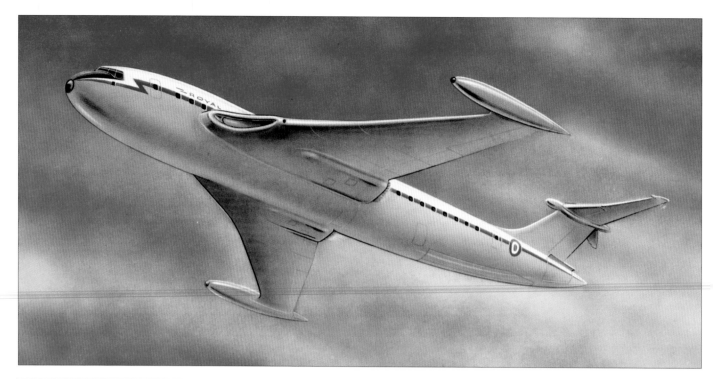

tips. HP.111 did have split and blown flaps and was readily convertible for any of the following roles:

1. Large capacity single-deck freighter
2. Two-deck freighter
3. Two-deck mixed freighter/personnel
4. Two-deck all-personnel transport

There was also the potential to adapt the HP.111 as a 168-seat passenger airliner. High- and low-speed wind tunnel models were being made to check the new fuselage, and Handley Page stated that three aircraft would be required to complete the C(A) trials programme. If the project was started in 1958 the designers expected a first flight in early 1961. Service entry could take place by the end of 1962.

The HP.111 came under consideration along with several other projects including a turbo-prop design from Shorts called the Britannic. The Air Staff favoured a turbojet design very much but political situations and decisions affected the issue, not least a lack of work at the government-owned Short Brothers factory in Belfast. The order duly went to Shorts and the firm's turboprop eventually entered service as the Belfast. In September Handley Page proposed the HP.111C civil variant with 21,000 lb (93.3kN) thrust Conway 42s, and this was followed in January 1960 by the HP.111C freighter but the project's opportunity had gone.

Artwork showing the HP.111 in RAF Transport Command colours. Handley Page Association

Artist's impression of the Handley Page HP.111 transport project of 1958. The late Jack Meaden

Model of the HP.111 on display at one of the SBAC Farnborough shows. The late Jack Meaden

Chapter Four

Service History

Background to Service

The V-Bomber Force was intended to deliver the British nuclear deterrent and had begun its existence in January 1955 with the entry into service of the Vickers Valiant. The Valiant was joined by the Avro Vulcan in June 1957 and the Victor completed the trio of types with its entry into squadron service in 1958. As with the two earlier types, the Victor's intended role was the delivery of nuclear weapons from high altitude, operating above the level attainable by the fighters or missiles used by the opposition. The initial specification had called for a ceiling of 50,000ft (15,240m) over the target, and as the bombers were developed efforts were made to better this figure. For example the Mk.2 received the more powerful Rolls-Royce Conway turbofan to achieve a higher service ceiling, although Handley Page would have preferred to use later versions of the Sapphire to attain an even greater height. As with the earlier V-Bombers, the Victor relied on the Navigation and Bombing System (NBS), although provision was made for the use of an optical T.4 bombsight as an alternative. The optical sight was soon withdrawn from use on operational Victors. The NBS was described in more detail in the companion volume on the Avro Vulcan, as was the overall role of Bomber Command and descriptions of its infrastructure and *modus operandi*, so will not be repeated here.

The Victor perhaps suffered somewhat from being the last of the V-Bomber types to be delivered. Being the last into production, it was the easiest to target when overall production had to be cut back. Thus, while the initial service versions (B Mk.1) of both types were produced in similar numbers, in comparison to the number of eighty-two Avro Vulcan B Mk.2s that entered service, only fifty-nine of the Victor B.2 version were ordered, and twenty-five of this smaller quantity were ultimately cancelled. This did not prevent the Victor from achieving very long service with distinction but perhaps its smaller numbers imprinted its unique shape less on the public mind than that of the iconic Vulcan.

Much of the credibility of a 'deterrent' relies on one's enemy believing that the deterrent really exists and will function as intended. Therefore the Victor joined with the earlier V-Bombers in exercises and deployments to show that RAF Bomber Command was a 'force in being' that could readily operate from diverse locations at short notice and deliver the nuclear weapons that it was capable of carrying. The Victor followed the pattern previously established whereby part of the force was maintained at permanent readiness at its normal bases. In times of tension the force could be ordered to proceed to dispersal bases, where groups of two or four aircraft remained at readiness to take off within the limit of four minutes from receipt of a missile attack warning. During the peak strength of the V-Force the Victor served with six Squadrons of Bomber Command, at Cottesmore, Honington and Wittering, in addition to having its own Operational Conversion Unit at Gaydon and providing a small number of aircraft for the Radar Reconnaissance Flight at Wyton. The intention was that in a major emergency the V-Force would disperse to selected airfields all over the UK that had runways of sufficient length and strength to operate its aircraft.

The dispersal routine was regularly practised during exercises. Dispersal gave the potential enemy a larger number of targets to hit, as well as allowing the whole force to become airborne in its allotted launch time of four minutes from receiving a warning of missile attack, since each runway had to launch only two or four aircraft. In practice, crews from each of the normal bases dispersed to the same small group of allotted dispersals to ensure that aircrews and

XA927 of No 10 Squadron – white overall with toned-down roundels, serial number and No 10 Squadron fin markings, and showing the small Orange Putter tail-warning radome. Phil Butler

XA933 of No 232 OCU at its Gaydon base during the Battle of Britain Day display on 17th September 1960. It has the Orange Putter radome and wears its serial number repeated on the nose-wheel doors. Phil Butler

XA933, still with No 232 OCU, but now coded 'A', at Coltishall in September 1961. Phil Butler

A later shot of XA933, now in the toned-down markings but still 'A' of No 232 OCU. Phil Butler

their supporting ground staff maintained familiarity with these locations. For example the dispersal at Burtonwood always received Vulcans (usually from Scampton), while that at Llanbedr always received Victors (usually from Wittering). Other dispersals used by the Victor squadrons included Boscombe Down, Bruntingthorpe, Lyneham, St Mawgan and Thurleigh.

The Victor joined the Valiant in forming the equipment of No 3 Group, Bomber Command (the Vulcan force served with No 1 Group). No 3 Group, in addition to managing and supporting the Valiant and Victor squadrons, also covered the Bomber Operational Conversion Units, No 231 (Canberras) and No 232 (Valiants and Victors). No 230 OCU operated in No 1 Group for some years before later transferring to No 3 Group. No 232 OCU was formed at Gaydon in February 1955 as the Valiant Operational Conversion Unit. The role of an OCU was primarily the training of complete crews on a different type of aircraft. In the case of the V-Bombers, which had a crew of five, this meant taking aircrew with a variety of experience from different sources. The new role of Air Electronics Officer was introduced at this time because the V-Bombers used the Navigational Bombing System which was more complex than anything previously available on an RAF bomber. The Victor joined the Valiant with No 232 OCU in November 1957 when the first example entered RAF service, and it remained with the unit until June 1965 when the OCU was disbanded following the withdrawal from service of the Valiant. Victor operational training then continued with the Tanker Training Flight at Marham, which specialised in the aircraft's new role as a refuelling tanker.

Although several of the first Victor crews to graduate from the Gaydon OCU went on to form No 10 Squadron, others moved on to Wyton to fly Victor B.1s with the Radar Reconnaissance Flight (RRF), which actually received its first aircraft before the first delivery to No 10 Squadron. The RRF was involved in the development of radar reconnaissance techniques, although it also had an operational role using Yellow Aster, a slightly modified version of the NBS, for maritime reconnaissance activities. Strategic reconnaissance was considered an important role for the V-Force. The second Valiant squadron to form had been No 543 which was also based at Wyton as a strategic reconnaissance unit, so perhaps it was no surprise that the first 'operational' Victor unit to form had a similar role, even if it was only a few days in advance of a true 'bomber' squadron.

The initial Victor base, apart from the Operational Conversion Unit at Gaydon and the small RRF at Wyton, was established at Cottesmore and occupied by Nos 10 and 15 Squadrons. (No 15 Squadron, by tradition, more usually identified itself as XV Squadron.) The Cottesmore Wing was initiated with the formation of No 10 Squadron on 15th April 1958 from some of the first crews to graduate from the OCU at Gaydon. No XV Squadron joined the Wing on 1st September 1958 and the two Squadrons served at Cottesmore until 1964. The Victors were allowed to fly only within the British Isles until this limitation was cancelled in March 1958.

The second operational base was Honington, where No 57 Squadron formed on 1st January 1959. After a delay of over a year, No 57 was joined by a re-formed No 55 Squadron on 1st September 1960 to bring the Wing up to its planned strength. The delay arose from the upgrading of the existing B.1 Victors to B.1A standard, many of these conversions being made by Handley Page from undelivered B.1 airframes that were retained at the factory until the extensive modifications could be incorporated. No 55 Squadron's formation was therefore delayed until the B.1A version was available, although No XV Squadron at Cottesmore in fact became the first unit to re-equip with the B.1A.

The Victor B Mk.2 followed the B.1 into service with the formation of the Wittering Wing and its dependent Nos 100 and 139 Squadrons in 1962, this Wing having aircraft equipped to carry the Blue Steel stand-off bomb. The first B.2 was delivered to the RAF on 1st November 1961. No 139 Squadron formed on 1st February 1962 from an Intensive Flying Trials Unit based at Cottesmore, with No 100 Squadron following on 1st May 1962. The Wittering Wing continued until the disbandment of No 139 Squadron at the end of 1968, No 100 having been disbanded in September of that year. The Victor B.2 flew with the Blue Steel stand-off weapon in parallel with the similarly equipped Vulcan B.2s of the Scampton Wing. A Victor B.2 (XL161) had flown with No 4 Joint Services Trials Unit during the development and qualification of the weapon over the Woomera ranges in Australia. The Blue Steel was declared to be 'available for use' in September 1962, although it was not formally operational until February 1963, and even at that point there were some limitations on its availability and use until more experience had been gained in the logistics of servicing and maintaining what was a very sophisticated weapon. However, the various difficulties were overcome and the Wittering Wing continued to deploy Blue Steel until the disbandment of the Victor B.2 squadrons. Blue Steel continued for a while longer with the Vulcan B.2s at Scampton. It is understood that a total of fifty-seven operational rounds of Blue Steel were delivered to the RAF and these were split between the three Vulcan and two Victor squadrons that operated the weapon.

XA926, a later 'A' of No 232 OCU, at Coltishall in September 1962. Phil Butler

Almost Hot

The most significant event in the career of the V-Force was the Cuban Missile Crisis of October 1962, the point of greatest risk of the Cold War becoming 'hot'. The crisis arose because the Soviets began to install two types of ballistic missiles at launch sites in Cuba; these had the range to attack targets in large areas of the United States and were a clear strategic threat. The threat was identified by the US intelligence services in mid-October 1962 when the start of construction of such sites was observed, and the British were informed of the findings on 19th October. President Kennedy immediately countered the threat by denouncing the Soviet escalation and initiating American countermeasures, including putting forces on high alert and threatening action against Cuba and a blockade ('quarantine') to prevent the arrival of Soviet ships carrying missiles and equipment. By 26th October Kennedy had declared that if assurances were not received within forty-eight hours regarding the withdrawal of the missiles from Cuba, America would act "to destroy the missile sites by bombing or invasion or both".

At this point the British Service Chiefs were summoned to a meeting with Prime Minister Harold Macmillan. Since a full deployment of V-Bombers to their dispersal bases would have become known to Soviet intelligence and would have contributed to a major escalation of tension, British precautionary measures were deliberately kept 'low key'. Therefore, no public announcements were made, but Bomber Command key personnel were kept available on their stations. This represented 'Alert Condition Three', Precautionary Alert, which was put in place at 13.00 hours on 27th October 1962. Key personnel were required to remain on their stations, with Operations Room staff to be available at short notice. Unobtrusive preparations were to be made to permit rapid 'generation' of aircraft should that be required. ('Generation' was a term describing the preparation of aircraft for take-off, fuelled, armed and in a fully operational condition.)

The Medium Bomber Force then comprised seventeen squadrons, eight of Vulcans, six of Victors and three of Valiants, not counting the Operational Conversion Units and four Valiant squadrons dedicated to in-flight refuelling, electronic countermeasures or strategic recon-

XA932 of No 10 Squadron with the original markings (not toned down) and also wearing the squadron crest below the cockpit. Phil Butler

XA938 of No 10 Squadron at Gaydon on 20th September 1958. Phil Butler

XA934, yet another 'A' of No 232 OCU, wearing the toned-down markings. This aircraft crashed near Gaydon on 2nd October 1962, so the photo probably shows it not long before it was lost. Phil Butler

Victor K.1 XA932 of No 214 Squadron. Phil Butler

naissance. A ninth Vulcan squadron was in the process of forming, and in reality two of the recently formed Vulcan units and the Victor B.2 Wing at Wittering were still 'working up' and not at full strength. At that point Bomber Command was able to realistically deploy approximately one hundred and twenty operational V-Bombers, after accounting for aircraft undergoing servicing or modification, involved in trials or on overseas deployments. In normal circumstances (Alert Condition Four), seventeen aircraft were maintained on 'Quick Reaction Alert' (QRA) at fifteen minutes readiness. On 28th October the number of QRA aircraft was increased (probably doubled) with effect from 08.00 hours the following day, and eight Vulcans on detachment to Malta were recalled to their UK base at Waddington. The Bomber Command Thor missile force (sixty ICBMs operated from fixed sites in eastern England) was also brought to fifteen minutes readiness, although it was normal practice for forty-five to fifty missiles to be in that state in any case. The overall state of readiness of both the missiles and the V-Force was maintained until 5th November 1962, by which time the stand-off between John Kennedy and Nikita Khrushchev had subsided.

The higher Alert Conditions were 'Two – Generate Aircraft' and 'One – Disperse Aircraft'. Alert Condition Two required the preparation of the maximum number of aircraft to combat serviceability. Aircraft allotted for take-off from their main bases (normally four from each) would be on standby at fifteen minutes readiness. Aircraft allotted for dispersal would be armed and prepared for take-off to their dispersal airfields. Operations Rooms and other vital support services would be fully manned twenty-four hours per day. The target was to generate 75% of the available force, which equated to about one hundred and twenty out of the one hundred and sixty or so aircraft on hand.

Alert Condition One required aircraft due to proceed to their dispersal airfields and to be 'regenerated' on arrival, to be prepared for take-off, with crews on standby at fifteen minutes readiness. Aircraft at main bases were to remain at fifteen minutes readiness. The Readiness States could also be fine-tuned by changing to 'Zero Five' or 'Zero Two'. Readiness 'Zero Five' required aircraft to be airborne

Victor B.1 XA936, 'A' of No 232 OCU, at Leuchars in September 1963. Tony Buttler

A line-up of No 10 Squadron Victors on the main runway at RAF Cottesmore not long after the unit's formation. Handley Page Association

XA928 of No 10 Squadron 'air-to-air' with flaps and air brakes extended. Crown PRB 15705

XA923 of the Radar Reconnaissance Flight at Wyton. It wears the early white colour scheme (no toned-down markings) with a (green) lightning-flash marking on its nose ahead of the cockpit glazing. The Valiant behind wears the markings of No 543 Squadron. Tony Buttler

within five minutes, while 'Zero Two' required aircraft to start engines and taxi to take-off positions. 'Ready' aircraft could then be ordered to SCRAMBLE. The 'Zero Five' and 'Zero Two' states were qualified by the availability of ground facilities and aircraft modifications. During the Cuban crisis not all of the V-Bombers had received the modifications to allow simultaneous starts of all four engines, nor were all the main and dispersal bases provided with operational readiness platforms at the end of the operational runway, although work on both of these aspects was advancing. Therefore, not all aircraft would have been able to meet the five- or two-minute target times. The V-Force was never brought to the higher Alert Conditions 'in anger' at any time, although the routines were frequently practised in planned exercises. Similarly, the Royal Air Force never implemented an 'airborne alert' state such as that planned by the USAF's Strategic Air Command, whereby armed bombers would actually be kept airborne with their targets programmed, during times of high alert. (Note: This account is based on that given by Clive Richards of the Air Historical Branch (RAF) in the Journal of the *Royal Air Force Historical Society* in 2008 and is quoted with his permission. It corrects several previously published accounts that were based on incomplete access to primary sources.)

XH589 of No 15 Squadron (with 'XV' marking on fin) at Farnborough in September 1960. Phil Butler

XH592 of No 15 Squadron at a USAF Armed Forces Day display. Phil Butler

XH587 here shows the enlarged radome of the B.1A version, containing the Red Steer tail-warning radar. Phil Butler

Three white Victor B.1As on an operational readiness platform, ready to give a 'scramble' demonstration at an air display. The two nearer aircraft are XH619 and XH594. Phil Butler

New Roles

The role of the Victor has changed several times. The first was the move from high-altitude delivery of its nuclear weapons to the low-level profile made necessary by developments in the Warsaw Pact defensive systems. This involved a low-level approach to the planned target, followed by 'toss-bombing' of the weapon until such time as the weapons were developed and cleared for release at low-level. This change resulted in the white V-Bombers forsaking their 'anti-flash' paint and pastel roundels/unit markings/serial numbers for camouflaged upper surfaces during 1964. The switch resulted in much design analysis to confirm the fatigue-life implications of the much more stressful flight regime in the denser and more turbulent air at lower levels, installation of Terrain-Following Radar, and clearance of all combinations of weapon loads for low-level release. No sooner had these changes begun to become familiar to the crews than the Vickers Valiant had to be withdrawn from service because of structural problems arising from the punishing low-level role.

The Victor had been identified as the more suitable of the surviving V-Bombers to replace the Valiant as a tanker, and a Victor B.1 had been carrying out role trials at Boscombe Down for some time before the decision had to be made on the withdrawal of the Valiant. The role of the Honington Wing was therefore changed to that of in-flight refuelling and its squadrons were soon moved to the base of the former Valiant flight-refuelling squadrons at Marham. Some of the individual aircraft histories actually show allotments to former Valiant squadrons (e.g. No 90 Squadron) but it is not clear if one or two Victors were actually briefly transferred to grounded Valiant squadrons at this time.

The change also brought about the formation of No 214 Squadron to join the refuelling task, a move enabled by the transfer of Victor bombers from the Cottesmore Wing for conversion to tankers. The converted aircraft were initially designated BK Mk.1 or BK Mk.1A but within a year this had changed to K Mk.1/K Mk.1A after their bombing role had been abandoned. As noted in Chapter Two, the first Victors so treated were two-point tankers (refuelling from the pods on their outer wings) but three-point tankers became available after an additional pod had been fitted below the fuselage.

XH592, with the markings of the Tanker Training Flight, was photographed at Marham. Phil Butler

Victor K.1A XH593 of the Tanker Training Flight. Phil Butler

Victor B.1A XH594 of No 232 OCU, photographed at Marham. Phil Butler

Victor K.1A (and K.1s) of Nos 57 and 214 Squadrons at RAAF Butterworth in Malaya, on detachment to give in-flight refuelling practice to Far East Air Force (FEAF) fighter squadrons. Handley Page Association

Opposite page:

Victor K.1A XH590 of No 55 Squadron formating with a Fleet Air Arm Blackburn Buccaneer and de Havilland Sea Vixen at a Farnborough air display. Phil Butler

A receiver's-eye view of a Victor tanker taken during the trials with XA918 at Boscombe Down. Handley Page Association

This page:

Victor K.1A XH614 of No 55 Squadron. Phil Butler

Victor K.1A XH648 of No 57 Squadron. Phil Butler

Victor B.2 XH669 at Farnborough in September 1960. At the time its serial number was worn only on the crew entry door. Phil Butler

This page:

Victor B.2 XH669 of the Wittering Wing carrying a Blue Steel at Coltishall in September 1964. Phil Butler

B.2 XH670 seen in this air-to-air photo was a trials aircraft that served only with the A&AEE and Handley Page. An intended conversion to K.2 standard did not proceed, although the aircraft was flown to Woodford. Phil Butler

Victor SR.2 XH672 of No 543 Squadron in formation with two Wyton-based English Electric Canberras of the Central Reconnaissance Establishment. Terry Panopalis

Opposite page:

Victor SR.2 XH674 of No 543 Squadron on a dispersal at Wyton. Inter Air Press via Phil Butler

Victor B.2 XL160 of the Wittering Wing. Tony Buttler

Victor SR.2 XL161 at Wyton in August 1966. Tony Buttler

Six 'two-point' tankers were delivered pending formal service clearance of the central refuelling pod on the trials aircraft XA918. These distinctions are sometimes shown by the designations K.1A(2P) or K.1/K.1A(3P).

The role of the Victor B Mk.2 continued unchanged at this point and the Wittering Wing continued to serve alongside the Vulcan with its Blue Steel stand-off weapons for some years. The Victor B.2 was also selected to replace the Valiant B(PR)K.1 in the strategic reconnaissance role, with a number of Victors being converted to the SR.2 version for service with No 543 Squadron at Wyton, replacing that unit's Valiants. Pending the conversion of the SR.2, some Victor B.1s joined No 543 in the interim. These aircraft were used for maritime reconnaissance, with various enhancements to their NBS and navigational aids to suit them for this role. The prime task was to carry out surveillance of sea areas in the Atlantic and the Mediterranean to monitor shipping movements, using cameras and the recording of radar images. Previously, somewhat similar work had been carried out by Victor B.1s of the Radar Reconnaissance Flight from 1958 to 1961. A single Victor SR.2 could survey 400,000 square miles in an eight-hour flight, or four aircraft could cover the whole of the North Atlantic in six hours. The Victors involved in the maritime reconnaissance role were equipped with SRIM 2305 (Yellow Aster), an enhancement of their NBS equipment.

A further task was the sampling of fallout from nuclear explosions, for which several of the Victor SR.2 conversions carried pods to sample the atmosphere when flying through clouds generated by nuclear tests. For example, these Victors conducted a number of operations to monitor French tests conducted in the South Pacific, including Operation Web in 1968, Operation Alchemist in 1970 and Operation Attune in 1971, occasionally operating from Lima in Peru as well as from US bases in Hawaii. After the disbandment of No 543 Squadron in 1974 the nuclear monitoring role was continued by the Victor Flight at Wyton until October 1975.

The maritime surveillance role was eventually taken over by the Vulcan B.2[MRR] aircraft which were converted to this task when the Victor SR.2s were needed for conversion to K.2 standard. The Vulcans flew with a re-formed No 27 Squadron rather than directly replacing the Victors of No 543. The K.2 was required to replace the K.1/K.1A fleet as the earlier version consumed their permitted airframe lives. The K.2 aircraft took over from the K.1/K.1As in Nos 55 and 57 Squadrons, while No 214 Squadron disbanded, there being insufficient Mk.2 airframes to re-equip three squadrons.

Unlike the Avro Vulcan, the Victor was never permanently based with any unit overseas. However, the type took its share of temporary overseas deployments in the bomber role to the Near, Middle and Far East, as well as on occasion joining the Vulcan in Strategic Air

Opposite page:
Victor B.2 XL164 taken at Radlett in June 1963 while undergoing trials with Handley Page for the low-level role of the type. Handley Page V1198-1 via Handley Page Association

Victor B.2 XL189 of the Wittering Wing, camouflaged and carrying a Blue Steel, making a slow flypast with airbrake extended. Phil Butler

Victor B.2 XL192, white and wearing the fin marking of No 100 Squadron, at Leuchars on 15th September 1962. Phil Butler

This page:
Victor K.2 XL233 of No 232 OCU, refuelling Lightning F.6s XR724 and XR769 of No 11 Squadron in 1974. MoD PRB 3645/9 via Phil Butler

Victor B.2 XL512 of No 139 Squadron in the toned-down white scheme. Tony Buttler

Victor B.2 XL512 carrying a Blue Steel after the V-Force had adopted a low-level role and received camouflage in place of the white anti-flash colours. Handley Page Association

Left: **The last Victor B.2 to be built, XM718, photographed in 1963 in the white scheme with toned-down markings and the badge of No 100 Squadron.** J. A. Todd via Phil Butler

Below: **A line of No 543 Squadron Victors at Wyton. Several wear the Wyton station badge with the markings of the resident units on their noses.** Handley Page Association

Inset: **The shield device worn by Victors of No 543 Squadron, showing the badge of RAF Wyton and the logos of the resident units (Nos 51, 543 and 39 Squadrons).** Phil Butler

Opposite page:
A Victor K.2 refuelling two Panavia Tornado GR Mk.1s in May 1983. Handley Page Association

Victor B.1 7844M (the former XA924) at RAF St Athan after retirement to No 4 School of Technical Training. Phil Butler

Command Bombing Competitions in the USA, and carrying out low-level role training in Canada. The B.1/B.1A squadrons maintained extended deployments to the Far East, to RAF Tengah (Singapore) or the RAAF base at Butterworth in Malaya during the 1962-1965 period as Exercise Chamfrom and Exercise Spherical. The Victor also shared in deployments 'showing the flag' in many countries, taking part in air displays and ceremonial events – with the ever-present agenda of reminding anyone who cared that the British nuclear deterrent was very much a force in being. Overseas deployments continued when the aircraft became a tanker, since any RAF fighter unit based overseas needed to maintain its currency with air-to-air refuelling practice.

None of the V-Bombers was sold to another country's air force. However, in October 1961 consideration was being given by the South African Government to the purchase of a number of Victor B Mk.2s. If agreement had been reached these aircraft would have been constructed out of the components made redundant by the reduction of the RAF B.2 order, by twenty-five, in August 1960. There were rumours that South Africa was interested in acquiring a fleet of eight Victors, and it was even said that the South African Air Force SAAF serial numbers 8001-8008 were reserved for

such aircraft. But while there seems little doubt that there was some genuine interest from South Africa (resulting in visits to Handley Page by SAAF personnel), it appears likely that political considerations related to the 'apartheid' regime then in power in that country would have blocked any possibility of a deal. The eventual outcome was the purchase of Blackburn Buccaneer S.50 strike aircraft by South Africa and that contract was the subject of much controversy at the time, a potential 'follow-on' Buccaneer contract being blocked.

The Victor in the end had a longer and more versatile career with the Royal Air Force than the other two V-types – although it entered service last (with No 232 OCU in November 1957) it remained in service until October 1993, a period of thirty-six years, and took part in the Falklands War and the first Gulf War in its in-flight refuelling role. The Victors were only retired as their airframe lives became exhausted, leaving the BAC VC-10 and Lockheed Tristar to replace them in their tanking duties.

Falklands and Gulf

The most famous operation performed by the Victor was certainly the type's involvement in 'Operation Corporate', the recovery of the Falkland Islands that followed the Argentine invasion in April 1982. The extensive in-flight refuelling process that enabled a single Vulcan to bomb the Port Stanley airport runway and return safely to Ascension Island could not have been possible without the Victors. The Operation involved the deployment of fourteen Victors to Wideawake Airfield on Ascension Island. The 'Black Buck' bombing missions, during which single Vulcans flew to the Falklands and back, typically involved support flights by no fewer than eleven of the Victors for each outward flight, with four more Victor sorties required to refuel the return. The refuellers in the most southerly stages of the outward leg needed to be themselves refuelled en route to the Falklands and on return to their base on Ascension Island. The first 'Black Buck', in which Vulcan XM607 hit the Port Stanley runway with its stick of 1,000 lb (454kg) bombs on 1st May 1982, was supported by Victors XH669, XH672, XL162, XL163, XL188, XL189, XL192, XL232, XL511, XL513 and XM717.

Some of the Victor force was required to remain based at Marham to support the refuelling of the reinforcing aircraft (Lockheed Hercules, McDonnell Phantoms, Hawker Siddeley Harriers, etc.) on their way to Ascension. The Ascension Island-based Victors themselves made flights as far as the Falklands and South Georgia (refuelled by other Victors) to carry out reconnaissance tasks in support of the overall operation. One maritime reconnaissance sortie to the vicinity of South Georgia by XL192 on 20th April 1982 involved flying a total of over 7,000 miles (11,263km) in 14 hours 45 minutes, then a record endurance for an operational flight. Similar flights by XL163 (on 22nd/23rd April) and XL189 (24th/25th April) concluded the 'MRR' sorties that assisted Operation Paraquat, the recapture of South Georgia from the Argentine forces. (RAF Hawker Siddeley Nimrods later made even longer reconnaissance flights.)

The final swansong of the Victor was in the first Gulf War: the removal of the Iraqi forces that had invaded Kuwait. Between December 1990 and March 1991 a detachment of tankers (by then all operated by No 55 Squadron) were deployed to the Persian Gulf to carry out air-to-air refuelling of RAF and other Coalition aircraft involved in Operation Desert Storm. Eventually eight of the Victors were based at Muharraq, Bahrain, primarily to refuel RAF SEPECAT Jaguars and Panavia Tornados and also carrier-based aircraft of the US Navy, and they flew almost three hundred sorties. The aircraft involved were XH671, XH672, XL161, XL164, XL190, XL231, XM715 and XM717. A list of the squadrons and other units equipped with the Victor, together with their formation and disbandment dates and bases, is included in Appendix Two.

The Vulcan refuelling plan for the first 'Black Buck' operation in the Falklands War in 1982. The plan involves three waves of Victor tankers:

'Wave 1 (Outbound) – Red Formation'
Red 1 refuels Red 2, which continues towards the Falklands, Red 1 returns to Ascension.
Red 3 refuels Vulcan twice and then returns to Ascension.

'Wave 2 (Outbound) – Blue Formation'
Blue 1 refuels Blue 2 and returns to Ascension.
Blue 2 continues south and refuels Vulcan, Blue 4 and Vulcan again, then returns to Ascension.
Blue 3 refuels Blue 4 and returns to Ascension.
Blue 5 refuels Blue 6 and returns to Ascension.
Blue 4 refuels Blue 6, then Red 2.
Blue 6 refuels Vulcan twice, Red 2, then returns to Ascension.
Red 2 refuels Vulcan, then returns to Ascension.

'Wave 3 (Recovery) – White Formation'
White 1 refuels White 2 and returns to Ascension.
White 3 refuels White 4 and returns to Ascension.
White 2 refuels Vulcan.
White 4 stands by as airborne reserve for White 2.

That was the plan. In the event there was some exchanging of roles due to equipment problems. Later 'Black Buck' missions had slightly simpler Victor support profiles, arising from experience gained on 'Black Buck One'.

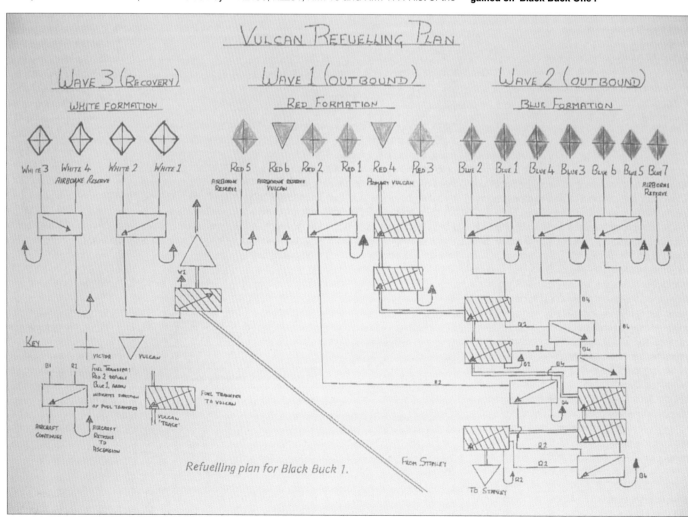

Refuelling plan for Black Buck 1.

Chapter Five

Trials Aircraft

This chapter would normally detail a large number of experimental aircraft used by Test Establishments and the industry for trials and experimental work. For the Victor such aircraft are few in number because many possible test applications had already been explored by the earlier V-Bombers – of necessity, because much of the equipment requiring experiments, tests or qualification had already been fitted to the Valiant and/or Vulcan.

RATOG

An exception to this trend was the trial of the de Havilland Spectre rocket-assisted take-off gear (RATOG). A constant-thrust assisted take-off version of the Spectre rocket motor from de Havilland, an 8,000 lb (35.6kN) thrust D.Spe.4, was made available for the Victor. Two would be installed and they were intended to provide assisted take-off to reduce runway length requirements at high all-up weight and/or for operation in high ambient temperatures. Such trials had been carried out on a Valiant and were also intended to be made on a Vulcan. The Vulcan trials only progressed as far as live firing on a test rig representing the structure of a Vulcan, but those for the Victor included RATOG take-offs, made by XA930 at Hatfield in

1959, before the requirement for the RATOG installations on all three V-Bombers was cancelled in August of that year. The intended use of XA921 for these trials did not take place and this facility was never used by production Victor Mk.1s. On XA930 each of the two jettisonable Spectre motors was mounted beneath the centre of the wing roots and installed as a self-contained unit within a releasable nacelle that was then dropped after firing. This nacelle had its own parachute gear to allow the engine to be recovered for repeated use. The motors gave a combined thrust of 16,000 lb (71.1kN) and during the take-off trials they lifted the bomber into the air after a run of just 550yd (503m), compared to the usual take-off distance of more than double that figure.

Similarly, the Conway engine for the Victor Mk.2 had been tested on the Vulcan, this being a simpler solution than the possible reworking of a Mk.1 Victor centre section to accommodate the Conway engine for trials, the air intakes for the Conway by-pass engine being significantly larger than those for the Sapphire-powered Mk.1.

So the experimental work carried out on the Victor was confined to the RATOG trials above, In-Flight Refuelling, the Blue Steel installation

Victor B.1 XA930 taking off at Hatfield with assistance from de Havilland Spectre rocket motors mounted between the engine nacelles under each wing. Handley Page Association

and launching tests, the Photographic Reconnaissance installation and various electronic equipment fits. To complete the story, however, we need to mention that, prior to the first flight of the HP.80, a Handley Page Hastings had been fitted with two Armstrong Siddeley Sapphires, partly for Handley Page (and test pilot Sqn Ldr Hazelden) to gain operating experience with the engine, and for performance measurements of the new engine, which had flown only in other test beds prior to the HP.80 first flight. Details of these trials are given in Chapter Two, and the airframe history is included in Appendix One.

In-Flight Refuelling

The first set of in-flight refuelling trials involved clearance of the type as a receiver of fuel from a Valiant tanker. This work was done at Boscombe Down in 1961 using XA930. It had been planned that XA921 should be the first aircraft to test the IFR probe mounted over the cabin but in fact it was XA930 that became the

A shot of XA918 during the final phase of the A&AEE refuelling trials, now as a three-point tanker.
Phil Butler

A further shot of XA918 during the final phase of the A&AEE refuelling trials as a three-point tanker.
Phil Butler

This shot of XA930 shows it fitted with underwing fuel tanks and an early version of the air-to-air refuelling probe that later became a standard feature on the Victor B.2.
Phil Butler

first to be so equipped. As such it flew from Radlett with the probe installed (plus underwing tanks) on 27th August 1958. Through the following year XA930 was used to test probes of three other different lengths before a decision was made in 1960 that selected the standard to be operated in squadron service. Wet in-flight refuelling for the Mk.1A was cleared during September 1960 and the first probe installation to be added to an operational aircraft, a Mk.1A, was made retrospectively in March 1962. XA930 was also used to carry out the clearance of the underwing fuel tanks that became a standard fit on the B.2/SR.2/K.2 versions of the Victor. Although XA930 was a B.1, these big external tanks were used only by the various Mk.2s.

With the perceived risk that the Valiant tanker fleet might have to be withdrawn prematurely, the Victor was selected as the most suitable replacement aircraft. Thus in 1963 trials were made by B.1 XA918 at A&AEE to confirm its suitability for the role. Trials later commenced with flight refuelling Mk.20B pods under the outer wings as a two-point tanker and, following their success, continued with a Mk.17 hose/drum unit fitted towards the rear of the bomb bay, to provide a three-point version, clearing the type for entry into service. This was done in parallel with the start of work on the conversion of the existing B.1 and B.1A versions as tankers, with the first six conversions being 'interim' two-point versions, which retained the ability to return to a bomber role.

Blue Steel Installation

The main trials for the Blue Steel stand-off bomber were undertaken by Vickers Valiant and Avro Vulcan aircraft, prior to the Victor installation. These involved modifications to the aircraft to carry the weapon (including work with scale models as well as the various experimental and operational versions of the type). The aircraft modifications were largely carried out at A. V. Roe's Woodford works, although this was confined to the Valiant and Vulcan trials aircraft. Victors flew to Woodford on several occasions for compatibility tests in connection with the project, and all three of the V-Bombers took part in dropping various versions of the weapon, both powered and unpowered. The weapon itself was only intended for carriage in an operational mode by the Mk.2 versions of the Vulcan and Victor.

Another view of XA930. The supporting strut for the refuelling probe was later deleted and a shorter probe fitted. Phil Butler

A view of a Blue Steel test round fitted to Victor Mk.2 XH675 in July 1961, looking rearwards from the nose of the missile. Handley Page Association

An unidentified Victor B.2 (either XH675 or XL161) carrying a Blue Steel test round. (A photo of XH675 carrying a Blue Steel test round appears in the colour section, page 131.) Handley Page Association

This shot shows the fuel tanks and large photo reconnaissance 'crate' fitted to the Victor SR.2. The installation had been developed on Victor B.1 XA920. Handley Page Association

During the development phase the dropping of inert unpowered Blue Steels was carried out in the UK, before rocket-powered versions became available. Victors involved in trials with A. V. Roe at Woodford and the A&AEE at Boscombe Down were XH674 and XH675. XH674 was used to drop dummy weapons from 1961 onwards, and was finally involved at Woodford with tests related to the low-level launching of operational Blue Steels, until being returned to Handley Page in April 1964 for trials related to the QRA (Quick Reaction Alert) role. It is not clear if the latter tests also involved Blue Steel or if they were connected with the simultaneous engine-start procedures without external power sources that were required to reduce reaction time following receipt of an alert. Although XH674 was intended to move on to Australia to take part in the trials, this aircraft never did so. XH675 was involved in Blue Steel vibration testing and missile handling trials at Boscombe Down in 1961. Although it later flew to Australia and is noted in the records of No 4 JSTU, it is believed that its work was then related to the Strategic Reconnaissance role rather than Blue Steel.

Trials with powered versions of Blue Steel commenced in the UK, but as the development work proceeded it was progressively transferred to the Weapons Research Establishment at Woomera in Australia. The earlier stages of the work were carried out by the contractors involved (primarily A. V. Roe as the overall weapon designer and Elliott Brothers as

designer of its inertial guidance system), both in the UK and Australia. By 1959 the project had advanced sufficiently for No 4 Joint Services Trials Unit (JSTU) to be formed, involving RAF personnel responsible for clearance of the weapon for operational use. The JSTU moved from Woodford to Edinburgh Field in South Australia to perform launches over the Woomera ranges and continued to serve at Edinburgh Field for a number of years until all the necessary operational trials had been completed. Meanwhile, a separate JSTU (No 18) was formed in the UK from those personnel not required to transfer to Australia; it looked after the balance of trials still to be carried out in the UK. No 18 JSTU did not have any aircraft attached, effectively 'borrowing' Vulcans or Victors from operational squadrons as and when required. On the other hand, No 4 JSTU had its own Vulcan B.2 (XH539) and Victor B.2 (XL161) permanently attached to the unit at Edinburgh Field.

XL161 arrived at Edinburgh Field on 5th June 1962 and made its first flight carrying a development missile (Avro W.100A Blue Steel No 048) on 17th August. This flight almost ended in disaster, with a near repetition of the accident in which the first Victor B.2 (XH668) had been lost. Due to an instrument fault the two air-speed indicators gave different readings. Unfortunately the pilots believed the faulty instrument and took action that resulted in the Victor entering a spin. During the violent manoeuvres the missile parted from the aircraft and was lost. Fortunately the crew was able to regain control and return to base. In October XL161 made a successful launch (W.100A No 060) and other launches followed during 1963 and 1964, after which XL161

returned to the UK in October 1964 for conversion to SR.2 standard.

Photographic Reconnaissance

During the design phase of the V-Bomber projects, the Ministry of Supply had requested proposals for photo reconnaissance versions of all three types. Although PR versions of the Valiant were produced and were among the first V-Bombers to enter service (forming the equipment of only the second V-Bomber squadron), it seems that the Victor proposal found great favour, and it had been intended that one of the prototypes would be converted to PR configuration for service trials. This did not occur because of the loss of WB771. However, XA920 – the fourth production aircraft – was selected for modification in line with the original design proposal, after being used at Boscombe Down for the official performance trials for the Victor. The modifications included the installation of an impressive array of cameras and several options for additional fuel tanks in the bomb bay, with provision to carry photo flares for night photography. These trials laid the groundwork for the Victor SR.2 conversions that later replaced the Valiants in No 543 Squadron at Wyton. The PR fit for the SR.2 was combined with Yellow Aster which was a modification of the Navigational Bombing System tested by the three Victor B.1s of the Radar Reconnaissance Flight at Wyton.

Electronic Equipment

All of the V-Bombers received upgrades to their electronic equipment during their lives, especially in the areas of electronic countermeasures (ECM) and navigational aids. Most of these were fairly subtle, in the sense that they made little external difference to the look of the aircraft. The biggest visible change was perhaps the upgrade from the B.1 to the B.1A, where the original Orange Putter radar in the fuselage tail of the B.1 was replaced by the significantly larger Red Steer in the B.1A.

Another intended refit was the carriage of the Red Neck Side-Looking Airborne Radar (SLAR) in very long underwing pods. X-Band and Q-Band pods were to be developed, against OR.3595. The first installation of these for trials was made in the second production aircraft XA918. These were an assessment of the aerodynamic effects of the pods and were carried out by Handley Page at Radlett. Further trials were made with pods of a slightly different shape on B.2 aircraft, beginning with XL158 at A&AEE from May 1961. Another installation was made on XH672, here with a Red Neck pod under the port wing and a standard underwing fuel tank beneath the starboard wing in a decidedly asymmetric configuration. The Red Neck radar project was cancelled and never used operationally, although it was intended as an optional fit for the SR.2 version of the aircraft. Back in March 1961 Treasury approval was given for the installation of Red Neck, and at that point fixed fittings were to be installed in

The original mock-up of the Red Neck reconnaissance radar pods is shown here fitted to Victor B.1 XA918 taking off from Radlett.
Handley Page A36 246 via Handley Page Association

An airborne shot of XA918 fitted with Red Neck underwing pods. Handley Page Association

nine aircraft during 1963. However, the work was cancelled in February 1962 because the system capability of delivering radar data from 100 miles to each side of the aircraft did not justify the cost of the equipment.

Another aspect of the electronic equipment was the requirement for the B.2 versions of the Vulcan and Victor to be capable of automatic landing in low visibility. This resulted in the fitment of the Smiths Mk.10 Autopilot for trials to Victor B.2 XH672. The equipment included a coupled radio altimeter and automatic throttle control; ILS was already fitted. The first set of trials lasted from March until the middle of May 1964 and only minor problems were encountered. John Allam was the pilot and he remembers that after these trials were completed Handley Page was ready to offer the aircraft to A&AEE Boscombe Down for their appraisal. However, the company was now told that it had to demonstrate two hundred auto-landings straight through without a single failure. In due course over two hundred landings were made at five different airfields in very variable wind conditions and without any problems at all. These trials were successful but the requirement for 'Autoland' was then cancelled before XH672 began its Boscombe Down assessment, and before any other Victors were 'qualified' to undertake automatic landings. Nevertheless the Mk.10 Autopilot became a standard item of equipment.

This photograph shows the asymmetric installation on XH672, with a single Red Neck pod under the port wing and a standard underwing fuel tank to starboard. Handley Page V1119 via Handley Page Association

Another view of the Red Neck pod on the port wing of XH672.
Handley Page V1119-4 via Handley Page Association

Chapter Six

Detail Description

With the aircraft's crescent swept-back wing tapering in thickness from root to tip, the prototypes and early production Victors were basically as detailed in the original HP.80 B.35/46 brochure of May 1947. However, the structural and aerodynamic improvements that had evolved during the design process had been incorporated along the way and the result was a most graceful aeroplane. Much of the first part of this description comes from a company brochure of February 1951 which essentially describes the then unflown prototypes.

The honeycomb sandwich construction used in the wing was strong and light and was intended to ensure that an extreme accuracy of contour and aerodynamic smoothness in the loaded condition was achieved – in other words the wing was free from waves and buckles. The stiffness in the wing also eliminated flutter and other undesirable qualities and enabled the fuel tanks to be pressurised without any undue penalties in weight. In fact, the whole of the Victor's structure was characterised by a smooth external finish and both flush-riveting and spot-welding were used throughout.

The text has touched already on the theories and benefits of the crescent wing but the wing geometry itself was complex. Apart from the variation in sweepback over the span, the thickness/chord ratio, camber, dihedral and twist all varied across the span. The drag rise at high Mach numbers across the wing was thus offset by a gradual thinning of the section. The camber and twist variations were designed to effect a favourable lift distribution in cruising conditions and the proportions of the crescent sections were modified to conform to wind-tunnel results. The variations across the wing on the prototypes were:

Sweepback at ¼ chord
Root 47.5°, mid-wing 40.5°, outer wing 32°

Dihedral
Root -4.6°, mid-wing +0.6°, outer wing -1.0°

Thickness/chord ratio
Root 16%, mid-wing 10%, outer wing 8%

These figures were quite different from the B.35/46 proposal, indicating how much the process of design had affected the wing.

Victor B Mk.1s in final assembly at Handley Page's Colney Street works at Radlett. Examples visible include XH617 and XH618. The probable date is early 1959. Handley Page Association

Although in many ways it had dictated the aircraft's structural layout, Handley Page did not permit the crescent wing to introduce a weight penalty. This was exemplified by the arrangement of the ribs. It proved necessary to have a heavy rib at each kink in the wing, but at the inner kink the rib also picked up the main undercarriage while at the outer kink it also functioned as a 'pipe' joint and as a fuel tank bulkhead. The part between the fuselage sides – the centre section – was made integral with the rear fuselage. In the centre wing, where structure weight and stowage space were of primary importance, it was the high sweep angle that permitted the use of a 16% thickness. There were only eight major wing ribs on each side of the fuselage which were designed to interchange the bending and torsion moments at the wing kinks and to feed concentrated loads into the primary structure.

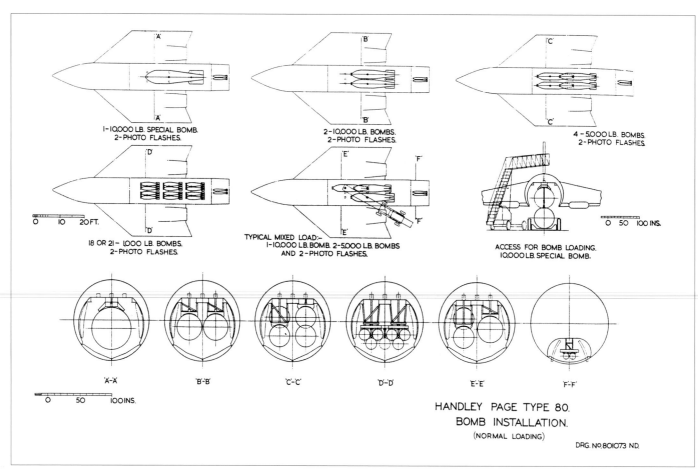

1-10,000 LB. SPECIAL BOMB.
2-PHOTO FLASHES.

2-10,000 LB. BOMBS.
2-PHOTO FLASHES.

4-5000 LB. BOMBS.
2-PHOTO FLASHES.

18 OR 21-1,000 LB. BOMBS.
2-PHOTO FLASHES.

TYPICAL MIXED LOAD:-
1-10,000 LB. BOMB, 2-5,000 LB. BOMBS
AND 2-PHOTO FLASHES.

ACCESS FOR BOMB LOADING.
10,000 LB. SPECIAL BOMB.

0   50   100 INS.

'A-A'   'B-B'   'C-C'   'D-D'   'E-E'   'F-F'

0   50   100 INS.

HANDLEY PAGE TYPE 80.
BOMB INSTALLATION.
(NORMAL LOADING)

DRG. No. 801073 ND.

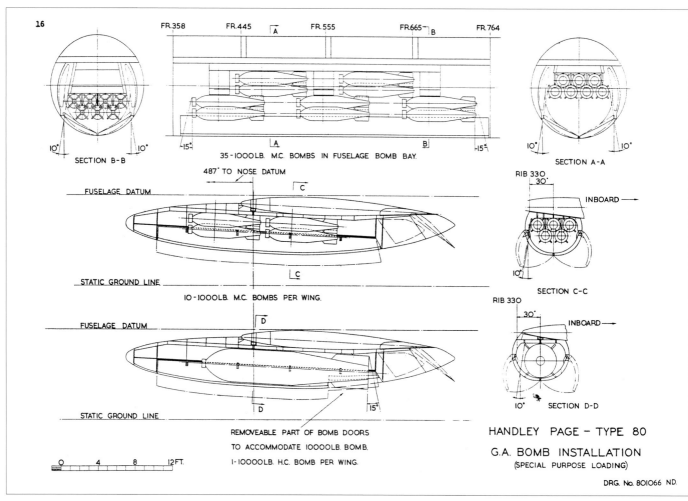

16

FR.358   FR.445   A   FR.555   FR.665   B   FR.764

SECTION B-B

35-1000 LB. M.C. BOMBS IN FUSELAGE BOMB BAY.

SECTION A-A

487" TO NOSE DATUM

FUSELAGE DATUM

STATIC GROUND LINE

10-1000 LB. M.C. BOMBS PER WING.

RIB 330

INBOARD →

SECTION C-C

FUSELAGE DATUM

STATIC GROUND LINE

REMOVEABLE PART OF BOMB DOORS
TO ACCOMMODATE 10000 LB. BOMB.
1-10000 LB. H.C. BOMB PER WING.

RIB 330

INBOARD →

SECTION D-D

0   4   8   12 FT.

HANDLEY PAGE – TYPE 80
G.A. BOMB INSTALLATION
(SPECIAL PURPOSE LOADING)

DRG. No. 801066 ND.

The wing was built of sandwich construction with multi-shear webs dividing it into a series of spanwise cells to carry fuel. The sandwich had an inner and outer skin of high-grade light alloy with a spanwise corrugated core of the same material but in a different grade. The outer skin was spot-welded to the core while the inner skin was attached by 'blind' riveting. Sandwich panels were formed by first fitting the outer skin into a sub-assembly jig and locating it using very accurate contour templates. The corrugated core was then added and held in position by service bolts. Next the complete panel was removed from the jig and dismantled, degreased and then reassembled before being trundled back and forth through a spot-welding machine. As stated, this assembly was very stiff and carried practically all of the normal wing bending loads, no spar booms having been necessary except for a short distance each side of the inner kink and on the rear web at

Opposite page, top: **Illustrations from a February 1951 HP.80 brochure showing the various types of bomb installation that could be carried by the aircraft.** Handley Page

Opposite page, bottom: **Second set of drawings from the brochure detailing the HP.80's bomb loads.** Handley Page

Below: **General arrangement drawing of the HP.80's wing from February 1951.** Handley Page

the fuselage side. The wing leading edges had double skins, the inner also having chordwise machined grooves to provide thermal de-icing. Double skins were also used on the 'droop'-type nose flaps which extended from the outer kink to the tip. Single skin construction with closely spaced chordwise stiffeners was used aft of the rear spar web.

To obviate tip stalling at low speed, these large leading-edge drooped nose flaps, extending at a predetermined wing lift co-efficient up to 20° of angle, had been fitted in the outboard wing sections for use in high-lift, low Mach number conditions. They were designed to droop at all angles of attack when the main flaps were extended, and stored compressed air was used to lower them in just one second. This was necessary because of the high peak power required and they could only be raised again when the air bottles had been recharged. Rearward-moving slotted main lift flaps, which had been proved during testing to be more effective than simple split or slotted flaps, were in place to give the aircraft a good take-off and landing performance. In addition, short, span contra-flaps, fitted between the outboard end of the main lift flaps and inboard end of the ailerons and which were to be operated during landing, were provided to give increased drag, a lower stalling speed and better stability at the stall.

The flying controls were entirely power operated and used fully duplicated and self-con-

tained units at each surface, and these had what Handley Page described as 'ideal' synthetic feel built in. This permitted the use of a tailplane with an elevator large enough to be regarded, for practical purposes, as an all-moving surface, and enabled Handley Page to state in its brochure that an unusually powerful elevator control had resulted. This, together with simple unbalanced controls with a small trailing edge angle (less than 11°), ensured that there was a reliable 'positive' response to control movements at high Mach numbers. To increase the useful range of tail incidence for down load at large angles of incidence, nose flaps were incorporated in the elevator. This additional trimming power was needed only when the main lift flaps were deflected. The selection of main flaps down would extend the elevator nose flaps which otherwise remained retracted during flight.

The tail unit consisted of a fin and rudder, swept back 45° at 35% chord, surmounted by a tailplane and elevators. The fixed tailplane's sweepback angle was 51.5° and on the elevators it was 38°, the surface's angle of dihedral being +15°. The fin, tailplane and elevator had single-spar structures with closely spaced ribs and single skins. In localised areas of the leading edges there was again double-skinning with machined grooves for thermal de-icing. In fact the horizontal tailplane served as an end-plate to the fin and rudder and thereby made

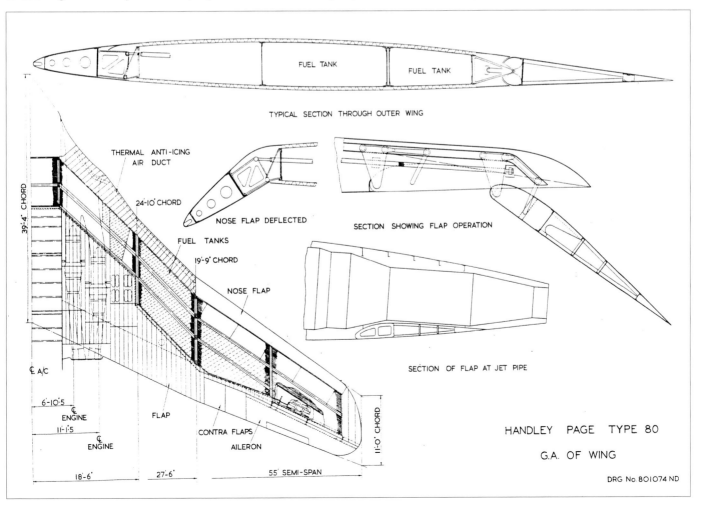

TYPICAL SECTION THROUGH OUTER WING

THERMAL ANTI-ICING AIR DUCT

24-10° CHORD

NOSE FLAP DEFLECTED

FUEL TANKS

19'-9' CHORD

NOSE FLAP

39'-4' CHORD

SECTION SHOWING FLAP OPERATION

SECTION OF FLAP AT JET PIPE

11'-0' CHORD

₵ A/C

6'-10'5
₵ ENGINE

11'-1'5
₵ ENGINE

FLAP

CONTRA FLAPS
AILERON

18'-6'   27'-6'   55' SEMI-SPAN

HANDLEY   PAGE   TYPE 80

G.A. OF WING

DRG No. 801074 ND

VICTOR: *Its Structure at a Glance*

UNRESTRICTED DATA

LENGTH: 114ft. 11ins.

SPAN: 110ft.

HEIGHT: 28ft. 1¼ins.

ENGINES: FOUR ARMSTRONG SIDDELEY SAPPHIRE TURBOJETS

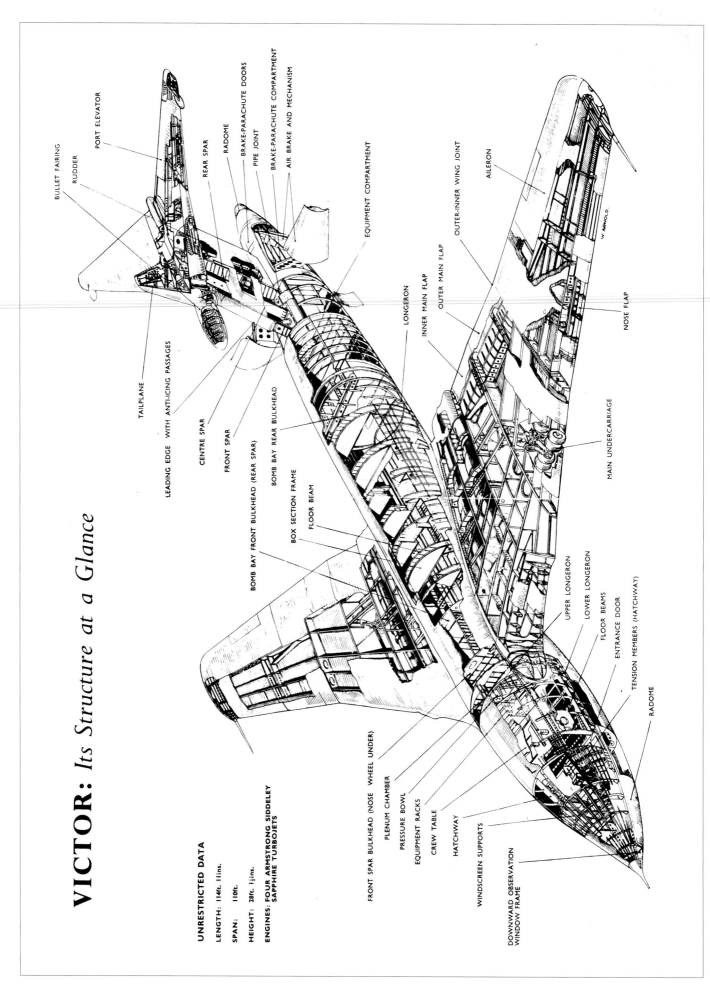

BULLET FAIRING

RUDDER

PORT ELEVATOR

REAR SPAR

RADOME

BRAKE-PARACHUTE DOORS

PIPE JOINT

BRAKE-PARACHUTE COMPARTMENT

AIR BRAKE AND MECHANISM

EQUIPMENT COMPARTMENT

OUTER-INNER WING JOINT

AILERON

TAILPLANE

LEADING EDGE WITH ANTI-ICING PASSAGES

CENTRE SPAR

FRONT SPAR

BOMB BAY FRONT BULKHEAD (REAR SPAR)

BOMB BAY REAR BULKHEAD

BOX SECTION FRAME

FLOOR BEAM

LONGERON

INNER MAIN FLAP

OUTER MAIN FLAP

NOSE FLAP

MAIN UNDERCARRIAGE

W. ARNOLD.

UPPER LONGERON

LOWER LONGERON

FLOOR BEAMS

ENTRANCE DOOR

TENSION MEMBERS (HATCHWAY)

RADOME

FRONT SPAR BULKHEAD (NOSE WHEEL UNDER)

PLENUM CHAMBER

PRESSURE BOWL

EQUIPMENT RACKS

CREW TABLE

HATCHWAY

WINDSCREEN SUPPORTS

DOWNWARD OBSERVATION WINDOW FRAME

the vertical surfaces more effective. This meant that their size could actually be reduced and that indeed proved to be the case, production machines having fins 20in (51cm) shorter than those on the Victor prototypes.

The four engines were buried in the wing roots. The Victor's inner wing had its primary structure concentrated forward and the engine bays were placed well behind the main load-carrying structure. Primarily this was a precaution against a fire or a burst engine causing critical damage to the structure but it also permitted easy maintenance and in due course simplified the conversion to more powerful engines. On the prototype the Sapphires were designed to give 7,960 lb (35.4kN) of static thrust at sea level and 1,087 lb (4.83kN) of cruising thrust when flying at 500 knots (576mph/926km/h) and 50,000ft (15,240m). The engine air intakes, which were located adjacent to the fuselage side, had a duct to carry away the fuselage boundary layer which would otherwise be drawn into the engines with a consequent loss of efficiency. Wind tunnel tests had shown that the Victor's arrangement of intakes and engine nacelles did not reduce the aeroplane's critical Mach number.

Opposite: **Handley Page Victor B Mk.1 structure detail.** Phil Butler

Top right: **A picture that appears in most books and articles describing the Victor, the unique image of B Mk.1A XH648 dropping its maximum load of thirty-five 1,000 lb (454kg) bombs during armament trials. This was the largest warload ever carried by a British military aircraft, the Victor being capable of a much larger load than the Vulcan or Valiant.** Phil Butler

Right: **Rolls-Royce Conway by-pass turbojet.** Rolls-Royce

Below: **XA940 landing at Brussels in 1964 with airbrakes and flaps deployed.** Handley Page

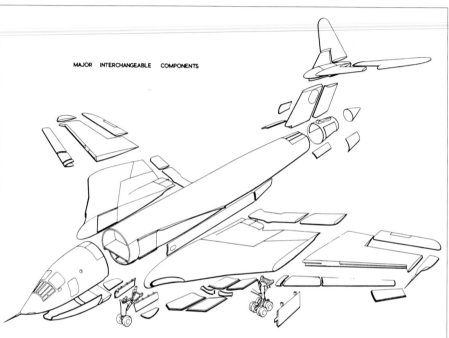

MAJOR INTERCHANGEABLE COMPONENTS

Hot air could be tapped from all four engine compressors to supply the de-icing system on the wing, tail and fin leading edges. The effects of the jet's efflux on the fuselage structure were catered for by the use of locally thicker skins on the lower fuselage side just aft of the bomb bay.

The fuselage shape, designed to give the same high critical Mach number as the wing, was the result of extensive pressure plotting. The size of the nose portion was dictated by the space needed to house the crew and much of the equipment, especially the radar. In the end the decision was made to blend the cabin into the main tube of the fuselage and have the radar protruding on the underside. This also allowed the nose wheels to be housed in the rear part of the underside bulge and to have the visual bomb-aiming station placed ahead of the radar in the aircraft's pointed nose. The Victor was not area-ruled because it came into existence before the area rule law had been established but in fact a graph of the aircraft's cross-section proved to be relatively smooth which meant that it did conform to the law in most respects.

Opposite page:

XA918 displays the massive drag chute that was so effective in reducing the bomber's landing run. Handley Page Association

The major interchangeable components on the Victor. Handley Page Association

Victor undercarriage and jet pipe detail. Handley Page Association

End fuselage and airbrake detail. Handley Page Association

This page:

Nose view of one of the Victor prototypes. Handley Page Association

For comparison, a similar view of a Mk.1 Victor converted to tanker configuration. Handley Page

And a Mk.2 displaying the much bigger intakes for the Conway engines. This photo shows a 543 Squadron aircraft at Wyton in the 1970s. Handley Page

The aircraft's front fuselage was built of light alloy skin stiffened by longitudinal stringers and frames and contained the crew's pressurised cabin above floor level and an unpressurised portion with the large H2S scanner in a removable dome below. The dielectric area beneath the cockpit floor was very large and there was another area of 'electric covering' under part of the lower rear fuselage. The rear fuselage included the wing centre section and extended back to the main fin pick-up bulkhead. Aft of the cabin and ahead of the bomb bay was a massive bridge which joined together the three spar webs that formed the two torsion boxes and made up the inner wing main structure and the torsion skin of the inner planes. Immediately aft of the rear spar web bulkhead was the bomb bay which was 32ft (9.75m) long and 7ft 3in (2.21m) high. To prevent buffeting when the doors were open there was a 7ft 6in (2.29m) long rear extension with a sloping roof. Above the bomb floor was a compartment to house the bag fuel tanks, and structurally the rear fuselage was built with longitudinal stringers

attached to hoop frames and a single skin. Heavy longerons at the bottom edges of the bomb bay were stabilised over the greater part of their length by the wing's lower surface and there were three heavy double-frames at the bomb-hoisting points which would carry all of the bomb loads.

The fuselage tail cone was detachable at the main fin pick-up bulkhead and carried the powerful hinged door airbrakes and the tail scanner. When closed the airbrakes formed part of the fuselage contour on each side immediately below the rudder; they extended rearwards and outwards, and any intermediate degree of opening could be selected. They were fitted at the rear of the fuselage in preference to a wing-mounted arrangement because it was expected that this was less likely to cause trouble at high Mach numbers. With the exception of one or two panels and the wing-spar bridge, there was no sandwich structure within the fuselage, the curvature of the skin and the load concentrations allowing normal manufacturing practice to be used. Production Victors had a

46ft (14.02m) diameter ribbon-type braking parachute fitted in the rear fuselage which was generally used on all landings to reduce the run by around 50%, from 6,000ft (1,829m) down to about 3,000ft (914m). However, early Victors used a cluster of four smaller brake chutes. This latter interim arrangement was employed while the large single chute was being designed but it gave problems because the individual chutes had a tendency to wrap around one another.

The Victor's very considerable bomb bay gave enough space for the internal stowage of a maximum of thirty-five 1,000lb (454kg) bombs with a special carrier beam installed, and this could be increased to 55,000lb (24,948kg) with external loads. The bay was made bigger than the Vulcan's, its size having been determined by the anticipated dimensions of the atomic bomb. In fact the resulting weapon came out smaller than expected but this did mean that the Victor was always able to carry more bombs than its great rival from Avro. There were no obstructions from structural

Opposite page:

Forward cockpit and pilot's controls and instruments in either one of the Victor prototypes or an early production aeroplane.
Handley Page Association

This page:

Three photos showing the underwing in-flight refuelling pod developed for the Victor tanker. In fact, the production model had just the two blades at the front. Handley Page Association

A 1967 picture showing a Vickers VC-10 refuelling from Victor tanker XA918 during trials.
Handley Page Association

members and the bay could carry every type of bomb currently under development in the early 1950s. The bomb doors retracted internally and no loading ramps or pits were required for even the largest bombs. Trials on early Victors indicated that loading a 10,000 lb (4,536kg) bomb would take about fifteen minutes, while a full internal load of 1,000 lb (454kg) bombs needed about thirty minutes. Hoisting was effected by a hydraulic jack lowered from an overhead gantry on top of the fuselage. On the prototypes provision was made for a small 'flap' at the forward end of the bomb bay (if required) to give a satisfactory bomb flight path after release.

Flexible fuel tanks occupied the wing centre section, the upper part of the fuselage above the bomb bay and wing compartments outboard of the engine and undercarriage installations. Overloads up to a maximum take-off weight of 150,000 lb (68,040kg) were to be achieved by carrying additional fuel in fixed fuselage 'overload' tanks and in drop tanks, or by having the 20,000 lb (9,072kg) of extra bombs housed in nacelles beneath the wings.

The crew's cabin, in fact the largest flight deck of the three V-types, was air-conditioned and pressurised to provide 8,000ft (2,438m) conditions when flying at altitudes of up to 47,000ft (14,326m). However, on operations the cabin's normal pressure would be altered to the equivalent of 25,000ft (7,620m) in case

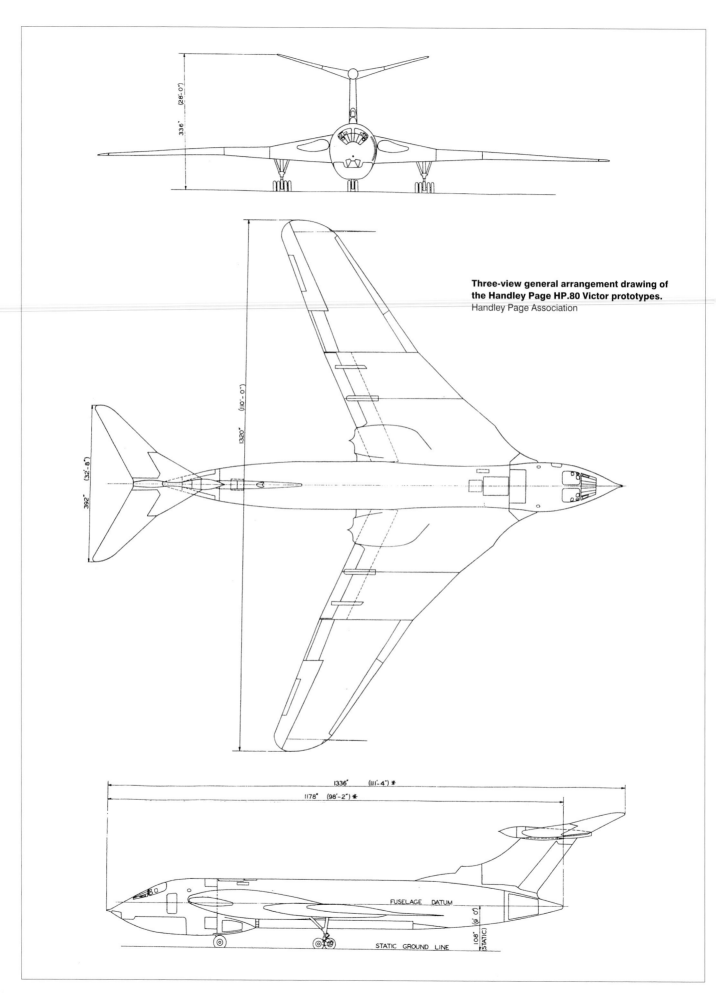

Three-view general arrangement drawing of the Handley Page HP.80 Victor prototypes.
Handley Page Association

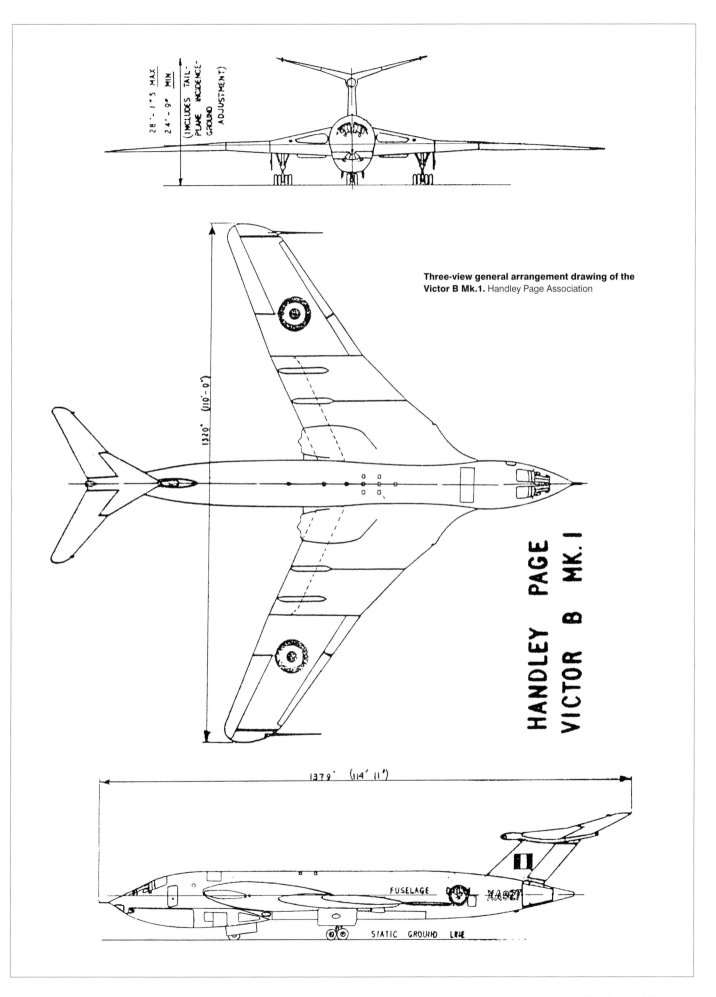

Three-view general arrangement drawing of the Victor B Mk.1. Handley Page Association

HANDLEY PAGE
VICTOR B MK.1

28″-1·5 MAX
24′-9″ MIN
(INCLUDES TAIL-
PLANE INCIDENCE-
GROUND
ADJUSTMENT)

1320″ (110′-0″)

1379″ (114′ 11″)

FUSELAGE DATUM XA927

STATIC GROUND LINE

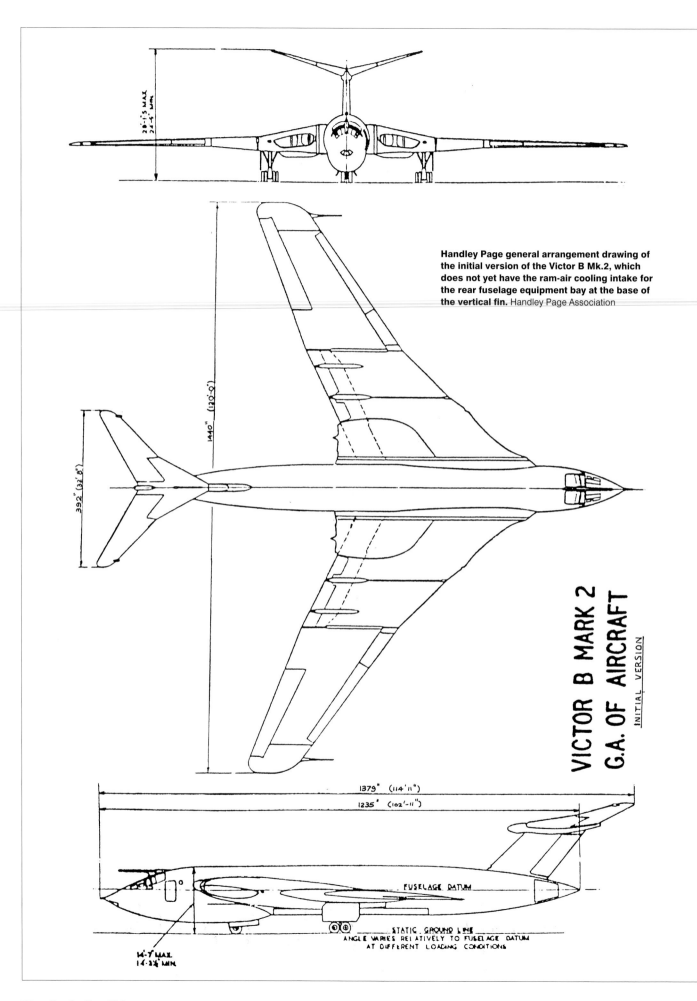

Handley Page general arrangement drawing of the initial version of the Victor B Mk.2, which does not yet have the ram-air cooling intake for the rear fuselage equipment bay at the base of the vertical fin. Handley Page Association

28·1·5 MAX
24·4 MIN

1440" (120'-0")

392" (32'8")

VICTOR B MARK 2
G.A. OF AIRCRAFT
INITIAL VERSION

1379" (114'11")
1235" (102'-11")

FUSELAGE DATUM

STATIC GROUND LINE
ANGLE VARIES RELATIVELY TO FUSELAGE DATUM
AT DIFFERENT LOADING CONDITIONS

14·7 MAX
14·2¾ MIN

Drawing of the Victor Mk.2's emergency equipment and exits. Handley Page Association

enemy damage brought an explosive decompression. There were usually five people on board – first pilot/captain, co-pilot, navigator/plotter/bomb aimer, navigator/radar operator and air electronics officer (AEO) – but a sixth seat for a crew chief could be added behind the pilots' ejection seats. The pilots were seated side by side, and the Victor's crew was standard with the other V-Bombers. However, unlike Valiant and Vulcan where captain and co-pilot were placed on a level rather higher than the other three crew members, here they were almost all on the same level. The rearward-facing crew were seated just a little higher than the pilots and their entrance hatch was placed on the port side. At the time of the V-Bomber's entry into service this hatch was known within Bomber Command as the 'pilots' entry and crew exit door', and the order of operating position from this door was the AEO, the navigator/plotter and then the navigator/radar operator on the far side. In the original 1947 project all five crew members had been shown facing forwards.

Between the two pilots there was a gangway to provide access to the prone bomb aimer's station. The pilots' ejection seats were Martin-Baker Mk.3s but for a normal emergency escape the rest of the crew had to use the side door, which had a built-in windbreak to provide them with protection when they jumped out. If the aircraft had to ditch, however, then the captain would jettison the canopy and all would hopefully escape through the roof hatch. Of the three V-Bombers, the Victor was considered to have the best all-round view; the pilot's windscreen was made of flat, dry-air-sandwich glass panels. There was also a direct vision window on each side and the cabin windscreens were heated electrically to prevent ice formation. Unlike the Vulcan that had a fighter-type stick, the Victor retained the traditional spectacle control column normally associated with large aircraft.

The Victor had a tricycle undercarriage that was designed and produced by Electro-Hydraulics Ltd. in close collaboration with Handley Page. There were eight tyres on each main bogie leg forming four double wheels and these gave a good spread of the aircraft's weight to allow it to operate from a variety of different airfields. High-grade steels and high-strength light alloys were used in the undercarriage to provide an excellent strength/weight ratio. The short nose gear had two wheels and a 175° castoring angle and could be steered hydraulically through 90°.

Space was provided for radar jamming and for defensive equipment to detect enemy missiles as they were launched from the ground and to fuse them before they were close to the

Mk.2 front fuselage structure. Handley Page Association

aircraft. Signals from the Red Steer tail warning radar (which replaced the original Orange Putter radar used on early production Victors) were passed to the pilots and the signaller both visually and aurally when aircraft or missiles were detected approaching from the rear of the bomber. The installation of the Electronic Warfare (EW) suite, which also included receivers and pulse analysers capable of assessing various enemy radio and radar transmissions, turned the B Mk.1 into the B Mk.1A, and the jammers that were designed to disrupt the

operation of enemy fighter radars were placed around the tail cone. The communications bay had HF and VHF radio, the Instrument Landing System (ILS) equipment and a radio compass and the radar bay contained GEE and a radar altimeter. B Mk.1 Victors used DC electrics but the B.2 introduced an AC system that was better suited to the electronic warfare equipment.

Long-range dead-reckoning navigation was aided by H2S Mk.9, the NBC Mk.2 Navigation and Bombing Computer and Green Satin equipment. Operating with an air-mileage unit

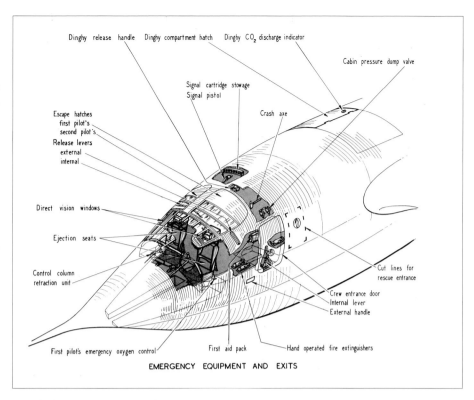

Dinghy release handle · Dinghy compartment hatch · Dinghy CO_2 discharge indicator

Cabin pressure dump valve

Signal cartridge stowage
Signal pistol

Crash axe

Escape hatches
first pilot's
second pilot's
Release levers
external
internal

Direct vision windows

Ejection seats

Control column
retraction unit

Cut lines for
rescue entrance

Crew entrance door
Internal lever
External handle

First pilot's emergency oxygen control · First aid pack · Hand operated fire extinguishers

EMERGENCY EQUIPMENT AND EXITS

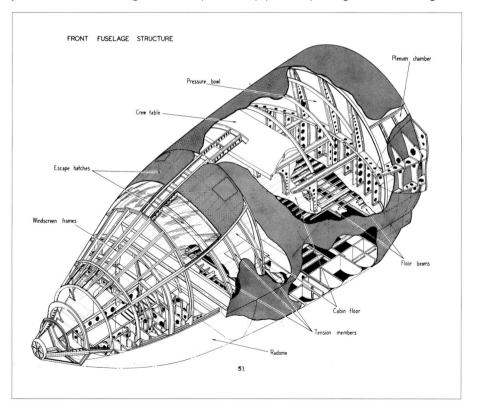

FRONT FUSELAGE STRUCTURE

Plenum chamber

Pressure bowl

Crew table

Escape hatches

Windscreen frames

Floor beams

Cabin floor

Tension members

Radome

51

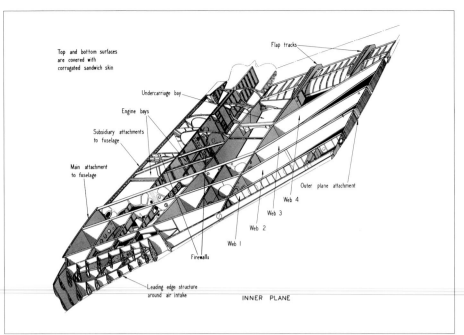

Top and bottom surfaces are covered with corrugated sandwich skin

Flap tracks

Undercarriage bay

Engine bays

Subsidiary attachments to fuselage

Main attachment to fuselage

Outer plane attachment

Web 4

Web 3

Web 2

Web 1

Firewalls

Leading edge structure around air intake

INNER PLANE

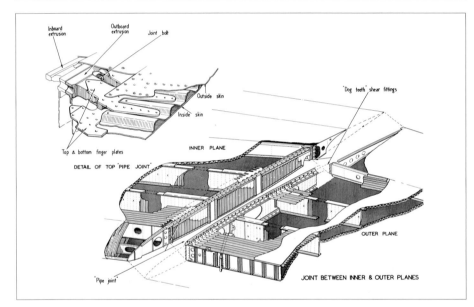

Inboard extrusion

Outboard extrusion

Joint bolt

Outside skin

Inside skin

'Dog teeth' shear fittings

Top & bottom finger plates

INNER PLANE

DETAIL OF TOP 'PIPE' JOINT

OUTER PLANE

'Pipe joint'

JOINT BETWEEN INNER & OUTER PLANES

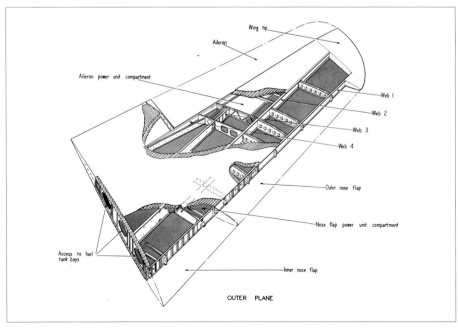

Wing tip

Aileron

Aileron power unit compartment

Web 1

Web 2

Web 3

Web 4

Outer nose flap

Nose flap power unit compartment

Access to fuel tank bays

Inner nose flap

OUTER PLANE

Mk.2 inner plane structure.
Handley Page Association

Detail of the joint between the Mk.2's inner and outer planes. Handley Page Association

Victor Mk.2 outer wing plane.
Handley Page Association

and remote-indicating G4B compass, the H2S/NBC system gave continuous track and radar map information, while a direct measurement of true ground speed and drift was given by the Green Satin system, which was a self-contained Doppler navigation aid designed for the V-Bombers. A periscopic sextant and direct-reading magnetic compass were installed in case the main systems failed. The H2S/NBC also gave the aircraft its radar bombing system. Accepting information from the visual sighting head, it offered the means of carrying out accurate visual bombing at heights up to 50,000ft (15,240m). A radio altimeter duplicated the height-finding function of H2S and would also give bomb-aiming information in the event of a full or partial failure of the aircraft's equipment. The ILS and Identification Friend or Foe (IFF) equipment were fitted as standard.

One notable feature in the Victor's design was the quantity of metal forgings used in its structure. A large proportion of these were manufactured in the 'hard' (high-strength) DTD.683 (Hiduminium 77) aluminium-zinc alloy which was one of the strongest aluminium alloys yet developed. The relatively short life of military aeroplanes in terms of their flying hours in theory made it possible to use such a strong material without incurring difficulties with fatigue. However, problems were later experienced with Hiduminium 77 on several aircraft, not least on the Vickers Valiant which was eventually withdrawn from service due to fatigue cracks in the wing. One suspects neither the RAF nor Handley Page expected the Victor to stay in service for so long but Hiduminium 77 was eventually taken out of the aircraft. Slightly lower strength aluminium-copper alloy was used in the pressure cabin and for other secondary components, while magnesium-zirconium castings were employed for control levers and some structural items. The then still very expensive titanium alloy was used where it showed advantages to offset its cost, such as in the engine-bay ribs (which acted as horizontal firewalls) and for a selection of bolts.

The B Mk.1 was essentially similar to the prototypes except for a 42in (106.7cm) longer fuselage and a slight change in the fin area from the shorter fin. There were the four 11,000lb (48.9kN) sea-level static thrust Armstrong Siddeley Sapphire A.S.Sa.7 Mk.202 turbojet engines and other changes comprised one-piece leading edge flaps, fuel-flow modifications in the wings and fuselage, and the addition of ECM equipment ahead of the nose gear which included a chaff dispenser to jam the enemy's radar. Other visible external differ-

Structure of the B Mk.2 fin.

Tailplane and elevator structure.

Main undercarriage unit on the Victor Mk.2.

Mk.2 nose undercarriage unit.
All Handley Page Association

ences between prototype and production Mk.1s were a straight leading edge to the swept fin of a notably cleaner design – the equipment-cooling intake and the dorsal fillet that housed it having been removed – and a revised 'acorn' at the junction of fin and tailplane. There were also subtle alterations in the modelling of the intakes, the fuselage profile and the crescent wing. Vortex generators, twenty-three in all, were added to each wing and these stretched from just inside the nose flaps right out to the wing tips.

Very early in the production run an in-flight refuelling facility was introduced which included a probe mounted in the top of the fuselage which projected directly above the cabin. From this a 4in (10.2cm) pipe led aft through the crew cabin into the fuel system near the ground refuelling point. A refuelling rate of 600gal/min (2,728lit/min) could be achieved and the weight penalty for installing this facility was just 110lb (50kg).

Changes introduced on the B Mk.2 were essentially the installation of the far more powerful Rolls-Royce Conway R.Co.11 engines, the larger intakes and trunking that they required plus an increase to the wingspan. The latter was lengthened by 10ft (3.05m), made up with extended wing tips, including inset aileron outer ends, plus an additional 18in (45.7cm) section to each wing root. The Conways were supported on trunnion mountings and the B.2 also had inside its extended starboard stub wing a Blackburn-Turboméca Artouste auxiliary power unit (APU) that was fed by a retractable air scoop. This was available for low pressure air starting of the Conways, when nec-

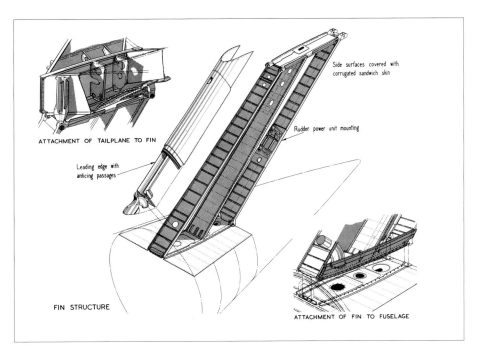

ATTACHMENT OF TAILPLANE TO FIN

Leading edge with anticing passages

Side surfaces covered with corrugated sandwich skin

Rudder power unit mounting

FIN STRUCTURE

ATTACHMENT OF FIN TO FUSELAGE

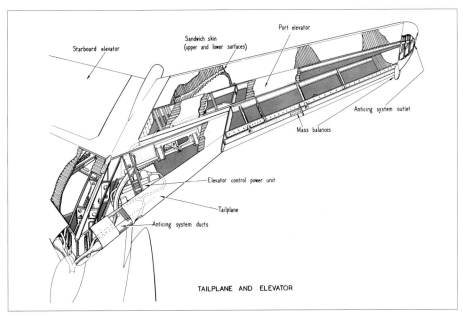

Starboard elevator

Sandwich skin (upper and lower surfaces)

Port elevator

Anticing system outlet

Mass balances

Elevator control power unit

Tailplane

Anticing system ducts

TAILPLANE AND ELEVATOR

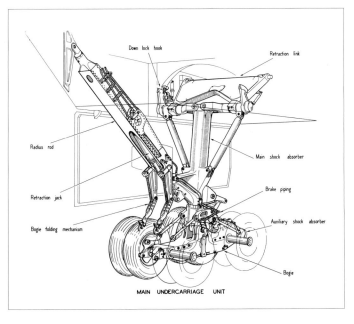

Down lock hook

Retraction link

Radius rod

Main shock absorber

Retraction jack

Brake piping

Bogie folding mechanism

Auxiliary shock absorber

Bogie

MAIN UNDERCARRIAGE UNIT

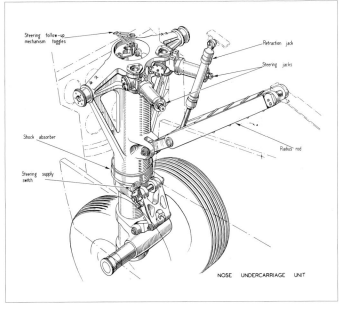

Steering follow-up mechanism toggles

Retraction jack

Steering jacks

Shock absorber

Radius rod

Steering supply switch

NOSE UNDERCARRIAGE UNIT

essary to provide power on the ground and for emergencies. The port side extended stub wing housed a Freon glycol cooling unit for the electronic countermeasures equipment. There were also two alternators for supplying emergency power – each of these was driven by an air turbine spun by one of a pair of large ram inlets that opened on each side of the dorsal fin.

The B.1's yaw damper was replaced on the B.2 by a yaw/roll damper to meet the increased problems of stability brought about by the later mark's greater operating altitude. In due course the most obvious physical change on the Mk.2 was the new ram-air cooling intake for the rear fuselage equipment bay which was moved to the base of the vertical fin (this was not fitted in the first Mk.2 XH668). The fuel system was revised, the underwing slipper tanks were made standard and the EW equipment was based around that employed by the B.1A but improved and updated. As described in Chap-

ter Three, in the early 1960s fixed drooped outboard leading edges replaced the original leading edge slats and the conversion work was usually carried out at station level. This alteration was made to both B Mk.1A and B Mk.2 aircraft and became standard for the Victor.

Looking now at the in-flight refuelling Victors, all of them had essentially the same storage and fuel transfer systems which comprised two 16,000 lb (7,258kg) capacity tanks in the former bomb bay, a seven-tank group mounted in the fuselage containing another 36,000 lb (16,330kg) of fuel, and ten tanks in the wings holding 32,000 lb (14,515kg) in all. The fuel jettison position was placed right at the end of the rear fuselage in place of the Red Steer ECM previously housed in the rear dome and now removed. As explained in Chapter Two, some of the early Mk.1As were adapted into B(K) Mk.1A two-point tankers with a Mk.20B flight refuelling pod on a new pylon underneath each wing.

However, all of the other conversions had three delivery points with the third hose in the lower fuselage. A self-contained package comprising tank, hose reel and drogue was hoisted into the bomb bay by means of the standard bombing-up equipment. The equipment installed in the SR Mk.2 reconnaissance Victors is outlined in Chapter Three.

The Victors were assembled in Handley Page's Colney Street factory at the southern end of the Radlett site. Major components such as the wings and fin were manufactured at the Cricklewood factory and then moved by road to Radlett, and Handley Page worked hard to ensure that each item was kept relatively small to ensure the job of transporting them was reasonably simple. Some large sub-assemblies like the front fuselage were built at Colney Street, while other items came in from the factory at Woodley near Reading, which until 1948 had been the home of Miles Aircraft until that company was taken over by Handley Page. Eventually all of these components and sub-assemblies went into the main jigs at Colney Street to be turned into complete airframes, and then the various items of equipment could be installed. After painting, each Victor was then prepared for its first flight. Finally, Handley Page's facilities included the Park Street site at the northern end of Radlett which was concerned with all aspects of research and development, and the experimental flying of new aeroplanes. Park Street's facilities included a large structural test frame plus a high-speed wind tunnel fed with air from three Rolls-Royce Nene turbojet engines.

Technical Data

	Span ft (m)	Length ft (m)	Height ft (m)	Gross Wing Area ft² (m²)	Gross Weight lb (kg)	Powerplant lbst (kN)	Max Level Speed mph (km/h) / ft (m)	Max Internal Fuel gal (lit)	Ceiling ft (m)	Military Load lb (kg)
HP.88	40' 0" (12.2)	39' 10" (12.1)	12' 8" (3.9) tail up	286 (26.6)	13,197 (5,986)	1 x 5,000 (22.2) RR Nene R.N.2	594 (956) at 36,000 (10,973)	– –	– –	None
HP.80 Prototype	110' 0" (33.5)	111' 4" (33.9)	28' 0" (8.5)	2,406 (223.8)	104,000 (47,174)	4 x 7,960 (35.4) Armstrong Siddeley Sapphire Sa.6	– –	8,420 (38,285)	–	2 x 10,000 (4,536), 4 x 5,000 (2,268) or 35 x 1,000 (454) bombs, 15 x 2,000 (907) 'A' Mk.9 mines or 1 x Blue Danube nuclear store. 2 x 10,000 (4,536) bombs* or 20 x 1,000 (454) bombs* or 12 x 2,000 (907) 'A' Mk.9 mines*
Victor B Mk.1	110' 0" (33.5)	114' 11" (35.0)	26' 9" (8.2)	2,406 (223.8)	180,000 (81,648)	4 x 10,500 (46.7) AS Sapphire Sa.7 Mk.202 or 11,050 (49.1) Sa.9 Mk.207	645 (1,038) at height	10,558 48,006	55,000 (16,764)	1 x 10,000 (4,536) or 35 x 1,000 (454) bombs, 1 x Blue Danube store, 1 x 7,000 (3,175) Yellow Sun Mk.1 nuclear store
Victor B Mk.2 †	120' 0" (36.6)	114' 11" (35.0)	26' 9" (8.2)	2,597 (241.5)	233,000 (105,689)	4 x 17,250 (76.7) RR Conway Co.11 Mk.103 or 20,500 (91.1) Co.17 Mk.201	645 (1,038) at 40,000 (12,192)	circa 10,475 47,625	60,000 (18,288)	1 x 10,000 (4,536) or 35 x 1,000 (454) bombs, 1 x 14,640 (6,641) Blue Steel air-to-surface nuclear missile, 1 x 7,250 (3,289) Yellow Sun Mk.2 nuclear store

* These munitions were housed in two special containers. One of these containers was fitted under each wing on the drop-tank mounting;
† Span for the K Mk.2 Tanker was 117ft 0in (35.7m).

Chapter Seven

What Was It Like?

One of the Victor prototypes caught by the official cameraman. Handley Page

Authors can write as much as we wish about the history of the Victor but, never having flown in an example, it becomes very difficult to portray to the reader a feeling of just what the aircraft was like to operate and to work with – to live with in fact! For that we need to speak to one or two of those who were there, and the following gentlemen have very kindly allowed us to tap into their memories. Please note that the navigation side of operating the Victor bomber was in almost all respects similar to the Vulcan and a detailed description of that side is given by Wing Commander 'Jeff' Jefford in the sister volume covering that aircraft. The navigation equipment in both types was the same, as were the operating procedures, so the differences (if there were any) would have been very minor and of no significance to a book like this.

Flight Lieutenant John Allam OBE

John Allam was the Handley Page test pilot who flew more Victors than anyone else – the second prototype and pretty well all of the production aeroplanes. He joined the RAF in 1943 but never got his chance to fly operationally before World War Two reached its conclusion. In 1950 he passed through the ETPS test pilots'

course and then, from 1951 to 1953, flew with A&AEE at Boscombe Down on the heavy aircraft test squadron. In August 1954 he joined Handley Page and stayed with the company until it closed in 1970, having in the latter stages been heavily involved with the Jetstream commuter aircraft. Several of the following paragraphs have been adapted from a lecture John presented on the Victor.

"The first Victor prototype WB771 was lost a few weeks before I joined the company, but I did get to fly WB775. As you may know, this aeroplane could land itself – that is if the conditions were right and the pilot had set the aircraft up nicely. The wind had to be blowing directly down the runway because even a small amount of side drift could push the Victor off line, but with everything just right you could take your hands off and leave the aircraft to touch down. Production aircraft could not perform this trick because their tailplanes were closer to the ground, which increased the ground effect on the tail and thus prevented the correct round out for touchdown. However, the Victor was always an easy aircraft to land.

"In fact, it was a nice aircraft to fly in just about every respect. There were hardly any sig-

nificant handling difficulties at all, although Dutch roll was a problem on the prototypes. That is where the aircraft swings or oscillates from side to side, although in fact the nose would make a 'Figure of 8' movement, and it was due to the aircraft having too much lateral stability and insufficient directional stability. The Victor could still be flown without allowing it to Dutch roll, but this was tiring for the pilot because he had to concentrate all of the time. Clearly the aircraft could not enter service with a weakness like this and the problem was cured by the addition of an artificial stabiliser called a yaw damper. This worked immediately and in fact two yaw dampers were fitted to production Victors to ensure there was a back-up if one of them failed.

"The Victor's in-flight characteristics and high-speed handling for an aircraft of its size were extremely good and that made life very easy for the pilot. It could cruise straight and level on maximum continuous power at 0.93 Indicated Mach Number, although this was not the most economical cruising speed but was

An early B Mk.1 Victor receives attention prior to another test flight. Handley Page

An unidentified Victor B.1 poses on the runway. Handley Page

much faster than today's civil airliners. The most economical cruise came at around Mach 0.83 IMN, at which speed the aircraft performed excellently and its engines were running nowhere near to maximum continuous power. It was also a pretty rugged aeroplane and I don't think there was anything about it that one could really point out as a bad feature.

"February 1954 was the date when we opened the bomb doors in flight for the first time. The Victor's bomb bay was big (almost certainly the biggest in any bomber at that time) and it was anticipated that there might be high levels of buffet when the doors were open. To alleviate this potential problem a set of gills or deflector plates was arranged at the forward end of the bomb bay to deflect the air downwards and thus reduce the volume of air entering the bomb bay. When the bombs doors were selected to open, these gills would automatically open rather like the old-fashioned radial piston engine gills. Testing at all heights and speeds showed that the degree of buffet was surprisingly light throughout the whole range and especially at high Mach numbers when the indicated speed was low.

"In May 1955 we took WB775 along to Boscombe Down for night-flying trials. Aero-

planes fly perfectly well at night, but their cockpit lighting systems need evaluating – especially in regard to reflections in the windscreen. The English Electric Canberra, for instance, had a real problem with its all-Perspex domed canopy, and on the approach to land at night, there were no fewer than six flare paths stacked up, one above the other, in front of the pilot. All of them were bright and clear but, although we knew that the bottom one was the one to land on, trying to land in wet weather was difficult because they tended to merge together. However, although appearing curved the Victor's windscreen was actually made up of optically flat panels and consequently there were no problems with undesired reflections either from the outside or from the internal lighting.

"In 1957 bomb-dropping trials commenced at Orfordness. The first trials involved dropping 1,000 lb (454kg) bombs over the ranges, and dropping these stores from various stations in the bomb bay showed that they all fell away cleanly without any problems. The release of a single 1,000 lb (454kg) bomb from the Victor could not be felt by the crew members, whereas in an aircraft like the piston-powered Avro Lincoln the release could be felt distinctly. This led on to the carriage and dropping on one

occasion of a dummy 10,000 lb (4,536kg) Blue Danube nuclear store, which again fell away cleanly and, in this case, was felt by the Victor's crew.

"On occasion I flew the Victor supersonically, which was no problem at all for the aircraft. Other pilots over the years have had a go at doing this because all you had to do was to put the aeroplane into a shallow dive and you would reach Mach 1 with ease. In fact, this shallow dive – 19° nose down starting at 40,000ft (12,192m) – was rather less steep than the dive required by a Hawker Hunter fighter to become supersonic, and it was just enough to create a good sonic bang.

"With the Mk.2 Victor and its Conway engines we acquired the capability of flying up to 60,000ft (18,288m), rather higher than the Mk.1, and at 55,000ft (16,764m) the Mk.2 could make steep (60° bank) 2g turns at Mach 0.93 without trouble. This was a pretty exceptional achievement at that height and that time and I think very few other types of aeroplane could do it. When the Mk.2 was being assessed by A&AEE at Boscombe Down the Establishment was visited by a couple of American test pilots who were evaluating several British aeroplanes. In due course, they were taken up to 55,000ft (16,764m), one at a time, in the Victor to be shown the aircraft's manoeuvring capability at that height. As the first of the Americans climbed down the ladder after his flight, he said to his chum, "Gee, Al, this ship's got manoeuvre capability at 50,000ft." This was spoken in such a way that it was clear there was nothing available in the United States that could achieve, at altitude, what the Victor was capable of.

"The Conway 11 first installed in the Mk.2 gave a static thrust of 17,500 lb (76.7kN), which meant some 25,000 lb (111.1kN) more thrust

was now available to the Victor than from the Mk.1's Sapphire. However, the definitive engine that came along later was the 20,500 lb (91.1kN) thrust Conway 17, which gave a total of 82,000 lb (364.4kN) for the aeroplane. Although the ground testing of the 11s coupled with a Mk.2 intake went very smoothly and successfully, when they were installed in a Victor for the first time it was a different story. Severe compressor surging was experienced right at the start of the high-power checks, and the bangs produced could be heard well over a mile away from the aircraft. Some modifications were made to the intakes prior to the first flight which did provide an improvement but the problem was far from being resolved. We did fly XH668 in this condition but handled the engines with some care.

"We had the same problems in flight when accelerating the engines quickly to high power settings – the surges produced very heavy thumps on the aircraft but fortunately they never produced a flame out. A lot of time was spent trying to solve this problem, both in the air and on the ground, and it eventually required several intake modifications and a lot of engine modifications to cure. Once the problem was solved, however, I found the Conway 11 to be an excellent engine – probably the best jet engine I have ever had the pleasure to handle. It was impossible to mishandle it in flight, it had excellent acceleration times and would relight from cold at altitudes up to 55,000ft (16,764m). I am sure that there was no other engine offering that capability at that time. The Conway 17 was never quite as good. Although its general handling was perfectly satisfactory, relighting could not be achieved above 40,000ft (12,192m). However, whilst the Victor could climb to 60,000ft (18,288m) with the Conway 11s, this was much easier to achieve with the 17s.

"In fact the extra power of the 17s was stunning! We found that by opening the engines up on the runway against the wheel, and then releasing the brakes as the aircraft wanted to move forward, it was possible from brake release to take off and climb through 20,000ft (6,096m) in two minutes and eight seconds, and to be out of 40,000ft (12,192m) in eight minutes! For that time this was quite astounding for an aircraft of the Victor's size.

XA921 with everything down prepares to land at Wyton in 1958. The very small radome at the very end of the rear fuselage covers the Orange Putter tail-warning radar. Handley Page

An early production Victor is brought to a halt by its tail parachute. To begin with the first prototype WB771 used a single 13ft (3.96m) diameter chute but this was found to be unsatisfactory. The arrangement was therefore replaced by a set of three or four 8ft (2.44m) chutes. However, in June 1959 it was established that there was a 9% failure rate of the multiple breaking parachutes, so the larger single chute shown here was designed as a substitute. Handley Page

XH621, a Victor B Mk.1A, was flying with No 57 Squadron when this picture was taken. It shows the original tail unit marking adopted by the unit. Handley Page

"As a result of the loss of the first B Mk.2 XH668 we had to perform a series of special trials at 55,000ft (16,764m) to investigate the variant's high-speed, high-altitude handling and manoeuvring characteristics at speeds up to Mach 0.95 Indicated. It was thought that some of these flights could be a little dangerous and so only the two pilots would go on each sortie – they had ejection seats and so could get out in an emergency when the rear crew did not have such facilities. The selected trials aircraft, XH670, had an observer's control panel installed at the co-pilot's station in place of the normal instrument panel. Peter Baker and I flew alternative flights while Harry Rayner, after being trained to operate the observer's panel, flew on every flight as a pilot/observer.

"In the meantime the Ministry concluded that, in case we got into trouble, we would need a chase plane to monitor these flights and a few weeks before the trials got under way they asked us which type would be the most suitable. After some thought we concluded, quite genuinely, that the only aircraft capable of flying chase at that altitude would be another Mk.2 Victor, an observation that was not well received by the Ministry because they imagined that two more Mk.2 Victors might be lost. In the end they selected the Gloster Javelin delta wing jet fighter, which in fact was incapable of climbing much above 48,000ft (14,630m) and had very little manoeuvre capability when it got there. Consequently, during those tests we had a chase plane sitting at around 7,000ft (2,134m) beneath us and pretty well incapable of observing anything worthwhile in the event of an emergency. In addition the Javelin could stay on station only for around forty minutes when our time on test condition was often around two hours, so three Javelins in sequence had to cover each test flight.

"We at Handley Page never agreed with the findings of the official inquiry into the crash of XH668 but after this tragedy some people within the Air Force and the Ministry were worried about the Mk.2's safety. We thought that XH668 had got into trouble at around 52,000ft (15,850m) but it was because of the findings

Head-on pass of an Interim Blue Steel Victor B Mk.2. This may in fact be XH675 in July 1961. Handley Page Association

This Victor B Mk.2 lacks its rear fuselage serial number. It may in fact be the first full production B.2 XH669, which indeed flew without its serial painted on. Handley Page

Another unidentified B Mk.2, seen flying at Farnborough. This may be XH669 again because the aircraft took part in the 1960 Show. Handley Page

that we had to check out several aspects in regard to the aircraft's flying characteristics at 55,000ft (16,764m). We had to assess if they had contributed to or were the cause of the accident. In the end this set of trials was concluded in about thirty flights without any problems being experienced, and we found nothing wrong with the aircraft at all.

"The Mk.2 Victor also introduced, in due course, a very slight fixed droop to the leading edge of the wing. To begin with all of the Mk.2s (and all of the Mk.1s) were fitted with leading edge flaps but the fixed leading edge which replaced them (set at a very small droop angle) did not upset the aircraft's performance in any way. It also took out some of the complication because the mechanism required to operate the leading edge flaps had been relatively complex and was now no longer required, and removing that also saved quite a bit of weight in the airframe.

"When selected, the original nose flaps would extend to the maximum position instantly. We referred to the nose flap extension as 'dumping' and the maximum Indicated

Mach Number at which they could be deployed was 0.97. There were no significant trim changes but when they were deployed the Mach number fell almost instantly to 0.93. Trials flying established that there were no fears of any problems should they be inadvertently extended at any speed during flight. In January 1959 we made the first flight with the fixed droop leading edges on WB775, the first aircraft so modified, and the reason for this change stemmed from an RAF requirement to improve the serviceability problems that they were having with the nose flaps. The drooped leading edge wings provided satisfactory handling qualities over the cleared flight envelope and the performance penalty was minimal. In February 1962 XL159 became the first Mk.2 to fly with the Conway 17 and fixed droop leading edges and the new wing fitting behaved just as well on the Mk.2 as it had on the Mk.1.

"Another modification made in 1962 was the fitting of pods to house window (chaff) and flares which took the form of 'Kuchemann carrots' or 'Whitcombe's Bodies', one being placed at about mid-span on each wing of a Mk.2. (Richard Whitcombe had been responsible for the formulation of the 'area rule' in America.) The first flight with these was made in December of that year and as far as I remember they did not affect either the handling or the performance of the aircraft.

"One area I did not specialise in was the in-flight refuelling tanker developments of the Victor – 'Spud' Murphy was the Handley Page test pilot who did most of the development flying on those. However, in the limited flying I did complete on these versions, both Mk.1 and Mk.2, I found that carrying all of that fuel made no difference to the Victor's flying characteristics. This was of course because the fuel storage tanks had been installed in lieu of the bomb

XH669 on show at Coltishall in September 1964 for Battle of Britain Day, complete with wing fairings, Blue Steel and camouflage.

load. Streaming the drogues behind the aircraft also gave us no problems – in fact as a pilot you could not really tell they were there. We could not see them of course but one of the rear crew would be able to look at the fighters or other types taking on fuel from the rearward-facing periscope we had in the crew cabin. ('Spud' Murphy had to eject with his co-pilot from Victor XL159 at 500ft [152m] after the bomber had entered a deep stall and developed a flat spin, and from which recovery was not possible. His back was broken but after many months recovering he was able to return to flying.)

"I would like to raise one point about the tankers. The Mk.1 Victor bombers were converted to tankers by Handley Page and subsequently there was no difference in their handling qualities. The Mk.2 bombers were converted to tankers at Manchester after Handley Page went out of business. Because of the way this conversion was done (which was not the way that Handley Page would have done it [see Chapter Three]), the Mk.2 tanker's handling characteristics were not anything like as good as the original Mk.2 bomber Victors. Nor was the Mk.2 altitude performance as good. This was brought about because the wing tips had been clipped, which reduced the wing area and changed the relationship between the centre of gravity and the centre of pressure, thereby upsetting the longitudinal stability. In fact, the centre of pressure had moved forward and was now too close to the centre of gravity. This is important because some former Victor pilots who only ever flew the Mk.2 tanker may not have such a rosy picture of the aircraft's handling qualities as a Victor bomber pilot.

"Of course, in regard to the Victor's capability as a tanker the loss in altitude did not matter because in-flight refuelling took place at lower heights anyway, and the Mk.2 tanker still flew quite well at high altitudes but not so nicely. However, above about 40,000ft (12,192m) the autopilot had a problem coping with the change in longitudinal stability. With the centre

of pressure so close to the centre of gravity it was not difficult to get a pilot-induced oscillation (PIO) going.

"I also flew both the Vickers Valiant and the Avro Vulcan but not really enough to make an in-depth comparison with the Victor. The Valiant was an extremely good aircraft, which incidentally Vickers did a fantastic job with on its development in a very short time and to a tight schedule. It was, however, not quite in the same class as either the Victor or Vulcan. I do feel that in many respects the Victor was a better aircraft than the Vulcan – and I am not saying that just because I worked for Handley Page. It is a fact that the Victor could fly faster than the Vulcan, and for a given bomb load it could fly higher and for around another 200 miles (322km) further. The Victor did have the edge when it came to performance, while from the point-of-view of manoeuvrability at altitude I would say the two bombers were pretty similar."

Air Vice-Marshal M. M. J. Robinson

Air Vice-Marshal Mike Robinson volunteered to serve in the RAF in May 1944. After a six-month short course at Oxford University in the spring and summer of 1945 he enlisted in the RAF as an Aircraftman Class 2. Graduating from the RAF College Cranwell with a Permanent Commission, his first operational flying came in Malaya where, from 1948 through to 1951, he flew the Bristol Beaufighter and then the Bristol Brigand light bomber. After that he went to the Central Flying School on instruction before going to Germany to the fly the English Electric Canberra – in fact the B(I) Mk.6 and B Mk.8 versions which he rated very highly. In the mid-1960s he was OC 100 Squadron at Wittering, flying the Victor Mk.2 with Blue Steel, and after that he spent time posted to the Far East before going to the Ministry as a Wing Commander. The next position was Station Commander at Lossiemouth when the base was operating Avro Shackletons, Fairey Gannets and SEPECAT Jaguars. After a period as Assistant Comman-

Above and right: **Victor XA930 is refuelled by Valiant WZ376 during trials.** Terry Panopalis

dant (Cadets) at Cranwell, and another spell at the Ministry as the Director for the Council of Organisation, he retired from the RAF in 1982.

"I will never forget the very strong impression I received when I first came aboard a Victor – this was the first occasion in which I had been in a pilot's seat where I was unable to see any other part of the aeroplane. The view forward was very good for take-off, landing and low flying but the pilots were seated so well forward, and the aircraft had such a pronounced sweep of the wings, that it was not possible to see any of the airframe behind the cockpit. The rear crew were also housed behind a black curtain and so it was really just the two pilots. There was a periscope for looking backwards but that could not be used by the pilot when he was in his seat. If I were involved in display flying at strange airfields, particularly civilian, when taxiing I would always have a member of the rear crew at the periscope to confirm that the wing tips were clear of obstacles such as parked aircraft. It was also quite difficult to ease into the pilot's seat because one had to wear an immersion suit, Mae West and overalls. And then once seated there were fourteen connections to make, including leg-restrainer straps, parachute harness, seat harness, normal and emergency oxygen and, of course, the radio. Strapping in was quite a process!

"The take-off in the Victor was very straightforward. The co-pilot handled the throttles and checked that the power from the four Conways came up evenly. Any tendency not to go straight, say because of a crosswind, was countered by using the nose wheel steering until sufficient speed was obtained to give authority to the rudder. Raise the nose at about 140 knots (161mph/260km/h), and lift-off a moment or two later depending on aircraft weight. For air displays one raised the nose at 140 knots and went immediately into a steep climb at that speed. By the end of the runway,

the aircraft was going through 1,000ft (305m) and the rate of climb meter was off the clock but one used the speedometer as the pitch indicator. One nice moment occurred at a New Zealand Air Force display when the Commander of a Republic F-84 Thunderjet fighter squadron also taking part in the event, a USAF Colonel, asked if I had reheat on my engines. I replied in my best Empire voice: "No, do you think I need any extra power!" A little unkind since he had blown off the dust at the start of the runway, revving up before taking off the brakes, and then more dust as he got airborne just before the end of the runway. For the display itself he reduced his fuel load to fifteen minutes to give him a comparable take-off 'appearance'.

"I only flew the Mk.2 Victor with the Conway but thanks to those engines the aeroplane had plenty of power. I understand that these brought a great improvement over the Mk.1 with its Sapphires because that version did suffer from a complaint known as 'centre-line closure' (see Chapter Three). During the two years or more that I flew the Victor on 100 Squadron I only experienced a single engine failure. This was when the oil pressure disappeared 'off the clock' on the leg from Perth to Darwin in Aus-

tralia. The Conways each gave over 20,000 lb (88.9kN) of thrust for take-off, which itself was a straightforward procedure, and the Conway was a much more powerful and reliable engine than the Sapphire.

"At height the Victor's handling was good. Perhaps the only worry was in one corner of the flight envelope which involved a process of zigzagging as we approached a target. When we were near to coming within range of the 'enemy's' surface-to-air missiles we would turn to the left, then turn sharp right to take us back across our original track, and then left again. At the extreme heights we were flying the Victor could get snappy in these turns and it was quite easy to get into a stall. Consequently the pilot hadn't to be too ham-fisted in this manoeuvre, otherwise the Victor could make it very evident that it was near to stalling. The Victor's controls were well balanced and there was nothing too heavy about them.

"When flying at low speeds on the run in to land, the Victor's speed controls could be temperamental. Speed management, i.e. adjusting the speed according to weight on the approach, could be slightly difficult so we devised a technique of selecting half airbrake for the final stages of the approach and this

Victor XA918 refuels English Electric Canberra WH878. Terry Panopalis

the time I would have had more faith delivering a gravity-dropped Yellow Sun free-fall nuclear weapon rather than a Blue Steel, which was essentially a 'trials' weapon that had to be rushed into operational use once Gary Powers and his Lockheed U-2 had been shot down. The American U-2 was a reconnaissance aeroplane designed to fly at very high altitude and when Powers' aircraft was downed over the Soviet Union in May 1960 by a surface-to-air missile, the V-Bombers and other high-altitude types had suddenly become very vulnerable. In theory, Blue Steel would allow a V-Bomber to make a nuclear attack on a target well outside the range of its defensive missiles but it had serious limitations. For example when carrying a 'live' weapon (in the sense of having its motoring powers aboard), and if we had to divert away from Wittering for whatever reason, we could only go to a limited number of airfields in the UK which had the necessary large water tank for subsequent unloading and submersion of the weapon. One of the principles of air power is its flexibility and Blue Steel did not always meet that criterion.

"It was during my time on Victors that the Cuban Missile Crisis blew up. If I remember correctly, from about 2.30pm on one Saturday (in fact the day before the Soviet ships turned around) we were kept sitting in our aircraft fully fuelled at 'Category 05' – i.e. cockpit readiness with five minutes to take-off. We stayed at that status for two to three hours before moving back to 'Category 15', which meant fifteen minutes to take-off. At that point we were able to get out of the Victor and return to the crew room but we still had to stay close together so that we could respond again should the crisis have deepened. Fortunately it never did.

"There are one or two interesting points about the Victor which you will never find in a reference book. For example when the wings were fully fuelled the tips were 14in (35.6cm) lower than if the wings were completely empty. The wings themselves would often extend beyond the edge of the taxiway, and the span of the tailplane was more than the main wingspan of a number of high performance jets, like the Hawker Harrier, the General Dynamics F-16 Fighting Falcon and the SEPECAT Jaguar, that were in service at the same time as the Victor.

"I flew tanker Victors with No 1 Group, which included on one occasion taking some Buccaneers across the Atlantic to Alberta so that they could perform live weapon practice over there. The speed we flew the tanker was always set by the speed of the receiving aircraft, although we were usually flying at between 230 and 250 knots (265 to 288mph/426 to 463km/h). The altitude was also based on what was comfortable for the receiver, and in fact everything we did as a tanker crew went towards ensuring the safety of the receiving aircraft. An example of

dampened the tendency for the speed, as indicated on the speedometer, to 'jump about'. So the landing was straightforward and the deployment of the tail parachute, once the nose wheel was on the ground, gave a dramatic and reassuring deceleration which saved quite a lot of wear on the brakes. However, if it had not been folded correctly the chute would sometimes not deploy properly. I thought that the Victor's undercarriage was an amazing and beautiful piece of engineering which seemed to have the ability to fold into itself. As it retracted forward it appeared to curl up and then disappear into what looked like a much smaller space inside the wing. The double nose wheel could be steered, which meant moving on the ground was easy – there was no need for differential engine power to change direction which had been the case with the earlier aeroplanes I had flown.

"So you can see that the Victor was a nice aircraft to fly but it did have a few quirks. As mentioned I later flew the Vulcan, not enough to make an in-depth comparison but sufficient to make some observations. The Vulcan was a totally amiable beast without any quirks at all,

and because of that big wing it was very difficult to make a hard landing in the delta bomber. Again you could not see out of the aircraft – except forward – but it too had plenty of power and balanced controls. In fact, the aircraft was almost viceless. From a pilot's point-of-view, I felt that the Vulcan was just a little bit better than a Victor – perhaps slightly more of a 'pilot's aeroplane'. Although others may dispute this, I consider that their speed, range and height were pretty similar, and at high altitudes you could outmanoeuvre most contemporary fighters in either – provided they kept a level playing field and did not introduce air-to-air missiles to the game. I once did a spiral climb in a Victor while being chased by a Gloster Javelin fighter, and he gave up when he realised he had reached the point where he could go no higher. We just carried on climbing!

"We only ever flew with a 'training' version of the Blue Steel onboard. However, later on while flying from Wittering my ex-co-pilot did launch a 'live' round over the range in Wales but I believe this was the only occasion an example was fired once the Blue Steel proving trials had been completed in Australia. To be honest, at

XA918 carrying out more refuelling trials – first with Blackburn Buccaneer XN976 and de Havilland Sea Vixen XN685; second with the Sea Vixen plus English Electric Lightning XN728. Terry Panopalis

Avro Vulcan B Mk.1 XA892, Vickers Valiant B Mk.1 WZ373 and Handley Page Victor B Mk.1 XA919, all in silver finish, pose for publicity pictures. A&AEE via Terry Panopalis

flew the K Mk.2, the last version in service. The OCU conversion course lasted for a little over five months and was very thorough indeed and I joined 55 Squadron just a few weeks before the Falklands began. Therefore, as a very new co-pilot I was off to Ascension Island and became involved with the 'Black Buck' raids. During the conflict we also flew in-flight refuelling sorties for Nimrods on reconnaissance and air cover duties, and for Lockheed Hercules aircraft which were performing 'Cadbury Drops' – that is dropping equipment and stores to troops on the ground. The IFR operations themselves were fairly straightforward because the procedures involved were by this time long established and finely tuned. By now the Victor itself was, of course, quite an elderly aeroplane and we also had to keep a close watch on the airframe's fatigue index. The operations connected with the Falklands, involving sorties with very heavy loads, did take their toll on what was left of the fatigue lives of some Victors.

"One memory from this period stands out and concerns a flight refuelling sortie in XL233. This took place in fact just after the Falklands War had ended. During the war, we had been carrying very high fuel loads, as much as we could cram into the Victor, and as a result such constant operations had left their mark on the bag tanks in XL233's wings. The wing tank's fuel gauge had been damaged and was indicating full when in fact only about 20,000 lb (9,072kg) of fuel had been taken into the wing (the tank actually held over 30,000 lb [13,608kg]). After completing our in-flight refuelling operation we began to climb and found that we were 'using' fuel at a far greater rate that we should have been. We also found that our communications equipment was giving problems and that we were stuck over the South Atlantic without an HF radio.

However, our Air Electronics Officer (AEO), Ray Holloway, was a real expert and he managed to get a Morse code message reporting our problem through to Ascension by using the sideband. Another crew on the island was dragged straight out of the bar and, led by 55 Squadron's Commanding Officer Wg Cdr Seymour, a Victor was launched to try and get some fuel out to us. In the meantime, Steve Jones, our captain, was flying straight for home with the objective of getting us as close to base as possible before we had to leave XL233. The guys in the back were getting ready to bale out and we expected to have to eject, but in the end the radar at Ascension was able to vector the CO's aircraft onto us. By that time we were flying on three engines, and in fact we completed the IFR on three engines (which I understand had not been done before) taking on 35,000 lb (15,876kg) of fuel in the process. After regaining our composure, we landed at Ascension."

this was the route taken during a refuelling operation. We worked on the principle of something going wrong at the worst possible moment, something that might prevent the delivery or receiving operation from working properly so that the receiver would be unable to take on any fuel at all. This meant, for example, that an Atlantic crossing would be taken much further north than would normally be necessary, to ensure that the receiver was close enough to Greenland or Iceland to divert safely should he have to.

"The operation itself was not easy and involved a closing speed into the drogue of not more than 4mph (6.5km/h) – and that required very skilful flying. When you were refuelling another big aircraft – perhaps Victor to Victor – to the pilot of the receiver the tanker would look very big and very close, so concentration throughout was vital. The pilots who flew the Vulcan raids over the Falkland Islands in 1982 had to make quite a number of in-flight refuellings to get there and back, and all of the time with water beneath them. Someone described it as like flying from London to Bombay and back but with the nearest land some way off. To my mind these flights were a fantastic feat of arms and concentration and the Victor K.2 force was heavily involved throughout.

"I did not notice much difference between the bomber and tanker Mk.2s. The smaller wing would have been necessary to give greater strength for carrying the heavy underwing tanks and, indeed, with full fuselage and wing tanks, the Mk.2 tanker was heavier than the bomber. As a result its take-off run was a bit longer, rate of climb lower and performance slightly reduced but not in a dramatic way. Handling was not really a worry and the problems above 40,000ft (12,192m) highlighted by John Allam probably came close to the edge of the flight envelope. When refuelling, and for general flying, the tanker would be operating in the middle of the flight envelope. In addition, the tanking operation itself would rarely if ever be done above 30,000ft (9,144m) because it was more difficult to receive fuel at that height. It was also inefficient because the receiver had to climb to that higher altitude and use some of its fuel to get there."

Flight Lieutenant Andy Pugh

After joining the RAF in 1979 and completing his training, Flight Lieutenant Andy Pugh joined No 232 OCU at Marham in November 1981 to convert onto the Victor tanker. In April 1982 he joined No 55 Squadron just in time for the Falklands Conflict. Later he moved on to No 101 Squadron flying Vickers VC-10 tankers, this time taking part in the 1991 Gulf War which involved refuelling aircraft from other services, including the US Navy. This was followed by a spell with Strike Command before he left the RAF to become a civil airline pilot.

"The Handley Page Victor was my first Squadron type in the RAF, although I only ever

Contracts and Airframe Histories

The data used to compile this appendix is derived from the Air Ministry 'Form 78s' (Aircraft Movement Cards) held by the MoD Air Historical Branch, supplemented by the equivalent Royal Australian Air Force records for aircraft tested at Woomera and Ministry of Defence (Procurement Executive) records for aircraft flown at experimental establishments in the UK.

SCALE MODEL AIRCRAFT

Two HP.88 prototypes to Contract 6/Aircraft/2243/CB.6(a), serial numbers allotted 5.4.48

VX330
21.7.51	First flight at Carnaby
26.8.51	Crashed at Stansted due to structural failure on its 28th flight (Sqn Ldr D. J. P. Broomfield killed)
2.1.52	Accepted Off Contract and Struck Off Charge

VX337
	Cancelled on 14.10.49

Note: The fuselage of the HP.88 was that of a Supermarine Attacker modified to accept the swept-back wing under Supermarine Type No 521. The prototype was assembled by Blackburn & General Aircraft at Brough under Blackburn designation Y.B.2

ENGINE TEST BED
SAPPHIRE HASTINGS

TE583
17.1.47	Arrived at Boscombe Down from Radlett
23.4.47	Returned to Radlett
31.7.48	Accepted Off Contract – to AFEE, glider-towing trials
14.6.49	To Radlett. H.P. – installation of Sapphire engines
13.11.50	First flight with Sapphire engines in outer nacelles
30.5.51	Arrived at NGTE, Bitteswell
3.5.52	To Radlett – pending conversion to standard
5.6.52	Allotted for Victor crew escape development
15.10.53	To Boscombe Down – tests of Victor escape door
25.8.54	Boscombe Down to Defford. Red Cabbage and Passive Q-Band development
23.4.58	Ground radar target at RRE and flying training aircraft
11.4.63	TSR.2 SLAR trials
25.5.64	To A&AEE. Radar trials
28.7.64	To Pershore. Continuation of trials
7.4.65	To Manston. MoD Fire-fighting training

Handley Page Victors
Two prototypes, 50 production B.1/B.1A, 34 production B.2 completed, 25 B.2 cancelled
Two prototypes to Contract 6/Aircraft/1875/CB.6(a), serial numbers allotted 11.3.49

WB771
19.9.52	Damaged by fuselage fire during assembly at Boscombe Down

A view of the HP.88 taken at Carnaby in June 1951. Henry Matthews

24.12.52	First flight at Boscombe Down, (0:17), Sqn Ldr H. G. Hazelden
25.2.53	Ferried from Boscombe Down to Radlett
15.7.53	Flypast at RAF Odiham during the Coronation Review
5.9.53	Loaned to firm to appear at the SBAC Show at Farnborough
31.12.53	Leading edge flap lost during approach to Radlett
-.2.54	Grounded for major inspection and modifications
14.7.54	Crashed at Cranfield after loss of tailplane during PE tests (Remains taken to RAE for investigation)

WB775
11.9.54	First flight at Radlett, then later a flypast at the SBAC Show
14.3.55	Delivered to A&AEE Boscombe Down for 'preview' trials
-.7.55	Flypasts at Paris Air Show
5.9.55	Loaned to firm to appear at the SBAC Show at Farnborough
15.11.56	Accepted Off Contract (commencing a new contract, 6/Aircraft/14201/CB.6(a), for flight trials)
22.8.59	Fuselage taken by road to RAE Farnborough for decompression tests (relating to the crash of XH668 on 20.8.59)
22.6.60	Struck Off Charge at RAE

XA917 to XA941 (25 aircraft). Contract 6/Aircraft/8441/CB.6(a). Serial numbers allotted 22.7.52. All built as B.1. Conversions to BK.1 (redesignated K.1 in June 1967) were XA926-928, 930, 932, 936-939, 941. None were converted to B.1A.

XH587 to XH594, XH613 to XH621, XH645 to XH651, XH667 (25 aircraft), all built as B.1. All except XH617 converted to B.1A. Contract 6/Aircraft/11303/CB.6(a). Serial numbers allotted 21.9.54. Conversions to BK.1A (redesignated K1A in June 1967) were XH587-591, 614-616, 618-621, 645-651, 667. XH615, 620, 646-648 and 667 were initially two-point (K2P) tankers but all became K3P three-pointers after the central hose-unit installation was cleared for use.

XH668 to XH675, built as B.2 (balance of 8 aircraft on contract as above). XH672, 674 converted to SR.2. XH669, 671-673, 675, converted to K.2.

XL158 to XL165, XL188 to XL193, XL230 to XL233 (18 aircraft). All built as B.2. Contract 6/Aircraft/12996/CB.6(a). Serial numbers allotted 3.1.56. XL161, 165, 193, 230 converted to SR.2. XL158, 160-164, 188-192, 231-233 converted to K.2.

XL511 to XL513 (3 aircraft) to Contract 6/Aircraft/12996/CB.6(a). Serial numbers allotted 27.2.56. All built as B.2, and all later converted to K.2.

XM714 to XM718 (5 aircraft) to Contract 6/Aircraft/15596/CB.6(a). Serial numbers allotted 29.1.58. Built as B.2. Further aircraft XM719 to XM721, XM745 to XM756 and XM785 to XM794 (25 aircraft) cancelled. Contract later changed to KD/C/08. XM715, 716, 718 converted to SR.2. XM715, 717 converted to K.2.

To summarise: SR.2 conversions were XH672, 674, XL161, 165, 193, 230, XM715, 717 and 718. XM717 served with No 543 Squadron as a crew trainer, not an SR.2. K.2 conversions were XH669, 671-673, 675, XL158, 160-164, 188-192, 231-233, 511-513, XM715, 718 (total 23). Intended K.2 conversions XH674, XL165, XL193 and XM718 were cancelled.

PRODUCTION AIRCRAFT

Victor B Mk.1

XA917
8.2.56	AW/CN
1.4.56	To C(A) Charge
12.4.60	A&AEE. Autopilot trials
2.3.61	Damaged beyond repair in heavy landing at Radlett
15.1.64	Sold to Air Ministry. To 7827M at RAF Wittering (allotted 13.12.63) (Nose survives in storage with an enthusiast)

XA918

29.3.56	AW/CN
23.6.56	Transfer to C(A) Charge
31.8.57	Loan to firm to appear at SBAC Show at Farnborough until 9.9.57
8.3.63	A&AEE. Trials re tanker role conversion (Contract KD/C/0181/CB.6[c])
18.4.63	Returned to Radlett
6.10.64	A&AEE. Flight refuelling trials
8.10.64	Handley Page
19.10.64	To A&AEE
22.10.64	Returned to Radlett
2.2.65	To A&AEE
17.2.65	Returned to Radlett
12.4.65	To A&AEE. C(A) Release trials for two-point tanker role
21.5.65	Returned to Radlett
21.9.65	To A&AEE
18.11.65	Transferred to Handley Page at Boscombe Down
8.12.65	Returned to Radlett for further company trials
18.8.66	Authority to go to A&AEE for three-point tanker trials, returned to Radlett 25.8.66
18.10.66	To A&AEE
10.8.67	To Handley Page. Further trials, until released 1.11.68
20.7.70	Struck Off Charge. Sold for scrap to Bradbury & Co, Bournemouth

XA919

25.3.57	AW/CN
28.3.57	To A&AEE. Radio trials
1.4.57	Loan to C(A)
16.5.61	To RAF Locking, Cat. 5 (GI), (allotted 7724M on 16.6.61)

XA920

22.6.56	AW/CN
31.7.56	Loan to C(A)
20.3.57	Transfer to C(A) Charge
15.10.57	To A&AEE. Official performance trials
5.1.59	To Handley Page. PR role trials (Contract 6/Aircraft/14537/CB.6[c])
17.8.60	To A&AEE. PR role trials
15.9.63	From RAE Farnborough to Stansted for vulnerability trials

XA921

12.7.56	AW/CN
10.7.56	Loan to C(A)
18.7.56	Allotted for autopilot, drop tank and RATOG trials
14.3.57	Transfer to C(A) Charge
17.9.57	To A&AEE. Armament trials
13.10.60	To Radlett for minor inspection
25.1.61	To A&AEE. Armament clearance trials
14.10.62	To RAF for disposal. Cat. 5(s)

XA922

29.11.57	AW/CN
29.11.57	Handling Squadron, Boscombe Down
19.4.58	Transfer to C(A). To Radlett
26.9.58	To RAE. 'Special armament' trials. (i.e. nuclear weapons)
3.5.66	To Handley Page. Flight strain gauging trials.
8.4.70	Transferred to Hawker Siddeley, Woodford. Transient voltage tests
27.4.73	Struck Off Charge for sale as scrap

XA923

31.1.58	AW/CN
4.2.58	232 OCU
14.4.58	Radar Reconnaissance Flight, Wyton
16.10.61	232 OCU
22.10.62	Handley Page. Major servicing
7.2.63	Ex M/S
12.3.64	Disposal Account, surplus
27.5.64	Cat. 5 (GI) for RAF Cosford as 7850M

XA924

24.1.58	AW/CN
27.1.58	232 OCU
21.3.58	Radar Reconnaissance Flight, Wyton
9.10.61	232 OCU
24.7.62	Handley Page. Major servicing on site
10.10.62	Ex M/S
11.1.63	Disposal Account, Cat. 3R. RoS by 71 MU
11.2.63	232 OCU
28.6.63	10 Squadron
2.3.64	Disposal Account, surplus
20.4.64	Cat. 5 (GI) for No 4 SoTT, St Athan. Allotted 7844M. Later RTP

XA925

28.2.58	AW/CN
4.3.58	232 OCU
16.4.58	Radar Reconnaissance Flight, Wyton
15.9.61	232 OCU
3.9.62	Handley Page. M/S on site
11.12.62	Ex M/S
26.6.63	15 Squadron
9.3.64	Disposal Account, surplus
20.3.64	Arrived at Handley Page, Radlett
28.4.64	Sold to Ministry of Aviation. Bird-strike investigation
14.7.66	Struck Off Charge for corrosion investigation

XA926

14.3.58	AW/CN
17.3.58	232 OCU
28.2.61	Cat. 3R. RoS Handley Page
15.3.61	232 OCU
13.6.61	Cat. 4 M/S on site. Handley Page
23.11.61	Ex M/S
17.9.64	Handley Page. Conversion to BK.1 (redesignated K.1 6.67)
22.3.66	57 Squadron
22.3.68	Handley Page. Mods
8.5.68	57 Squadron
3.6.74	55 Squadron
17.6.74	57 Squadron
26.5.76	St Athan. Cat. 5. Non-Effective Aircraft
22.11.76	SoC. Cat. 5(s)

XA927

16.4.58	AW/CN. 10 Squadron
3.7.62	Cat. 4 M/S on site
18.10.62	Ex M/S
20.5.64	15 Squadron
17.9.64	Handley Page. Conversion to BK.1
29.9.66	Ex conversion
4.10.66	214 Squadron
3.7.68	Loaned to A&AEE at Marham for drogue test
5.7.68	Returned to 214 Squadron
1.2.77	SoC at RAF St Athan as Cat. 5(s)

XA928

25.3.57	AW/CN
29.3.57	Loan to C(A)
19.8.57	Handley Page. Embodiment of C(A) Release Mods
5.5.58	10 Squadron
2.3.64	Disposal Account, surplus
10.9.64	Handley Page. Conversion to BK.1
8.3.66	57 Squadron
9.8.76	214 Squadron
16.12.76	SoC as Cat. 5(s) at St Athan

XA929

23.6.57	AW/CN. 10 Squadron
8.9.59	232 OCU
6.1.60	10 Squadron
14.8.61	Handley Page. M/S on site
30.1.62	Ex M/S
16.6.62	Overshot on abandoned take-off at Akrotiri, destroyed by fire
2.8.62	SoC as Cat. 5(s)

XA930

30.9.57	AW/CN
9.10.57	Loan to C(A). To A&AEE, operational reliability trials
30.6.58	To Handley Page for temporary storage
25.3.60	To A&AEE. Flight refuelling receiver and drop tank trials
22.6.60	Returned to Radlett
14.7.60	Authority to transfer to de Havilland, Hatfield, for RATOG
16.8.60	Despatched from Radlett to A&AEE. RATOG trials
23.6.61	Handley Page. C(A) Release Mods
10.9.63	10 Squadron
15.9.64	232 OCU
18.3.65	55/57 Squadrons
1.9.65	Loan to MoA. Transfer from Honington to Radlett
20.9.65	Arrived at A&AEE for flight refuelling trials
29.10.65	Despatched to Honington, on return to 57 Squadron
10.5.66	Handley Page. BK.1 conversion
3.4.67	55 Squadron
1.8.67	214 Squadron
15.3.68	Handley Page. Mods
5.5.68	214 Squadron
9.7.74	St Athan. Non-Effective Aircraft
17.4.75	Struck Off Charge. Cat. 5(s)

XA931

28.11.57	AW/CN. 232 OCU
14.12.61	10 Squadron
30.8.63	232 OCU Gaydon
26.6.64	19 MU St Athan, for storage
1.4.70	Non-Effective Aircraft
30.4.74	SoC as Cat. 5(s)

XA932

11.2.58	AW/CN
13.2.58	232 OCU
29.7.59	10 Squadron
21.11.61	Handley Page. M/S on site
29.3.62	Ex M/S
2.3.64	Disposal Account, surplus
5.3.64	Loan to MoA. Arrived at Radlett. TI of radio, TACAN and aerial mods
18.12.64	To Boscombe Down. Tanker radio trials
3.2.66	To Handley Page. Radio compass investigation
2.9.66	Handley Page. Conversion to BK.1
11.8.67	214 Squadron
2.2.77	Allotted for Ground Instruction at Marham, allotted 8517M. Initially for static display, later for BDR training
10.11.87	Sold to Sweffling Engineering Co

XA933

25.2.58	AW/CN
3.3.58	232 OCU
24.2.59	Cat. 3R Flying Accident
2.3.59	Handley Page. Repair in Works
1.12.59	232 OCU
27.3.62	Handley Page. M/S on site
25.7.62	Ex M/S
22.5.64	Loan to MoA. Arrived at Radlett. TFR trials
27.8.64	Arrived at A&AEE. TFR trials
19.11.64	To Handley Page. Removal of instrumentation
30.4.65	Despatched to Honington
3.5.65	55/57 Squadrons
1.12.65	57 Squadron
23.8.66	VTF
26.4.67	19 MU St Athan
1.4.70	Non-Effective Aircraft
1.10.71	SoC Cat. 5(s)

XA934

21.3.58	AW/CN
25.3.58	232 OCU
2.10.62	Cat. 5(s) Flying Accident. Crashed near Gaydon after engine failed on take-off and two more failed on approach. Three crew killed
5.10.62	Struck Off Charge

XA935

2.4.58	AW/CN
9.4.58	10 Squadron
29.10.58	232 OCU
11.5.59	RAF Wyton
1.3.60	15 Squadron
9.5.61	232 OCU
1.11.61	10 Squadron
14.12.61	232 OCU
7.9.62	Categorised Cat.4 Rogue. Re-cat. 3R – RoS Handley Page
31.10.62	232 OCU
17.6.64	19 MU St Athan
1.4.70	Non-Effective Aircraft
30.4.74	SoC as Cat. 5(s)

XA936

23.5.58	AW/CN
28.5.58	10 Squadron
27.2.59	232 OCU
31.1.62	Handley Page. M/S on site
28.6.62	Ex M/S
11.1.65	Handley Page. Conversion to BK.1
29.11.66	Ex Conversion, delivered to No 214 Squadron
23.6.76	St Athan, Non-Effective Aircraft
20.9.76	SoC as Cat. 5(s)

XA937

31.5.58	AW/CN
4.6.58	10 Squadron
18.8.61	Handley Page. Re-spray
1.9.61	10 Squadron
16.5.62	Handley Page. M/S on site
30.8.62	Ex M/S
2.3.64	15 Squadron
9.3.64	Disposal Account, surplus
30.4.64	Handley Page for BK.1 conversion
26.11.65	Loan to MoA. Tanker 'Final Conference' and radio trials
14.1.66	To A&AEE. Radio compatibility trials
14.2.66	Despatched to 57 Squadron
3.10.66	214 Squadron
22.8.67	Handley Page. Mods
23.10.67	214 Squadron
7.2.77	St Athan. SoC as Cat. 5(s)

XA938

22.7.58	AW/CN
28.7.58	10 Squadron
2.3.64	15 Squadron
12.10.64	Handley Page for BK.1 conversion
28.9.66	Ex Conversion, delivered to No 214 Squadron
30.9.76	To Procurement Executive, for ground tests at RAE Farnborough

XA939

27.8.58	AW/CN. Delivered to 10 Squadron
2.3.64	15 Squadron
8.10.64	Handley Page for BK.1 conversion
5.7.66	Loan to MoA. TI of Mod. 4351
2.9.66	Handley Page. Trials related to Mod. 4351
22.11.66	214 Squadron
23.9.76	SoC Cat. 5 at RAF Catterick for fire-fighting training

XA940

9.9.58	AW/CN
10.9.58	10 Squadron
7.11.62	232 OCU
11.1.63	10 Squadron
2.3.64	15 Squadron
15.10.64	232 OCU
9.3.65	55/57 Squadrons
1.12.65	57 Squadron
14.12.66	Tanker Training Flight
8.6.67	Loan to MinTech. Arrived at A&AEE. Check servicing

XH590 on in-flight refuelling duty – in this case a pair of Blackburn Buccaneers. Tony Buttler

10.7.67	Handley Page. Trials of engines with strain gauged compressor blades
24.7.68	Despatched to 19 MU
9.2.72	Non-Effective Aircraft
31.8.73	SoC as Cat. 5(s)

XA941

11.9.58	AW/CN
17.9.58	15 Squadron
25.1.59	10 Squadron
8.9.60	55 Squadron
23.3.61	232 OCU
3.9.63	10 Squadron
2.3.64	15 Squadron
2.9.64	Cat. 3R Flying Accident. RoS by 60 MU in Far East
10.12.64	Ex RoS
2.2.65	55/57 Squadrons
13.5.65	Handley Page for BK.1 conversion
27.10.65	Loan to MinTech. TI of Mod. 3886
20.12.65	Handley Page. Continuation of BK.1 conversion
19.12.66	Ex Conversion, delivered to 214 Squadron
1.9.73	Disposal Account, Cat. 3R
15.8.74	St Athan, Non-Effective Aircraft
22.11.74	SoC as Cat. 5(s)

XH587

17.11.58	AW/CN. Loan to MoA. TI of RCM and radio equipment
17.8.60	To A&AEE. Trials of ECM equipment
6.4.61	Returned to Handley Page. Mods and conversion to B.1A
19.12.61	Ex Conversion
16.1.62	15 Squadron
6.10.64	Handley Page. Conversion to BK.1A
29.4.65	57 Squadron, ex conversion
16.7.74	St Athan. Non-Effective Aircraft
17.4.75	SoC as Cat. 5(s)

XH588

28.10.58	AW/CN
31.10.58	15 Squadron
1.8.61	Handley Page. Conversion to B.1A
22.5.62	Ex Conversion
1.6.62	55 Squadron
	55/57 Squadrons
25.11.65	Handley Page. Conversion to BK.1A
7.12.66	214 Squadron, ex conversion
1.8.67	55 Squadron
23.6.75	57 Squadron
30.7.75	RAF Machrihanish for fire-fighting & crash rescue training (no M number allotted)

XH589

21.11.58	AW/CN
1.12.58	15 Squadron
6.11.61	Handley Page. Conversion to B.1A
31.10.62	Ex Conversion
6.11.62	55 Squadron
	55/57 Squadrons

12.7.65	Tanker Training Flight
12.7.66	Handley Page. Conversion to BK.1A
28.4.67	55 Squadron, ex conversion to BK.1A
14.3.74	57 Squadron
25.3.74	55 Squadron
25.6.75	214 Squadron
6.5.76	St Athan. Non-Effective Aircraft
9.7.76	SoC for fire-fighting training at St Athan

XH590

26.11.58	AW/CN
1.12.58	15 Squadron
3.10.61	Handley Page. Conversion to B.1A
30.8.62	Ex Conversion
14.9.62	57 Squadron
1.12.65	Handley Page. Conversion to BK.1A
9.1.67	Ex Conversion
12.1.67	55 Squadron
25.2.74	57 Squadron
11.3.74	55 Squadron
16.6.75	SoC as Cat. 5(c)
3.7.75	RAF Manston for fire-fighting training (no M number allotted)

XH591

7.1.59	AW/CN
20.1.59	15 Squadron
16.1.62	Handley Page. Conversion to B.1A
31.12.62	Ex Conversion
6.2.63	55 Squadron
	55/57 Squadrons
1.12.65	57 Squadron
13.7.66	Handley Page. Conversion to BK.1A
28.4.67	Ex Conversion
2.5.67	55 Squadron
17.9.68	Loan to MinTech. Defect investigation at Radlett
21.1.69	Handley Page for repair
24.11.69	55 Squadron
23.6.75	57 Squadron
2.6.76	214 Squadron
5.11.76	St Athan. SoC as Cat. 5(s)

XH592

31.12.58	AW/CN
2.1.59	15 Squadron
1.9.61	Handley Page. Conversion to B.1A
30.6.62	Conversion
5.7.62	55/57 Squadrons
11.3.65	232 OCU
23.6.65	Tanker Training Flight
21.6.68	Handley Page. Re-spray
13.8.68	Tanker Training Flight
6.2.70	232 OCU
17.10.74	SoC as Cat. 5(GI). Allotted 8429M for No 2 SoTT, Cosford.
13.12.83	Re-allotted for display at RAF Museum, Cosford. Later scrapped but the cockpit survives at Bruntingthorpe, Leicestershire

XH593

26.1.59	AW/CN
28.1.59	15 Squadron
18.8.60	Handley Page. Conversion to B.1A
12.4.61	Ex Conversion
17.4.61	57 Squadron
	55/57 Squadrons
15.7.65	Tanker Training Flight
19.1.67	Handley Page. Mods
14.3.67	Tanker Training Flight
6.2.70	232 OCU
23.9.74	Disposal Account, surplus
17.10.74	SoC as Cat. 5(GI). Allotted 8428M for No 2 SoTT, Cosford
18.4.85	Sold to Solair Ltd., Wallsend, as scrap

XH594

31.1.59	AW/CN
5.2.59	15 Squadron
22.7.60	Handley Page. Conversion to B.1A
23.3.61	Ex Conversion
27.3.61	55/57 Squadrons
9.3.65	232 OCU
23.6.65	Tanker Training Flight
16.11.67	Handley Page. Mods
23.3.68	Tanker Training Flight
6.2.70	232 OCU
19.2.74	St Athan. Non-Effective Aircraft
31.5.74	SoC as Cat. 5(s)

XH613

27.2.59	AW/CN; Conversion to B.1A at Handley Page
14.7.60	Ex Conversion
18.7.60	15 Squadron
9.11.61	Handley Page. Re-spray
21.11.61	15 Squadron
14.6.62	Cat. 5(s) Flying Accident. Engines failed on approach to Cottesmore. Crashed 5 miles west of Castle Bytham, Lincs
15.6.62	Struck Off Charge

XH614

18.3.59	AW/CN
23.3.59	57 Squadron
30.9.60	Handley Page. Conversion to B.1A
27.4.61	Ex Conversion
28.4.61	55 Squadron
	55/57 Squadrons
10.8.65	Tanker Training Flight
3.9.66	57 Squadron
6.10.66	Handley Page. Conversion to BK.1A
11.8.67	Ex Conversion
15.8.67	55 Squadron
26.9.67	Loan to MinTech. Arrived at A&AEE, EMC trials during flight refuelling
3.1.68	Despatched to Marham
16.1.68	55 Squadron
25.2.74	214 Squadron
8.4.74	55 Squadron
23.6.75	214 Squadron
7.9.76	SoC as Cat. 5(s)

XH615

7.4.59	AW/CN
8.4.59	232 OCU
11.1.61	Handley Page. Conversion to B.1A
27.6.61	Ex Conversion
29.6.61	10 Squadron
6.10.64	55/57 Squadrons
10.3.65	Handley Page. Conversion to BK.1A
18.6.65	Ex Conversion
21.6.65	49/148/207 Squadrons
	55 Squadron
23.2.67	Handley Page. Mods
16.5.67	Tanker Training Flight
6.2.70	232 OCU
3.6.74	55 Squadron
14.6.74	232 OCU
23.7.74	55 Squadron
6.9.74	214 Squadron

4.10.74	Struck Off Charge. To RAF Leeming for fire-fighting practice

XH616

21.4.59	AW/CN
23.4.59	57 Squadron
6.4.61	Handley Page. Conversion to B.1A
19.9.61	15 Squadron, ex conversion
22.9.64	90 Squadron
18.3.65	232 OCU
23.6.65	Tanker Training Flight
18.8.66	Handley Page. Conversion to BK.1A
8.6.67	Ex Conversion
13.6.67	57 Squadron
25.7.67	Loan to MinTech. Drogue trials by A&AEE at Marham
26.7.67	57 Squadron
20.1.76	Struck Off Charge for fire-fighting training

XH617

19.5.59	AW/CN
29.5.59	57 Squadron
19.7.60	Cat. 5(s) Flying Accident. Caught fire in air. Abandoned, Oakley, Norfolk
20.7.60	Struck Off Charge

XH618

3.6.59	AW/CN; Handley Page. Conversion to B.1A
15.8.60	Ex Conversion. Delivered to 15 Squadron
4.2.63	Cat. 3R Flying Accident. Repair by No 103 MU
4.3.63	15 Squadron, ex RoS
16.9.63	Loan to MoA. Arrived at Radlett for low-level role trials
12.12.63	Despatched to A&AEE. Low-level role trials
10.8.64	To Radlett for conversion to BK.1A
12.1.66	Ex Conversion. Loan to MoA. Final 'Tanker Conference'
25.2.66	57 Squadron
3.5.66	Loan to MoA. Arrived at A&AEE. Mk.17 HDU trials
20.6.66	57 Squadron
30.6.66	Loan to MoA. Arrived at A&AEE. Further Mk.17 HDU trials
15.8.66	57 Squadron
24.10.67	Handley Page. Mods
19.12.67	57 Squadron
24.3.75	Cat. 5(s) Flying Accident. Collided with Buccaneer XV156 during refuelling. Broke up over the North Sea, 95 miles east of Sunderland
25.3.75	Struck Off Charge

XH619

24.6.59	AW/CN
25.6.59	57 Squadron
28.11.60	Handley Page. Conversion to B.1A
30.5.61	Ex Conversion
1.6.61	57 Squadron
	55/57 Squadrons
1.12.65	57 Squadron
9.6.66	Handley Page. Mods and conversion to BK.1A
9.3.67	Ex Conversion
12.4.67	55 Squadron
19.8.68	Handley Page. Refurbish
	55 Squadron
8.8.73	214 Squadron
23.6.75	Disposal Account as Cat. 5(c)
30.6.75	RAF Marham, for fire-fighting practice

XH620

20.7.59	AW/CN
21.7.59	57 Squadron
19.4.61	Handley Page. Conversion to B.1A
25.10.61	Ex Conversion
27.10.61	15 Squadron
4.2.64	90 Squadron
11.2.64	Handley Page. Conversion to BK.1A
22.4.65	Ex Conversion. 55/57 Squadrons
26.5.65	90/148/207 Squadrons
	55 Squadron
22.2.67	Handley Page. Mods
5.4.67	55 Squadron

1.5.67	57 Squadron
23.8.67	Tanker Training Flight
25.10.67	57 Squadron
4.12.67	Loan to MinTech. Arrived at A&AEE. Trials of autopilot malfunction during in-flight refuelling
8.12.67	Despatched to Marham
11.12.67	57 Squadron
8.6.71	Cat. 3R. RoS
23.6.72	Ex RoS. Returned to 57 Squadron
10.9.73	232 OCU
30.10.73	57 Squadron
20.5.74	55 Squadron
3.6.74	232 OCU
30.10.75	St Athan. Cat. 5
24.6.76	SoC as Cat. 5(s)

XH621

21.7.59	Handley Page. Conversion to B.1A
24.9.60	Ex Conversion
27.9.60	57 Squadron
	55/57 Squadrons
10.8.65	Cat. 3 (prov). Flying Accident
1.9.65	390 MU
24.9.65	57 Squadron
4.10.65	Handley Page for repair and conversion to BK.1A
30.11.66	Delivered to 57 Squadron, ex conversion
2.6.76	214 Squadron
22.12.76	St Athan. Cat. 5(s)

XH645

25.9.59	AW/CN
28.9.59	57 Squadron
27.1.61	Handley Page. Conversion to B.1A
7.7.61	Ex Conversion
12.7.61	55 Squadron
	55/57 Squadrons
1.12.65	Handley Page. Conversion to BK.1A
24.1.67	Delivered to 57 Squadron, ex conversion
14.2.74	St Athan. Non-Effective Aircraft
9.9.74	SoC as Cat. 5(s)

XH646

30.9.59	AW/CN; Handley Page. Conversion to B.1A
21.10.60	Ex Conversion
24.10.60	55 Squadron
	55/57 Squadrons
19.3.65	Handley Page. Conversion to BK.1A
7.7.65	Ex Conversion
8.9.65	55 Squadron
20.3.67	Tanker Training Flight
12.9.67	Handley Page. Mods
16.11.67	Tanker Training Flight
19.8.68	Cat. 5(s) Flying Accident. Collided with Canberra WT325 and crashed at Kelling Heath, near Holt, Norfolk
20.8.68	Struck Off Charge

XH647

19.11.59	AW/CN; Handley Page. Conversion to B.1A
24.11.60	Ex Conversion
29.11.60	57 Squadron
	55/57 Squadrons
16.2.65	Handley Page. Retrofit and conversion to BK.1A
2.6.65	Ex Conversion
3.6.65	49/148/207 Squadrons
	55 Squadron
17.1.67	Tanker Training Flight
8.5.68	Handley Page. Mod.
3.6.68	Tanker Training Flight
6.2.70	232 OCU
8.7.74	214 Squadron
29.7.74	232 OCU
28.8.74	57 Squadron
30.9.74	232 OCU
7.10.74	Disposal Account, surplus
26.11.74	Struck Off Charge for crash-rescue training

XH648

21.12.59	AW/CN
22.12.59	57 Squadron

26.10.60	Handley Page. Conversion to B.1A
10.5.61	Ex Conversion
12.5.61	15 Squadron
6.4.64	55/57 Squadrons
16.2.65	Handley Page. Retrofit and conversion to BK.1A
20.5.65	Ex Conversion, 55/57 Squadrons
26.5.65	49/148/207 Squadrons
	55 Squadron
18.3.67	Tanker Training Flight
1.5.67	55 Squadron
23.6.75	57 Squadron
2.6.76	Imperial War Museum, Duxford, where it remains on display

XH649

8.1.60	AW/CN; Handley Page. Conversion to B.1A
16.1.61	Ex Conversion
20.1.61	57 Squadron
	55/57 Squadrons
5.11.64	Handley Page. Conversion to BK.1A
19.5.66	Loan to MoA. Ground refuelling tests in conjunction with XL193
25.5.66	Handley Page
10.6.66	57 Squadron, ex conversion
17.7.67	Loan to MinTech. A&AEE refuelling trials at Marham
18.7.67	57 Squadron
10.11.75	St Athan
27.7.76	SoC as Cat. 5(s)

XH650

5.2.60	AW/CN; Handley Page. Conversion to B.1A
17.1.61	55 Squadron
	55/57 Squadrons
24.9.64	Handley Page. Conversion to B.1A
23.2.67	55 Squadron, ex conversion
22.4.74	214 Squadron
20.5.74	55 Squadron
23.6.75	214 Squadron
12.2.76	RAF Manston for fire-fighting practice. Cat. 5(s)

XH651

31.3.60	AW/CN
1.4.60	57 Squadron
13.2.61	Handley Page. Conversion to B.1A
4.8.61	Ex Conversion
10.8.61	15 Squadron
9.10.64	Handley Page. Conversion to BK.1A
9.1.65	Loan to MinTech. Fuel transfer gauging tests at Radlett
30.6.65	Handley Page
13.7.66	57 Squadron, ex conversion
2.6.76	214 Squadron
26.1.77	Struck Off Charge. Cat. 5(s)

XH667

31.3.60	AW/CN; Handley Page. Conversion to B.1A
31.1.61	Ex Conversion
3.2.61	57 Squadron
	55/57 Squadrons
11.2.65	Handley Page. Retrofit and conversion to BK.1A
29.4.65	Ex Conversion
30.4.65	55/57 Squadrons
29.5.65	49/148/207 Squadrons
	55 Squadron
14.3.67	Handley Page. Mods
26.4.67	55 Squadron
1.5.67	214 Squadron
16.10.68	Loan to MinTech. (A&AEE tests at Marham)
17.10.68	214 Squadron
21.8.69	Loan to MinTech. Arrived at A&AEE. Trials of SRIM 3594/3597

The first Victor B Mk.2 XH668 photographed over water in February or March of 1959. Tragically this aircraft crashed into the sea off Milford Haven on its first test flight following delivery to Boscombe Down, on the 20th August 1959. Peter Green

23.9.69	214 Squadron
23.9.75	Hal Far, Malta, for fire-fighting practice

Victor B Mk.2

XH668

3.6.59	AW/CN
14.8.59	Authority to go to A&AEE for preview trials
20.8.59	Dived into sea off Milford Haven after loss of pitot head caused loss of control on its first test flight after delivery to Boscombe Down
4.5.62	Struck Off Charge

XH669

6.8.59	First Flight
22.12.59	AW/CN; handed over to C(A) at Park Street
3.9.60	Loaned to firm for SBAC Display at Farnborough
17.6.63	Handley Page. Mods
8.7.64	100/139 Squadrons
15.3.66	Handley Page. Mods
21.6.66	Wittering OCU
10.10.68	Handley Page. Storage
3.6.70	Hawker Siddeley, Woodford K.2 conversion
20.1.77	57 Squadron
18.8.80	St Athan. Major servicing
12.11.80	57 Squadron
10.6.83	St Athan. Major servicing
31.8.83	57 Squadron
20.3.86	55 Squadron
26.6.87	St Athan. Major servicing
3.11.87	55 Squadron
21.6.90	Caught fire in air. Not repaired; to 9092M at Waddington. The cockpit survives with 'The Cockpit Collection'

XH670

2.11.59	First Flight
22.12.59	AW/CN; handed over to C(A) at Park Street
18.1.60	Landed at Thurleigh with hydraulic system fault
7.1.62	Arrived at A&AEE. Position Error calibration
9.2.62	Returned to Handley Page
9.6.64	Arrived at A&AEE. Low-level role trials
31.7.64	Returned to Radlett for inspection and fitting of APU
19.8.64	To A&AEE. Continuation of low-level trials
27.11.64	To Handley Page. Preparation for engineering flight trials
1.11.68	Storage pending K.2 conversion
1.5.70	Arrived at Hawker Siddeley, Woodford, for conversion
31.10.75	Struck Off Charge as source of spares
	The cockpit survives with 'The Cockpit Collection' (Reports of XH670 serving with No 543 Squadron are in error)

XH671

2.2.60	First Flight
4.5.60	AW/CN; despatched to Park Street on C(A) Charge
17.1.61	Despatched to A&AEE. Radio and navigation trials
4.3.63	Arrived at Handley Page, Radlett. C(A) Release Mods
20.3.64	Wittering Wing
12.4.65	Handley Page. Mods
22.6.65	100/139 Squadrons
12.2.66	Handley Page. Mods
24.5.66	100/139 Squadrons
4.4.67	VTF
29.1.68	Wittering Wing
8.1.69	Handley Page. Storage
9.4.70	Hawker Siddeley. K.2 conversion
6.8.76	57 Squadron
1.5.80	St Athan. Major servicing
18.8.80	57 Squadron
8.9.80	55 Squadron
21.4.83	St Athan. Major servicing
12.7.83	55 Squadron
30.11.84	A&AEE
18.12.84	55 Squadron
25.2.85	57 Squadron
25.6.86	55 Squadron
15.10.86	St Athan. Major servicing
24.2.87	55 Squadron
15.3.93	Damaged during cabin pressure test, Marham. Struck Off Charge

XH672

6.4.60	First Flight
26.5.60	AW/CN; despatched to Park Street on C(A) Charge
11.4.61	Arrived at A&AEE. C(A) Release handling trials
7.6.61	To Handley Page. Preparation for autopilot trials
25.4.62	Despatched to A&AEE. Autopilot trials
17.5.62	To Handley Page, Radlett
26.8.63	To A&AEE. Autopilot, radio altimeter Mk.7 and autoland trials
12.12.63	To Handley Page. Autoland trials
2.7.64	Handley Page. C(A) Release Mods and B.2(SR) conversion
13.8.65	543 Squadron
13.4.66	Handley Page. Mods
26.6.66	543 Squadron
19.3.74	Hawker Siddeley. K.2 conversion
24.5.78	57 Squadron
29.6.82	St Athan. Major servicing
12.8.82	57 Squadron
13.1.84	A&AEE Boscombe Down
23.2.84	57 Squadron
24.2.86	St Athan. Major servicing
26.6.86	57 Squadron

2.7.86 55 Squadron
26.3.94 To Cosford Aerospace Museum, allotted as 9242M
In the Cold War Exhibition from 2007

XH673
23.5.60 Production test flown
1.9.60 AW/CN; despatched to Park Street
5.12.60 Damaged in wheels-up landing at Waddington
27.10.61 Despatched from Radlett to A&AEE
2.4.62 Despatched to Radlett
12.4.62 Allotted to Handley Page. C(A) Release Mods
5.12.63 139 Squadron
25.6.65 Wittering OCU
16.7.65 100/139 Squadrons
6.9.65 Handley Page. Mods
12.10.65 100/139 Squadrons
10.10.68 Handley Page. Storage
4.6.70 Hawker Siddeley. K.2 conversion
17.12.76 57 Squadron
12.11.80 St Athan. Major servicing
16.2.81 57 Squadron
9.1.84 St Athan. Major servicing
26.4.84 57 Squadron
2.7.86 Allotted as 8911M for display at RAF Marham. Still present 2008

XH674
4.8.60 Production test flown
1.9.60 AW/CN; despatched to Park Street. Allotted for Blue Steel trials
2.9.60 Despatched to A&AEE for pilot training
13.10.60 Returned to Handley Page, Radlett
13.11.61 To A&AEE for dummy missile drop trials
23.11.61 Returned to Handley Page, Radlett
28.2.62 Despatched to A. V. Roe, Woodford, for check of Blue Steel missile 'cooling pack', and then returned to Radlett
30.7.62 To A&AEE, Blue Steel dummy drop
2.10.62 Arrived at Woodford from Radlett
5.4.63 From Woodford to A&AEE. 'Proving checks'
17.4.63 Returned to Woodford
28.5.63 Returned to Radlett (via Scampton) for fatigue life checks
2.8.63 Authority to go to Woodford, dummy drop trials
22.10.63 Allotment changed to Blue Steel low-level trials at Woodford
16.1.64 Despatched from Radlett to Woodford for above trials
29.4.64 Handley Page. Preparation for Bomber Command QRA trials
19.5.64 To RAF Wittering for QRA trials
14.7.64 Returned to Handley Page. C(A) Release Mods and SR.2 conversion
17.9.65 543 Squadron
21.6.66 Handley Page. Mods
15.11.66 543 Squadron
2.5.68 Handley Page. Mods and major servicing

4.7.68 543 Squadron
24.5.74 VTF
24.3.75 RAF Marham for disposal
15.10.75 St Athan. Cat. 5(s)
22.6.76 Struck Off Charge

XH675
late 9.60 Production test flown
8.3.61 AW/CN
24.7.61 To A&AEE. Blue Steel handling and vibration trials
2.11.61 To Handley Page, Radlett
14.6.62 To A&AEE. Photo reconnaissance role trials
24.9.62 Arrived at Edinburgh Field, Australia, for trials
13.2.63 Returned to UK for C(A) Release Mods with Handley Page
17.2.64 OCU Wittering
22.9.65 Handley Page. Mods
17.11.65 Wittering Wing (100/139)
20.10.66 Handley Page. Mods
20.1.67 100/139 Squadrons
4.10.68 Handley Page. Storage
15.6.70 Hawker Siddeley. K.2 conversion
30.3.77 57 Squadron
1.10.80 55 Squadron
4.2.81 St Athan. Major servicing
1.5.81 55 Squadron
18.4.84 St Athan. Major servicing
11.9.84 55 Squadron
30.6.91 Struck Off Charge

XL158
-.10.60 First Flight
30.12.60 AW/CN
3.1.61 To Handley Page at A&AEE. Engineering trials and assessment
20.4.61 Transferred from Handley Page to A&AEE charge at Boscombe Down
30.5.61 Red Neck trials at A&AEE
8.6.62 Handley Page. C(A) Release Mods
27.9.63 139 Squadron
31.5.65 Wittering OCU
9.6.65 100/139 Squadrons
25.4.66 VTF
18.5.66 100/139 Squadrons
8.11.68 Handley Page. Storage
6.5.70 Hawker Siddeley, Woodford. K.2 conversion
12.4.76 55 Squadron
7.6.76 57 Squadron
2.8.79 St Athan. Major servicing
5.12.79 57 Squadron
26.6.81 St Athan. Mods and major servicing
18.8.81 57 Squadron
23.8.83 St Athan. Major servicing
28.11.83 57 Squadron
14.3.85 55 Squadron
10.2.88 St Athan. Major servicing
14.7.88 55 Squadron
-.1.94 Struck Off Charge

XL159
late 11.59 First Flight
20.2.61 AW/CN. Allotted for flight trials of R.Co.17 engines
31.8.61 Allotted for C(A) Release trials
23.3.62 Stalled and crashed Stubton, Notts. (Handley Page & A&AEE crew)
31.10.62 SoC as Cat. 5(s)

XL160
-.12.60 First Flight
26.1.61 AW/CN. Arrived at Rolls-Royce, Hucknall, same day. R.Co.17 trials
27.7.62 From Hucknall to Radlett. Handley Page. C(A) Release Mods
17.1.64 100 Squadron
28.5.65 Handley Page. Mods
19.7.65 100/139 Squadrons
30.3.67 Handley Page. Mods
19.6.67 100/139 Squadron
26.10.68 Handley Page. Storage
21.5.70 Hawker Siddeley, Woodford. K.2 conversion
22.9.75 55 Squadron
4.11.78 St Athan. Major servicing
9.2.79 55 Squadron
2.10.80 57 Squadron
22.7.82 St Athan. Major servicing
26.10.82 57 Squadron
12.8.85 55 Squadron
8.1.86 57 Squadron
2.7.86 Allotted 8910M at Marham for Battle Damage Repair training
Nose survives at the Norfolk & Suffolk Air Museum, Flixton

XL161
-.1.61 First Flight
27.3.61 AW/CN. Preparation for Blue Steel trials
28.9.61 Arrived at Woodford. Blue Steel trials
23.2.62 Despatched to Radlett. Preparation for Blue Steel trials in Australia
26.4.62 Returned to Woodford
30.5.62 Despatched from Woodford to Edinburgh Field, Australia (arrived 4.6.62)
13.8.63 Transferred to No 4 JSTU
4.10.64 Returned to Handley Page, Radlett
29.10.64 Handley Page. C(A) Release Mods and conversion to SR.2
26.4.66 543 Squadron
8.5.67 Handley Page. Mods
10.5.68 543 Squadron
4.4.74 Hawker Siddeley. K.2 Conversion
20.3.78 55 Squadron
28.9.82 St Athan. Major servicing
18.11.82 55 Squadron
19.7.85 St Athan. Major servicing
6.11.85 55 Squadron
57 Squadron?, 55 Squadron
27.9.93 To Lyneham; allotted 9214M for crash-rescue training

XL162
-.2.61 First Flight
5.5.61 AW/CN
30.11.61 Arrived at A&AEE Boscombe Down. 'Special store' trials
4.6.62 Returned to Handley Page. Retrofit and Mods
22.8.63 139 Squadron
29.7.65 Handley Page. Mods
23.9.65 100/139 Squadrons
19.12.66 Handley Page. Mods
14.4.67 100/139 Squadrons
14.1.69 Handley Page. Storage
13.5.70 Hawker Siddeley. K.2 conversion
13.9.76 57 Squadron
12.11.79 St Athan. Major servicing

Victor tanker XH672 streams one of the in-flight refuelling drogues for the benefit of an air show audience. Tony Buttler

26.3.80 57 Squadron
16.12.80 55 Squadron
11.7.83 St Athan. Major servicing
30.9.83 55 Squadron
11.1.85 A&AEE
7.2.85 55 Squadron
1.7.85 57 Squadron
25.6.86 55 Squadron
3.11.87 St Athan. Major servicing
11.3.88 55 Squadron

XL163
-.3.61 First Flight
15.5.61 AW/CN
7.2.62 139 Squadron
4.7.63 100 Squadron
6.12.63 Handley Page. Mods
1.9.64 100/139 Squadrons
28.5.65 Handley Page. Mods
12.7.65 100/139 Squadrons
23.8.65 Wittering OCU
23.9.65 100/139 Squadrons
15.12.65 VTF
20.12.65 100/139 Squadrons
21.2.66 VTF
25.3.66 Wittering OCU
19.4.66 VTF
25.4.66 Wittering OCU
23.5.66 VTF
9.6.66 Wittering Wing (100/139 Squadrons and Wittering OCU)
27.1.67 Handley Page. Mods
31.5.67 100/139 Squadrons
14.1.69 Handley Page. Storage
20.5.70 Hawker Siddeley. K.2 conversion
4.10.74 232 OCU
3.7.75 55 Squadron
7.6.76 57 Squadron
18.10.76 55 Squadron
24.6.77 St Athan. Major servicing
22.9.77 55 Squadron
16.12.80 57 Squadron
30.7.81 St Athan. Major servicing
15.2.82 57 Squadron
8.1.86 55 Squadron
2.7.86 St Athan. Spares recovery
29.9.86 St Athan. Allotted as 8916M for Battle Damage Repair training

XL164
5.6.61 AW/CN
8.11.63 Arrived at A& AEE Boscombe Down. Low-level role acceptance trials
20.9.64 Returned to Handley Page, Radlett
4.1.65 To A&AEE. PTR 175 radio trials
27.7.65 To Handley Page
4.10.65 To A&AEE. Autopilot trials
5.11.65 To Handley Page. Mods
22.3.66 To A&AEE. TFR trials
22.3.67 To Handley Page for de-instrumentation
12.6.67 19 MU, St Athan
1.12.72 Hawker Siddeley. K.2 conversion
26.5.77 57 Squadron
1.2.79 RAF Wyton
13.3.79 57 Squadron
14.3.79 MoD(PE) – A&AEE. Trial of Blue Saga modification
24.6.79 MoD(PE) – A&AEE. Reduced take-off thrust trials, followed by EMC trials on the ground
14.11.79 57 Squadron
30.4.81 St Athan. Major servicing
30.7.81 55 Squadron
30.1.85 St Athan. Major servicing
29.4.85 57 Squadron
25.6.86 55 Squadron
27.9.93 Allotted as 9215M for crash-rescue training at Brize Norton. Nose to Gatwick Aviation Museum, Charlwood

XL165
9.6.61 AW/CN
8.11.61 232 OCU
31.10.62 100 Squadron
9.5.63 232 OCU
29.4.64 Handley Page. Retrofit
12.4.65 Handley Page. Conversion to SR.2
24.7.65 A&AEE. C(A) Release trials for SR and survey role
7.2.66 Despatched from A&AEE to Wyton
8.2.66 543 Squadron
7.6.66 A&AEE. Camera-crate heating trials
7.9.66 Handley Page. Repair and Mods
13.1.67 543 Squadron
3.7.68 Handley Page. Major servicing
8.10.68 543 Squadron
25.4.74 VTF
27.3.75 St Athan
30.10.75 SoC as Cat. 5(s)

XL188
3.7.61 AW/CN
2.11.61 IFTU Cottesmore
1.4.63 Wittering OCU (VTF)
14.4.64 Handley Page. Mods
2.3.65 232 OCU, Wittering
7.5.65 Handley Page. Mods
29.6.65 100/139 Squadrons
23.9.65 VTF
14.4.66 Wittering Wing
2.6.66 Handley Page. Mods
18.10.66 100/139 Squadrons
2.1.69 A&AEE. Braking parachute trials
25.7.69 Handley Page. Storage
3.9.69 MinTech. Radio interference trials at St Athan
24.3.70 Arrived at HSAL, Woodford
29.4.71 Hawker Siddeley. K.2 conversion
7.1.75 55 Squadron
5.2.79 St Athan. Major servicing
15.5.79 55 Squadron
20.6.79 Wyton
14.8.79 55 Squadron
17.3.83 St Athan. Major servicing
10.6.83 57 Squadron
18.12.84 55 Squadron
24.2.87 St Athan. Major servicing
29.6.87 55 Squadron
25.6.91 Allotted as 9100M for Battle Damage Repair training at Kinloss

XL189
4.8.61 AW/CN
16.12.61 IFTU Cottesmore
1.4.63 Wittering OCU
20.2.64 Handley Page. Retrofit
1.12.64 232 OCU
20.1.65 100/139 Squadrons
24.4.65 232 OCU
6.6.65 Handley Page. Mods
15.7.65 100/139 Squadrons
18.1.67 VTF
24.4.67 100/139 Squadrons
19.5.67 VTF
1.2.68 100/139 Squadrons
17.10.68 Handley Page. Storage
16.4.70 Hawker Siddeley. K.2 conversion
17.12.73 MoA Charge, in connection with K.2 development
17.7.74 Hawker Siddeley. Continuation of conversion
8.1.75 232 OCU
3.7.75 55 Squadron
16.9.77 St Athan. Major servicing
14.11.77 55 Squadron
8.9.80 57 Squadron
18.8.81 St Athan. Major servicing
8.10.81 57 Squadron
11.8.82 St Athan. Major servicing
6.10.82 57 Squadron
13.5.85 55 Squadron
20.3.86 57 Squadron
2.7.86 Allotted as 8912M, Cat.5 (GI) for RAF Waddington

XL190
14.9.61 AW/CN
3.5.62 139 Squadron
13.8.63 Handley Page. Retrofit
28.4.64 100/139 Squadron
4.7.66 Handley Page. Mods
19.10.66 100/139 Squadron
14.1.69 Handley Page. Storage
10.7.70 Hawker Siddeley. K.2 conversion
12.12.74 232 OCU
8.12.75 55 Squadron
31.5.78 St Athan. Major servicing
4.9.78 55 Squadron
8.10.81 St Athan. Major servicing
20.11.81 55 Squadron
30.9.83 St Athan. Major servicing
10.1.84 55 Squadron
19.12.84 57 Squadron
4.2.85 55 Squadron
27.9.93 Allotted as 9216M for crash rescue training at St Mawgan. Nose survives at the RAF Manston History Museum

XL191
20.9.61 AW/CN
13.6.62 139 Squadron
1.10.63 Handley Page. Mods
6.5.64 100/139 Squadrons
9.6.66 Handley Page. Mods
3.11.66 100/139 Squadrons
15.10.68 Handley Page. Storage
29.5.70 Hawker Siddeley. K.2 conversion
15.7.74 232 OCU
1.1.77 55 Squadron
20.1.82 St Athan. Major servicing
26.4.82 55 Squadron
11.9.84 St Athan. Major servicing
31.1.85 55 Squadron
19.6.86 Undershot and crashed at Hamilton, Ontario
7.7.86 SoC as Cat. 5(s)

XL192
26.6.62 AW/CN
28.6.62 100 Squadron
20.1.64 Handley Page. Retrofit
25.11.64 232 OCU
4.12.64 100/139 Squadrons
24.6.65 Handley Page. Mods
18.8.65 100/1139 Squadrons
17.6.66 VTF
6.7.66 100/139 Squadrons
8.7.66 VTF
9.9.66 100/139 Squadrons
11.10.66 VTF
1.2.68 100/139 Squadrons
28.10.68 Handley Page. Storage
23.6.70 Hawker Siddeley. K.2 conversion
8.7.70 Loan MinTech. Pilot familiarisation at HSAL
23.11.70 Hawker Siddeley. Returned to storage pending conversion
16.6.76 57 Squadron
12.2.80 St Athan. Major servicing
10.6.80 57 Squadron
21.1.83 St Athan. Major servicing
21.4.83 57 Squadron
1.7.86 55 Squadron
7.7.88 Marham for spares recovery. Allotted 9024M for crash-rescue training

XL193
24.8.62 AW/CN
30.8.62 100 Squadron
6.2.64 232 OCU
7.8.64 Handley Page. Retrofit and conversion to SR.2
16.5.66 Loan to MoA at Radlett. Ground refuelling trials with K.1A XH648
21.6.66 Delivered from Radlett to Wyton
22.6.66 543 Squadron
15.11.67 Handley Page. Major servicing

24.1.68	543 Squadron
24.5.74	Victor Flight, Wyton
3.4.75	St Athan
10.11.75	Struck Off Charge for spares recovery and scrapping

XL230

13.12.61	AW/CN
21.12.61	IFT OCU Cottesmore
1.4.63	OCU Wittering
28.5.64	Handley Page. Retrofit and conversion to SR.2
20.5.65	543 Squadron
14.11.65	Handley Page. Mods
7.1.66	543 Squadron
2.2.66	Handley Page. TI of air sampling Mods 4226, 4277
5.4.66	Delivered to Wyton
10.5.73	Crashed at Wyton; yawed during attempted overshoot

XL231

31.1.62	AW/CN
2.2.62	139 Squadron
8.11.63	Handley Page. Retrofit
20.7.64	100/139 Squadrons
14.10.65	Handley Page. Mods
29.11.65	100/139 Squadrons
9.9.66	VTF
11.10.66	100/139 Squadrons
8.5.67	Handley Page. Mods
11.7.67	100/139 Squadrons
8.1.69	Handley Page. Storage
28.4.70	Hawker Siddeley, Woodford. K.2 conversion
23.7.70	Handed over to MinTech. Main development aircraft for K.2 conversion
21.7.73	Despatched to A&AEE for trials
23.1.74	Returned to HSAL Woodford. Continuation of development work
25.3.74	Released to HSAL on completion of development work
11.7.77	57 Squadron
12.5.82	St Athan. Mods and major servicing
7.6.82	57 Squadron
25.4.85	St Athan. Major servicing
19.7.85	55 Squadron
12.8.85	57 Squadron
2.7.86	55 Squadron
25.11.93	Sold to Yorkshire Air Museum, Elvington. Still present 2008

XL232

9.3.62	AW/CN
13.3.62	139 Squadron
24.10.63	100 Squadron
17.12.63	Handley Page. Mods
7.10.64	232 OCU
16.11.64	100/139 Squadrons
25.5.65	Handley Page. Mods
5.7.65	100/139 Squadrons
8.1.69	Handley Page. Storage
24.1.70	Hawker Siddeley, Woodford. K.2 conversion
30.5.73	To MinTech charge at Woodford
3.5.74	Arrived at A&AEE for trials
18.12.74	To HSAL Woodford for Mods
21.8.75	Delivered to Marham
19.11.75	55 Squadron
8.12.75	232 OCU
7.6.76	57 Squadron
1.1.77	232 OCU
7.3.78	St Athan. Major servicing
8.6.78	55 Squadron
20.7.79	57 Squadron
25.4.80	55 Squadron
4.2.81	57 Squadron
3.3.81	55 Squadron.
13.8.81	57 Squadron
7.1.82	55 Squadron
15.10.82	Destroyed by fire at Marham after the engine blew up
13.10.83	SoC as Cat. 5 (scrap)

XL233

11.4.62	AW/CN. Free loan to Ministry of Aviation. C(A) Release trials, replacing XL159
28.6.62	Despatched to A&AEE. Trials of drooped leading edge
13.7.62	Returned to Radlett
30.8.62	To A&AEE Boscombe Down. Handling trials with fixed drooped leading edge
21.9.62	Returned to Handley Page, Radlett
20.5.63	To A&AEE. Handling trials of 'retrofit' aircraft without Blue Steel
24.7.63	Returned to Handley Page Ltd. C(A) Release Mods, completion of retrofit
10.4.64	100/139 Squadrons
29.3.66	VTF
26.4.66	Handley Page
15.7.66	Wittering. (100/139 Squadrons.)
24.4.67	VTF
19.5.67	100/139 Squadrons
13.6.68	To Handley Page. Fatigue crack investigation
21.6.68	Loan to MinTech re fatigue investigation
12.8.68	100/139 Squadrons
8.1.69	Handley Page
22.4.70	Hawker Siddeley, Woodford. K.2 conversion
8.5.74	232 OCU
1.1.77	55 Squadron
23.10.78	Loan to MoD(PE). Strain gauge recorder calibration
6.3.79	Trials completed, returned to 55 Squadron
27.11.81	St Athan. Major servicing and Mods
16.4.82	55 Squadron
4.3.83	A&AEE Boscombe Down. Aileron up-rigging trials
5.7.83	55 Squadron
22.5.86	A&AEE Boscombe Down
31.7.86	St Athan. Cat. 5 for Spares Recovery
25.9.88	Sold as scrap

XL511

14.5.62	AW/CN (but retained for retrofit)
26.7.63	139 Squadron
31.5.65	Wittering OCU
9.6.65	100/139 Squadrons
7.12.65	Wittering OCU, VTF (100/139 Squadrons)
19.12.66	Handley Page. Mods
31.3.67	100/139 Squadrons
5.11.68	Handley Page
1.7.70	Hawker Siddeley, Woodford. K.2 conversion
7.7.75	55 Squadron
17.8.78	St Athan
16.11.78	55 Squadron
7.1.83	St Athan. Major servicing
21.3.83	55 Squadron
1.7.85	57 Squadron
4.11.85	55 Squadron
29.1.86	57 Squadron
2.7.86	Manston for fire-fighting. Cat.5(FF) (no M number allotted)

XL512

29.6.62	AW/CN (but retained at Handley Page for retrofit)
8.11.63	139 Squadron
17.9.64	Wittering OCU
1.3.66	Handley Page. Mods
10.6.66	Wittering OCU (100/139 Squadrons)
2.1.69	Handley Page
22.12.69	Loan to MinTech. at Handley Page. Mock-up of K.2 conversion
25.6.70	Arrived at Hawker Siddeley, Woodford. K.2 conversion
13.2.76	55 Squadron
7.6.76	57 Squadron
26.4.79	St Athan. Major servicing
12.9.79	57 Squadron
18.11.82	St Athan. Major servicing
24.1.83	57 Squadron
12.3.85	55 Squadron
7.7.88	St Athan. Minor servicing
10.10.88	55 Squadron
-.3.94	Sold as scrap

XL513

31.8.62	AW/CN (but retained at Handley Page for retrofit)
30.12.63	139 Squadron
20.1.65	VTF, Wittering OCU
21.2.66	100/139 Squadrons
2.10.68	Handley Page
17.6.70	Hawker Siddeley, Woodford. K.2 conversion
20.3.75	55 Squadron
11.4.75	232 OCU
3.7.75	55 Squadron
28.9.76	Overshot and caught fire at Marham after bird strike on take-off. SoC as Cat. 5(c)

XM714

20.11.62	AW/CN
21.11.62	100 Squadron
20.3.63	Cat. 5 Flying Accident. Crashed. Stalled after take-off at Wittering, crew of five killed

XM715

31.12.62	AW/CN
4.3.63	100 Squadron
16.4.64	232 OCU
8.7.64	Handley Page. Retrofit. SR.2 conversion
23.6.65	543 Squadron
20.12.67	Handley Page
10.6.70	Hawker Siddeley. K.2 conversion
16.9.70	Loan to MinTech. Front fuselage mock-up work
3.9.71	Returned to Hawker Siddeley for storage pending conversion
15.5.75	232 OCU
3.7.75	55 Squadron
12.12.77	St Athan. Major inspection
8.3.78	55 Squadron
25.10.82	St Athan. Major inspection
11.1.83	55 Squadron
25.6.86	St Athan. Major inspection
15.10.86	55 Squadron
19.11.93	To Bruntingthorpe after sale. Still present 2008 with the Cold War Jets Collection

XM716

28.2.63	AW/CN
5.3.63	139 Squadron
23.10.63	100 Squadron
25.4.64	232 OCU
5.8.64	Handley Page. Retrofit. Conversion to SR.2
17.11.65	543 Squadron
29.6.66	Cat. 5(s) Flying Accident. Crashed at Warboys. Tail lost due to overstressing of airframe
30.6.66	Struck Off Charge

XM717

12.3.63	AW/CN
14.3.63	100 Squadron
20.3.64	Handley Page. Retrofit
25.1.65	Loan to MoA. Investigation of drop tank defects
9.2.65	100/139 Squadrons
7.1.69	543 Squadron
12.3.74	Hawker Siddeley. K.2 Mods
2.11.77	55 Squadron
12.2.85	57 Squadron
14.4.86	55 Squadron
	Nose to RAF Museum. Displayed at Hendon

XM718

30.4.63	AW/CN
3.5.63	100 Squadron
21.10.63	Cat. 4 Flying Accident
5.12.63	RIW Handley Page
1.4.65	Ex Repair
2.4.65	Loan, MoA. Camera heating trials
7.9.65	To A&AEE. Camera heating trials
3.1.66	Delivered to Wyton. 543 Sqn, ex conversion to SR.2
17.1.67	Handley Page. Mods
9.5.67	543 Squadron
24.1.68	Handley Page. Mods
14.3.68	543 Squadron
24.9.74	232 OCU
23.10.75	St Athan. Cat. 5(s)
31.3.76	Struck Off Charge

BLUE STEEL CONVERSIONS

The following Victor B.2s were modified to carry the Blue Steel missile after 'retrofit'.

XH669, XH671, XH673, XH675. XL158, XL160, XL162, XL163, XL165, XL188, XL189, XL190, XL191, XL192, XL231, XL232, XL233, XL511, XL512, XM717.

In addition XH674 and XL161 carried the missile for trials, but did not receive the full range of modifications needed to enter Squadron service.

GROUND INSTRUCTIONAL AIRFRAMES

Ground Instructional Airframes during the Victor era received new identities in a series of numbers commencing at 1M. These are often (incorrectly) called 'Maintenance Serials', although the letter 'M' was actually used because it was the last letter allotted for use with Royal Flying Corps serial numbers before the Royal Air Force was formed. Thus it was assumed that the last RFC serial number would be M9999, after which allocations would restart at 1A and run to 9999M. Grounded Instructional airframes therefore came to be re-numbered at the end of the intended range of letter/number combinations. The range of Ground Instructional numbers ceased to be used at 9344M and such airframes now retain their original identities. The term 'Ground Instruction' covered a wide range of uses, including airframes used in RAF (also Royal Navy and Army Air Corps) Schools of Technical Training, those used to train firemen at airfields, 'gate guardians', museum exhibits, and even aircraft sold to foreign air forces for their own Technical Schools.

7724M	XA919	16.6.61, No 1 Radio School, RAF Locking
7827M	XA917	13.12.63, RAF Wittering (aircrew emergency training). Cockpit section to Marham by November 1981. To Barnham exercise area in 1993, then to Crowland in 1994. To Cupar August 1995.
7844M	XA924	14.4.64, No 4 SoTT St Athan. RTP 19.6.75.
7850M	XA923	26.5.64, No 2 SoTT, Cosford. Scrapped March 1985.
8428M	XH593	19.9.74, No 2 SoTT, Cosford. Scrap 1987.
8429M	XH592	1.10.74, No 2 SoTT, Cosford. To the Aerospace Museum but scrapped Sept/Oct 1994 (nose to Bruntingthorpe)
8517M	XA932	14.1.77, RAF Marham, for display. Offered for sale Aug 1987 and remains removed from dump as scrap Nov 1987.
8910M	XL160	10.6.86. Marham, BDR Training, wfu 6.86 and to dump by To Barnham exercise area in 1993. Nose section to Blyth Valley Aviation Collection by June 1994. To Norfolk & Suffolk Aviation Museum, Flixton 29.7.05.
8911M	XH673	10.6.86. Marham, for display.
8912M	XL189	10.6.86. Waddington, for display. Scrapped 28.9.89 by S Calvert & Son Ltd., Carlton Miniott, Thirsk.
8916M	XL163	29.9.86. St Athan, BDR Training. To dump 28.11.86. SoC 20.3.90. Scrapped by Hanningfield Metals Ltd., Stock, Dec 1991

Victor B.2 XL162, one of the twenty-one 'Blue Steel retrofit' aircraft, photographed at Handley Page's Radlett factory airfield after service with No.139 Squadron, whose fin badge it wears, while awaiting conversion to K.2 standard.
via Phil Butler

XM715, the preserved Victor K.2 at Bruntingthorpe in the hands of the Cold War Jets Collection. This was photographed on 15th April 2007, wearing the 'hemp' camouflage that Victors wore during their last years of service.
Phil Butler

9024M	XL192	6.2.90. Marham, crash rescue training, having already been dumped there on 4.1.89.
9092M	XH669	1.3.91. Waddington, crash rescue training. Scrapped 12.5.95. Cockpit to N. Towler Cockpit Collection, Rayleigh.
9100M	XL188	29.5.91. Kinloss, crash rescue training. Arrived 25.6.91. Scrapped Sept 1997.
9114M	XL162	5.8.91. Manston, crash rescue training. Arrived 15.8.91. Gone by Aug 1995.
9214M	XL161	27.9.93, Lyneham, crash rescue training. Arrived 20.10.93, Sold and scrapped 21.8.95.
9215M	XL164	27.9.93, Brize Norton, crash rescue training. Arrived 11.11.93. Scrapped 8.95. Nose to Gatwick Aviation Museum, Charlwood, 12.12.95.
9216M	XL190	27.9.93, St Mawgan, crash rescue training. Arrived 19.10.93. Sold to Imperial Aviation Group, North Coates, 26.2.98. Sale fell through, resold to local scrap dealer Feb 1999. Nose survives at the RAF Manston History Museum, arrived 6.2.99.
9242M	XH672	26.9.94, Cosford Aerospace Museum. Cold War Museum, 2007.

The following examples were allotted for fire and rescue training and would normally have been allotted Ground Instructional numbers but were not, presumably as an administrative oversight.

XA939	Catterick	29.3.76
XH588	Machrihanish	30.7.75
XH589	St Athan	9.7.76

XH590	Manston	3.7.75
XH615	Leeming	4.10.74
XH616	Manston	20.11.76
XH619	Marham	30.6.75
XH647	Catterick	26.11.74
XH650	Manston	12.2.76
XH667	Hal Far	23.9.75
XL511	Manston	2.7.86

SURVIVORS

Cockpit Sections
XA917	Stored at Cupar, Fife
XH592	With Phoenix Aviation at Bruntingthorpe, Leics
XH669	At 'The Cockpit Collection', Rayleigh, Essex
XH670	Rayleigh (as above)
XL160	At the Norfolk & Suffolk Aviation Museum, Flixton, Suffolk
XL164	At the Gatwick Aviation Museum, Charlwood, Surrey
XL190	RAF Manston History Museum, Manston, Kent
XM717	RAF Museum, Hendon

Complete Aircraft
XH648	At the Imperial War Museum, Duxford, Cambridgeshire
XH672	At the Cold War Exhibition, RAF Museum, Cosford, Shropshire
XH673	Displayed at RAF Marham, Norfolk
XL231	At the Yorkshire Air Museum, Elvington, North Yorkshire
XM715	At the Cold War Jets Collection, Bruntingthorpe, Leicestershire

Victor Flying Units

TRIALS UNITS

Victor B.1 XA918, seen landing at the SBAC Show at Farnborough in 1957. via Phil Butler

RAE

The Royal Aircraft Establishment (RAE) was formerly the Royal Aircraft Factory at Farnborough, having its origins in the Balloon Factory established in the 19th century. It became the RAE on 1st April 1918 and was the main Government establishment for aeronautical research until finally closed down in 1994. Its headquarters was always at Farnborough but after World War Two, a separate organisation (the National Aeronautical Establishment or NAE) was set up at Thurleigh airfield, near Bedford. The Thurleigh organisation became part of the RAE in 1957. Experimental flying with the Victor took place at both the Farnborough and Bedford sites, with armament trials being a main activity at Farnborough, and the development of 'automatic landing' and other aerodynamic work at Bedford.

A&AEE

The Aeroplane and Armament Experimental Establishment (A&AEE) at Boscombe Down was the main centre for evaluation of aircraft, armament and equipment for use by the RAF and Fleet Air Arm. Its work continues today, although in 1992 it was renamed the Aircraft and Armament Evaluation Establishment. Formed from the earlier 'Aeroplane Experimental Establishment' at Martlesham Heath in 1924, the A&AEE remained there until moving to Boscombe Down on the outbreak of World War Two. The Handling Squadron, an RAF unit that prepared 'pilot's notes' and other aircraft documentation, was amalgamated into the A&AEE in 1954, having previously been associated with the Empire Central Flying School at Hullavington and then the RAF Flying College at Manby.

No 4 Joint Services Trial Unit

During much of the postwar period, operational trials and experiments with British guided missiles and other weapons systems were often carried out at the Long Range Weapons Establishment (otherwise titled the Weapons Research Establishment, WRE) at Woomera in Australia. This was run jointly by the British and Australian Governments. The headquarters of the Establishment was at a former explosives factory near Salisbury in South Australia but the associated bombing ranges and other facilities were spread over a wide area in several Australian states. The Royal Australian Air Force provided maintenance facilities for trials aircraft at Edinburgh Field, although many of the aircraft remained 'on charge' with the Royal Air Force or 'Ministry' establishments such as RAE or A&AEE. If 'Target' aircraft such as pilotless

Meteors, Canberras or Jindiviks were needed, these were provided by No 1 or No 2 Air Trials Units of the RAAF, while the weapons systems would be operated by numbered 'Joint Services Trial Units' (JSTUs) composed of military personnel from the Services involved with the equipment, often supported by civilian staff drawn from contractors and experimental establishments.

The Victor was involved as one of the 'carriers' of the Avro Blue Steel missile, the trials of which were the responsibility of No 4 JSTU. No 4 JSTU was formed at A. V. Roe's Woodford site on 1st September 1956 and left for Edinburgh Field in December 1959. Trial launches of Blue Steel from Valiant, Victor and Vulcan aircraft continued from 1960 to 1964 in Australia. The Victor B.2 flown by No 4 JSTU was XL161. Further trials were conducted in the UK by No 18 JSTU based at Scampton, with a small number of missiles being launched by aircraft from various Victor and Vulcan squadrons. No 18 JSTU (which was formed from the UK-based element of No 4 JSTU when the main group of No 4 moved to Australia) did not have any specific aircraft attached. Many of the 'JSTUs' were literally 'Joint Service' with involvement of other British and Australian Armed Services, but Nos 4 and 18 were composed of RAF personnel only, although they worked closely with representatives of A. V. Roe and Elliott Brothers (London) Ltd. of Rochester. The latter company made the Blue Steel's Inertial Navigation System.

RAF BOMBER COMMAND

No 3 Group

Cottesmore Wing

This Wing comprised the Victors of Nos 10 and 15 Squadrons, between 1958 and 1964.

Honington Wing

This Wing comprised the Victors of Nos 55 and 57 Squadrons, between 1959 and 1965. At this point the role of the squadrons changed to in-flight refuelling, following the demise of the Vickers Valiants that had previously performed that role, and these squadrons moved to Marham.

Marham Wing

Victors of the Marham Wing took over the former task of the flight-refuelling Valiants following the enforced withdrawal of that type. The Wing comprised Nos 55 and 57 Squadrons, transferred from their bomber role at Honington, and the re-formed No 214 Squadron. Victors continued to operate in this role at Marham from 1965 until 1993.

Wittering Wing

This Wing comprised the Blue Steel-equipped Victor B.2As of Nos 100 and 139 Squadrons from 1962 to 1968.

No 232 OCU

This was formed on 21st February 1955 at Gaydon as the Valiant Operational Conversion Unit. The Victor joined the Unit on 28th November 1957, with both types serving at Gaydon until 'C' Flight was transferred to Cottesmore on 1st April 1962 to become the Victor Training Flight as the training unit for the Victor B.2. (Victor B.1 training continued at Gaydon.) The OCU was disbanded on 30th June 1965 following the withdrawal of the Valiant from service. No 232 OCU re-formed at Marham on 6th February 1970 to bring together the Victor OCU at Marham and the Victor Training Flight at Wittering. It disbanded once more on 4th April 1986, after which time any necessary conversion training was carried out within No 55 Squadron, the only surviving Victor unit.

No 10 Squadron

Re-formed with Victor B.1s at Cottesmore on 15th April 1958, having previously flown English Electric Canberras until January 1957. Disbanded on 1st March 1964.

No 15 Squadron (XV Squadron)

Re-formed with Victor B.1s at Cottesmore on 1st September 1958, having previously flown English Electric Canberras until April 1957. Disbanded on 31st October 1964.

No 55 Squadron

Re-formed with Victor B.1As at Honington on 1st September 1960, having last operated de Havilland Mosquitos in 1946. Role changed to in-flight refuelling in March 1965 and moved to Marham in May 1965. Re-equipped with the Victor K.2 until disbanded at Marham on 15th October 1993.

No 57 Squadron

Re-formed with Victor B.1s at Honington on 1st January 1959, having previously flown Canberras from Coningsby until December 1957. In June 1966 its role was changed to in-flight refuelling and the unit moved from Honington to Marham where it later received the Victor K.2. Disbanded on 30th June 1986.

No 100 Squadron

Re-formed at Wittering on 1st May 1962 with Victor B.2s, until disbanded on 30th September 1968. No 100 had earlier flown the Canberra until September 1959.

No 139 Squadron

Re-formed at Wittering on 1st February 1962 from the Victor B.2 Intensive Flying Trials Unit. Disbanded on 31st December 1968.

No 214 Squadron

Re-formed on 1st July 1966 at Marham with Victor BK.1 (later redesignated K.1). Continued to operate the K.1 and K.1A tankers until disbanded on 28th January 1977.

No 543 Squadron

Received Victor B.1s at Wyton as an interim replacement for its grounded Vickers Valiants in May 1965, with Victor SR.2s replacing the B.1s in December 1965. Temporarily moved to Honington on 23rd March 1970 before returning to Wyton. Disbanded on 24th May 1974 when the remaining SR.2s were needed for conversion to K.2 tankers. A small cadre of the unit continued to operate from Wyton as the 'Victor Flight' for a time.

Intensive Flying Trials Unit (IFTU)

This unit flew Victor B.2 XL230 at Cottesmore from 21st December 1961 until 1st April 1962 when the Victor Training Flight was formed.

Victor Training Flight (VTF)

The VTF was formed at Cottesmore on 1st April 1962 from 'C' Flight of No 232 OCU to carry out conversion training on the Victor B.2. It moved to Wittering in March 1964 and disbanded on 6th February 1970 on the re-formation of No 232 OCU.

Tanker Training Flight (TTF)

The TTF was formed at Marham on 1st July 1965 from an element of No 232 OCU. It was also referred to as the Victor OCU in aircraft allotments shown on the Form 78s for individual aircraft. Disbanded on 13th October 1969 to form the Victor Training Unit.

Victor Flight

Formed at Wyton on the disbandment of No 543 Squadron (24th May 1974) to continue SR operations until it too was disbanded, on 15th October 1975.

Victor OCU

See Tanker Training Flight.

Victor Training Unit (VTU)

The VTU was formed on 13th October 1969 from the TTF, the Victor Training Flight and several ground-based training units. It was redesignated No 232 OCU on 6th February 1970.

Radar Reconnaissance Flight

The Radar Reconnaissance Flight was formed in 1951 as part of the Central Signals Establishment, equipped with the Avro Lincoln and later the English Electric Canberra, to develop radar reconnaissance techniques. While at Wyton it received its first Victor B.1 in March 1958 (shortly before No 10 Squadron received its first aircraft) and the unit moved to Gaydon on 1st September 1961 to become part of No 232 OCU. The main task of the Victors was development of the Yellow Aster system later used in the Victor SR.2 and Vulcan B.2[MRR] applications. The unit finally disbanded on 1st November 1963.

Victor K Mk.2 Conversion Programme

The programme for the conversion of Victor B.2 and SR.2 versions to K.2 tankers was originally scheduled to be carried out by Handley Page at Radlett but was transferred to Hawker Siddeley Aviation, Woodford, the former A. V. Roe factory. Hawker Siddeley carried out their own design work, resulting in some changes from those proposed by Handley Page. The most significant of these was to reduce the wingspan instead of providing wing-tip fuel tanks on the existing wings. These were alternative means of reducing stresses in the wing structure and thereby conserving its fatigue life. Although it had been planned to convert twenty-nine aircraft, the programme was cut back to twenty-four on financial grounds. The aircraft involved, in order of their 'Set' on the Woodford conversion line, are listed in the table, with dates of arrival, first flight after conversion and despatch to RAF Marham. Most of the aircraft except XL164 (which arrived by road from St Athan) were flown in from

Radlett where they had been in storage pending conversion. The other exceptions were XM717, XH672 and XL161, which flew in from Wyton.

XL232, XL189 and XL231 made earlier flights part way through their conversion for trials, with XL232 and XL231 making visits to Boscombe Down. These aircraft were then returned to the conversion line for the K.2 conversion to be completed. The dates in the table record their first flights after conversion was complete. Set 23 was originally XH670, which was used for some ground trials and then reduced to spares. Sets 25 to 28 were intended to be XM718, XH674, XL193 and XL165, respectively. XL161 was initially Set 29 but was renumbered as 23 after the conversion of Sets 25 to 28 and XH670 (the original Set 23) had been cancelled.

(With acknowledgements to George Jenks, A. V. Roe Heritage Centre)

No	Serial	Arrival	First flight	To Marham
1	XL232	21.4.70	24.10.75	18.11.75
2	XL189	16.4.70	16.12.74	7.1.75
3	XL233	22.4.70	1.3.74	7.5.74
4	XL191	29.5.70	13.6.74	12.7.74
5	XL163	20.5.70	27.8.74	3.10.74
6	XL190	10.7.70	20.11.74	11.12.74
7	XL513	17.6.70	4.2.75	20.3.75
8	XM715	10.6.70	10.4.75	9.5.75
9	XL511	1.7.70	16.6.75	4.7.75
10	XL160	21.5.70	19.8.75	19.9.75
11	XL188	25.3.70	5.11.75	6.1.76
12	XL512	25.6.70	13.12.75	12.2.76
13	XL158	6.5.70	17.3.76	9.4.76
14	XL192	23.6.70	25.5.76	15.6.76
15	XH671	9.4.70	9.7.76	5.8.76
16	XL162	13.5.70	1.9.76	10.9.76
17	XH673	4.6.70	11.11.76	16.12.76
18	XH669	3.6.70	22.12.76	20.1.77
19	XH675	15.6.70	4.3.77	29.3.77
20	XL164	1.12.72	27.4.77	25.5.77
21	XL231	28.4.70	23.6.77	8.7.77
22	XM717	13.3.74	8.9.77	1.11.77
23	XL161	3.4.74	5.1.78	17.3.78
24	XH672	20.3.74	14.4.78	23.6.78

Bibliography

A large amount of primary source material was consulted prior to the writing of this work, principally the original documents and project brochures held by the Handley Page Association, the National Archives at Kew and the RAF Museum at Hendon. The most important secondary (published) sources were as follows:

Aerodynamics of the Crescent Wing:
Report on lecture by G. H. Lee; *Flight,* 14th May 1954
British Experimental Jet Aircraft: Barry Hygate; Argus, 1990

Completing the Trio: The Aeroplane; 19th September 1958
Conway – The Evolution of the First Rolls-Royce By-Pass Turbojet: Flight; 15th January 1960
Handley Page HP.88: David Foster & Henry Matthews; *World X-Planes Volume 1,* 2005
Handley Page Aircraft since 1907: C. H. Barnes; Putnam, 1976
Handley Page Victor – Postwar Military Aircraft 6: Andrew Brookes; Ian Allan Publishing, 1988
Handley Page Victor – Warpaint 36: Steve Hazell; Warpaint Books, 2002

RAF Bomber Command and the Cuban Missile Crisis, October 1962: Clive Richards; *RAF Historical Society Journal No 42,* May 2008
RAF Flying Training and Support Units since 1912: Ray Sturtivant with John Hamlin; Air-Britain, 2007
Under the Victor's Skin: The Aeroplane; 5th September 1958
V-Bombers – Valiant, Vulcan and Victor: Barry Jones; Crowood, 2000
Victor – A Technical Description of Britain's Latest V-Bomber: Flight; 30th October 1959

Victors in Colour

Right: **The first Victor prototype was WB771; this shot shows the aircraft in the handsome black, red stripe and aluminium colour scheme given to the aircraft in August 1953.** Richard Curtis

Below: **Three views of the second prototype, WB775, photographed at Farnborough in its blue colour scheme at the SBAC Display in September 1955.** Mike Hooks

Opposite page:
The first production Victor B.1, XA917, after its heavy landing at Radlett on 2nd March 1961 – it never flew again but became a grounded instructional airframe at RAF Wittering.
Ken Nevinson

Close-up of the nose of Victor XA918 taken at Boscombe Down during in-flight refuelling trials.
Terry Panopalis

Victor B.1 XA918 refuelling A&AEE Canberra WH876 from its fuselage pod, again during the trials at Boscombe Down. Terry Panopalis

Another angle on XA918, this time refuelling a Harrier. Terry Panopalis

This page:
An early air-to-air shot of Victor B.1 XA922, which was used by the Handling Squadron and then transferred to the RAE at Farnborough for trials in connection with the carrying of nuclear weapons. Terry Panopalis

XA926 as a K.1 of No 57 Squadron at Abingdon on 15th June 1968. Gerry Manning

Victor K.1 XA926 of No 57 Squadron at Abingdon in June 1968. Mike Hooks

This page:

XA930, the development aircraft for drop tanks (shown here), photographed at the 1958 SBAC Display at Farnborough. Terry Panopalis

Victor B.1 XA933 of the Victor Training Flight, photographed at Marham on 31st August 1966. Terry Panopalis

Victor B.1 XA935 of No 10 Squadron at Cottesmore in 1957. Graham Hopkin

Opposite page:

Victor K.1 XA937 of No 214 Squadron at Marham in 1970. Terry Panopalis

Victor B.1 XH588 of No 15 Squadron, photographed at Farnborough in September 1960 before return to Handley Page in the following year for conversion to B.1A standard. P. H. T. Green

Victor K.1A XH588 of No 55 Squadron at Finningley for the Battle of Britain Day display on 20th September 1969. Phil Butler

XH588 of No 55 Squadron at its Marham base in April 1970. Gerry Manning

Victor K.1A XH590 of No 55 Squadron at Marham in April 1970. Gerry Manning

Victor B.1A XH592 of the Tanker Training Flight at Marham on 31st August 1966. This example was used for crew conversion training and was never converted to a tanker. Terry Panopalis

Victor B.1A XH592 in the markings of No 232 Operational Conversion Unit after being retired to RAF Cosford in 1974. It was officially 8429M when serving as an instructional airframe with No 2 School of Technical Training but by the time this photograph was taken in May 1989 it was on display in the Aerospace Museum. Gerry Manning

Victor B.1A XH593 of the Tanker Training Flight at Marham in May 1970. This was one of the aircraft to be used for crew training and was never converted into a tanker. Terry Panopalis

Victor K.1A XH615 of the Tanker Training Flight at Marham in May 1970. Terry Panopalis

Victor K.1A XH616 of No 57 Squadron at Marham in April 1970. Gerry Manning

Victor K.1A XH618 of No 57 Squadron at Marham in April 1970. Gerry Manning

Victor K.1A XH619 of No 55 Squadron taking off for its display at Leuchars on 6th September 1972. Gerry Manning

Opposite page:

Victor K.1A XH645 of No 55 Squadron at Leuchars, 16th September 1972. Gerry Manning

Victor B.1A XH648 of No 55 Squadron, photographed during an 'Open Day' in 1961. Terry Panopalis

XH648, now as a K.1A of No 55 Squadron, at Marham on 29th April 1970. Phil Butler

Opposite page:

Victor K.1A XH651 of No 57 Squadron seen at Leuchars on 20th September 1975. Gerry Manning

A view of Victor tankers at their dispersals at Marham on 29th April 1970. Gerry Manning

An XH-series Victor K.1A displaying at Wattisham on 18th May 1968, with two BAC Lightnings of No 29 Squadron in tow. Gerry Manning

This page:

Victor K.1A XH648 of No 55 Squadron at Marham on 29th April 1970. Gerry Manning

Victor K.2 XH671 of No 55 Squadron at Fairford on 21st July 1991. Gerry Manning

An air-to-air shot of XH675 carrying a Blue Steel test round during trials in the UK. Test rounds were painted black; later operational versions were white. George Jenks, A. V. Roe Heritage Centre

Opposite page:

Victor K.2 XH672 of No 55 Squadron, photographed after its participation in the first Gulf War. Cliff Knox via Phil Butler

Victor K.2 XH673 of No 57 Squadron at Mildenhall on 24th May 1981. Gerry Manning

Victor SR.2 XH674 of No 543 Squadron photographed in October 1969. Terry Panopalis

This page:

Victor K.2 XH675 of No 55 Squadron at Finningley on 19th September 1981. Gerry Manning

Victor K.2 XL160 of No 57 Squadron at Greenham Common on 29th June 1981. Gerry Manning

Victor K.2 XL160 of No 57 Squadron at Marham in April 1983. Tony Buttler

This page:

This page:

Victor SR.2 XL161 of No 543 Squadron, taken on 11th September 1966. Terry Panopalis

Victor B.2 XL164 taxying at Farnborough during the 1961 SBAC Display. Mike Hooks

This shot shows Victor B.2 XL164 carrying a Blue Steel. Mike Hooks

Opposite page:

XL164 as a K.2 of No 57 Squadron at Coningsby on 14th June 1986. Gerry Manning

XL164 was another Gulf War veteran when caught in this air-to-air shot. Cliff Knox via Phil Butler

Victor B.2 XL188 carrying a Blue Steel appeared in the static display at Coxyde/Koksijde in Belgium on 10th August 1968, shortly before the Victor B.2 was withdrawn from service with the Wittering Wing (100/139 Squadrons). Phil Butler

An anonymous Victor K.2 features in this striking head-on shot.
Cliff Knox via Tony Buttler

A line-up of No 543 Squadron Victor SR.2s taken in July 1966. Two aircraft wear a shield on their nose with badges of the units then resident at RAF Wyton – Nos 39, 51 and 543 Squadrons.
Terry Panopalis

Victor K.2 XL188 of No 55 Squadron, at Cottesmore on 14th July 1990. Gerry Manning

Victor K.2 XL190 of No 55 Squadron photographed shortly after take-off at Marham. Tony Buttler

Victor K.2 XL192 of No 57 Squadron seen at Finningley on 4th September 1976. Phil Butler

Victor K.2 XL192 of No 57 Squadron at Greenham Common on 22nd July 1983. Gerry Manning

Opposite page:

XL231 is now preserved at the Yorkshire Air Museum, Elvington. It was photographed there on 9th July 1997. Gerry Manning

Victor B.2 XL511 of No 139 Squadron carrying a Blue Steel and photographed at Wittering on 13th July 1968. Terry Panopalis

Victor K.2 XL512 of No 57 Squadron in the static display at Liverpool Airport on 19th August 1984. Gerry Manning

This page:

Another one of the surviving Victors is XM715, preserved with the Cold War Jets Collection at Bruntingthorpe and photographed in May 2007. Phil Butler

Victor B.2 XM717 of No 139 Squadron photographed in June 1968. Terry Panopalis

Victor K.2 XM717 of No 55 Squadron at Mildenhall on 22nd May 1991. Gerry Manning

This page:

An air-to-air shot of Victor K.2 XM717 of No 55 Squadron 'somewhere in the Gulf' in May 1993. Terry Panopalis

Gulf War-vintage nose art 'Lucky Lou' on the nose of XM717. Gerry Manning

Opposite page:

Unit marking of No 55 Squadron at Marham on 29th April 1970. Gerry Manning

Unit marking of No 57 Squadron on Victor XH651 in 20th September 1975. Gerry Manning

Line-up of No 55 Squadron Victor K.2s. Handley Page Association

Victor B.2 XL164 at Radlett where it spent its life with Handley Page on trials work prior to conversion to a K.2 by Hawker Siddeley. Handley Page Association

Opposite page:

Victor K.2 XL162 with parachute streamed on landing at Wideawake during the Falklands Conflict. Handley Page Association

Victor SR.2 XM715 in No 543 Squadron markings. Handley Page Association

Victor B.1 7850M at Cosford. Handley Page Association

This page:

Victor K.1 XA930 of the TTF. Handley Page Association

Victor K.2 XM717 refuels two Lightnings. Handley Page Association

Victor K.2 XH671 of No 55 Squadron. Handley Page Association

10 Sqn
B.1 1958

15 Sqn
B.1A 1959

15 Sqn
B.1A.1960

57 Sqn
B.1 c.1960

57 Sqn
B.1A 1961

57 Sqn
K.2 1986

57 Sqn
K.2 1987

55 Sqn
B(K).1A 1975

55 Sqn
K.2 1991

57 Sqn
K.1A 1974

57 Sqn
B(K).1A 1975

100 Sqn
B.2 1963

139 Sqn
B.2 1962

214 Sqn
K.1 1975

543 Sqn
SR.2 1973

RAF Wittering 139 Sqn
B.2R 1964

Tanker Training Flight
B.1. c.1969

232 OCU
B.1A c.1975

232 OCU
B.1A 1970-74

RAF Marham 'Pool'
B(K).1A 1975

This page features drawings of many of the varied unit markings worn by the Victor during its long service with the Royal Air Force. David Howley